Adrian Small
Dolton 24-11-10

THE PORTHOLE
MURDER
CASE

THE PORTHOLE MURDER CASE

THE DEATH OF GAY GIBSON

by
Denis Herbstein

Hodder & Stoughton
LONDON SYDNEY AUCKLAND TORONTO

British Library Cataloguing-in-Publication Data

Herbstein, Denis.
  The Porthole murder case.
  I. Title
  364.1

  ISBN 0-340-50157-X

Published by Hodder and Stoughton,
a division of Hodder and Stoughton Ltd,
Mill Road, Dunton Green, Sevenoaks, Kent TN13 2YA
Editorial Office: 47 Bedford Square, London WC1B 3DP

Photoset by E.P.L. BookSet, Norwood, London

Printed in Great Britain by St Edmundsbury Press,
Bury St Edmunds, Suffolk

*This book is dedicated to
Denis Hocking,
the West Country pathologist*

CONTENTS

ILLUSTRATIONS

CAST LIST OF THE 'PORTHOLE' STORY
(not in order of appearance)

James Camb, born Waterfoot, Rossendale Valley, Lancs, December 1916.

Bob, his father, and Lillie, his mother, who died within days of Jim's birth.

Cousins Jenny Haslam and Florrie Stone.

Camb's first wife, Margaret Clark McCombie, married Glasgow, September 1943.

Their daughter, Evelyn (Tootsie).

Camb's second wife, Irene Long, married Dewsbury, Yorkshire, March 1963.

Irene's daughter, Jackie, adopted by Camb.

Eileen Isabella Ronnie (Gay) Gibson, born Jamalpur, India, June 1926.

Her father, Joseph, and her mother, Ellen (Daisy).

Two older brothers, Joe junior and Paul.

Helena Baker, her cousin.

Mildred Jones, schoolfriend and correspondent of Gay Gibson.

IN THE A.T.S.
Brenda Rainford, friend of Gay's.
Peter Dalby, actor in 'Stars in Battledress'.
Evelyn Armour, paymistress.
Dr Ruth Haslam, army medical officer.

IN JOHANNESBURG
Henry Gilbert, British actor-manager.
Gilbert's wife, Dr Ina Schoub, hospital casualty officer.
Mike Abel, villain in *Golden Boy*.
Doreen Mantle, actress.
Eric Boon, boxing champion and aspiring actor.
Mrs Franton Taylor, Gay's singing teacher.
Charles Schwentafsky, Gay's Kenyan benefactor.

'DURBAN CASTLE'
Crew
The Master, Captain Arthur Patey.
Alec Hort, first officer.
Ollie Middleton, chief purser.
Nightwatchmen James Murray and Frederick Steer.
Eileen Field, Gay's cabin stewardess.
Bill Conway, bosun's mate and maintenance man.
Joe Chidgey and Bill Pott, first-class smoking-room stewards.
Dr Anthony Griffiths, ship's surgeon.

Passengers
Gay's table companions, Frank Hopwood, Union-Castle
    victualling official, and Wing Commander William Bray, RAF.
Wendy Noakes and her husband Bindy (at captain's table).

Sir Vernon Thomson, chairman and managing director of
    Union-Castle.

SOUTHAMPTON POLICE
Detective Sergeants Herbert Gibbons and John Quinlan.
Ex-Detective Constable Minden Plumley.

WINCHESTER ASSIZES
Sir Malcolm Hilbery, Judge of the King's Bench.

Counsel for the Prosecution
Geoffrey Dorling (Khaki) Roberts KC
    and his junior, Henry Elam, instructed by Edward Robey,
    solicitor for the Director of Public Prosecutions.

Counsel for the Defence
Joshua Casswell KC and Joseph Molony,
    instructed by Geoffrey Wells, of Woodford & Ackroyd.

Forensic Pathologists
Professor James Webster and Dr Denis Hocking (defence).
Dr Donald Teare (prosecution).

Peg Durrant of the Jurors' Office.

OFFICIAL LOG of the   M.V. "DURBAN CASTLE".

from   DURBAN.   towards SOUTHAMPTON

Date of the Occurrence entered with Hour.	Place of the Occurrence, or situation by Latitude and Longitude at Sea.	Date of Entry.	Entries required by Act of Parliament.	Amount of Fine or Forfeiture Inflicted.
	Continued	10/10/47	Immigration Officials and Port Authorities.	
			No. S/38. J King. Asst Pantryman.	
NOT DEDUCTED:			Wages earned = £23. 15. 4.	
INCOME TAX £2. 5. 0.			Deductions = 15. 7. 11.	LEAVE
			Balance of Wages. 8. 7. 5. Plus 9. 2.	PAY
			J. King. A. Rodolf, Master	
			Chief Steward. OC. Fiddleton Purser.	
10.10.47	Capetown	11/10/47	No. F/22. C. Wheeler. Greaser Cleaner. for	
			being absent from his watch on duty	
			between midnight Thursday and 4.00	
			a.m. Friday 10.10.47. is hereby fined the	
			sum of ten shillings (first offence)	10/.
			and he will forfeit half a days pay.	
			seven shillings. Upon this entry being	7/.
10/	Fines enforced and collected.		read over to C. Wheeler. he admitted the	
	Forfeiture enforced.		offence described and had nothing	
	7/.		more to say.	
			J. Pinkerson. A. Rodolf, Master	
			Chief Engineer. OC. Fiddleton Purser.	
9.57 AM	Lat. 11°34'N.	18/10/47	At 9.57 A.M. today Mr. H.H. Knight. Chief Steward	
18.10.47	Long 17 39 W.		reported to the Master that a first class	
			lady passenger from Cabin 126. named	
			Miss Eileen Gibson. could not be found.	
			She had failed to appear in the Dining	
			Saloon for breakfast.	
			The Master proceeded immediately to	
			make inquiries to satisfy himself that	
			an efficient search had been made.	
			and forthwith held an enquiry into	
			the disappearance of this lady. This	
			enquiry was held in the presence of	
			the Chief Officer. and the Purser. and	
			the Chief Steward	
			At 10.20 A.M. being satisfied that Miss	
			Gibson was not on board. the Master	
			gave orders for the ships course to be	
			reversed. with the intention of continued	

N.B.—Every entry in this Log Book required by the Act must be signed by the Master and by the Mate or some other of the Crew, and every entry of illness, injury or death must also be signed by the Surgeon or Medical Practitioner on board (if any); and every entry of wages due to, or of the sale of the effects of, any Seaman or Apprentice who has died must be signed by the Master and by the Mate and some other member of the Crew; and every entry of wages due to any Seaman who enters His Majesty's Service must be signed by the Master and by the Seaman or by the Officer authorized to receive the Seaman into such Service.

NOTE.—Reading over Entries of Offences.—The Master's especial attention is called to Section 228 (b) (c) and (d) of the Merchant Shipping Act, 1894, which will be found in Notice I. prefixed to this Log.

1

The Man from Waterfoot

James Camb was born in the small Lancashire town of Waterfoot nine days before Christmas 1916 in the middle of a
war-inspired slipper boom. The semi-detached house in which
this apparently unremarkable event occurred lay at the bottom
of a Pennine foothill from which had been quarried the mill-
stone grit used for the paving of Trafalgar Square. Neither the
village GP, Dr Sugden, nor the midwife attended the birth. A
swab was left inside the mother's body; it 'mortified', went
gangrenous, and she was dead within days. Lillie Camb is
nowadays dimly remembered as 'a real lady'. The boy was
healthy and well formed, but the abrupt disappearance of his
mother at so tender an age might account for the errant behaviour that marked the whole of his life.

As the Great War drew to its conclusion, Waterfoot was
contributing its fair share of humanity to the trenches.
Sharman's, the local grocer, offered to dispatch hampers of
roast hare, plum pudding, figs, six kinds of disinfectant soaps,
vermin powders and lemonade tablets 'suitable for warm cli-
mates', to friends or relatives in khaki. The Cambs were not
poor by the standards of those days, but any brother or son in
the forces would have been surprised to receive largesse more
appropriate for the officer class. Their home at No. 4 Lench
Street was without an indoor toilet, and they shared one at the
top of the street with their neighbours. The house was solid
enough, but poky, and Lillie Camb would hang the washing
out to dry on a line stretched across the street.

In their out-of-the-way corner of Lancashire Jim's cousins,
the Cambs and the Haslams, spoke to one another in the

dialect exemplified by Walter Hargreaves' poem of 1916:

Welcome to Rossendale's greit hills,
Its moors, its dales, its streams, its rills,
Wheer nature's music stirs an' thrills
Un allus charms yo'.
Though th'owd wind sometimes bites un chills
'Twill never harm yo'.

The widower, Bob Camb, a 'small, harmless' man, was a slipper clicker at the Globe shoe factory. He spent his free time at the Waterfoot working men's club. It would not have been difficult to find a new mother for Jim and his elder brother, Tom, from among the war widows and spinsters of the town. When pressed on the matter, Bob would explain that no one could replace his Lillie, but from an early age the boy was high-spirited and forever getting into mischief and Bob could not cope with him. On reaching school age, Jim was sent to live with one of his mother's sisters, Auntie Rosie Barlow in Lumb, a remote settlement three miles up the Burnley road from Waterfoot. A Lumb neighbour, Willie Howorth, remembers Jim as 'full of confidence, who mixed well with all the children, but he was too fast for them. He prodded for trout in Whitewell Brook, slept under the stars when the mood took him.'

By now Bob Camb had left Lench Street and moved to Glen Terrace, to a solitary house squeezed between a gloomy cliff and the railway line to Bacup. The sparse 'one up, one down' lacked even the few comforts they had enjoyed in Lench Street. With no woman to cook for him, Bob would get his midday meal at the chip shop at the bottom of nearby Townsend Street. In time Jim moved down from Lumb to be shared between his father and two Camb maiden aunts, who were strict but caring, in Miller Barn Lane. At play-time the two tiny figures in fawn coats, woollen caps, black woollen stockings and wooden clogs arrived at Waterfoot council school bearing Jim's lunch. They would peer through the railings into the playground below, hoping to catch a sight of their mercurial nephew. 'Our little joy', they called him, if he wasn't playing truant.

Jim's contemporaries saw him in a different light. One classmate, Edith Harris, remembers his 'dark shining eyes with an impish grin. He wasn't very tall, he was always clean and tidy. We always thought of him as very bright. But he was a terrible torment. He chased the girls and tried to tease them in a most unpleasant way. These days he might be thought of as slightly hyperactive.' Betty Bursnell, who lived at No. 3 Lench Street, recalls: 'He was a beautiful lad who won everyone over with his charm and good looks. He could be very polite and courteous when he wanted to . . . he would get up for you on a bus or at the doctor's surgery. But underneath that charming exterior was a little devil. The mothers used to go to the school gates to fetch their daughters because they were so frightened of him. They said he was feeling up their clothes.' Another contemporary, John Trickett, talks of Jim's 'very strange eyes, like Valentino. He had a habit of going up to other boys like me and tickling you under the chin. But he was never bothered by boys.' While the lads of his age roamed the moors or played cricket in the street, Jim went off on his own. Whether by design or personality, he was a loner.

His Sunday-school teacher at the Woodlea Conformist Mission, Robert Raikes, despaired of Jim passing his scripture exam. He hadn't been to a single lesson. The night before the exam, he came in, glanced over the book, and the next day, thanks to 'a natural gift of writing and the gab', came away with second prize. On the darker side, Jim did the rounds of the village asking for contributions to the 'Woodlea Mission Christmas Club', gave out pay cards and called each week to collect the money. This charitable cause was news to the church. And yet, recalls Robert Willetts, the present Mission secretary, 'he had this magnetic personality . . . you looked up to him.' One widely remembered scam was Jim's day out at the seaside. His father had been made temporarily redundant, and Jim, no older than ten, purloined his wages and cleared off to Morecambe. He could hardly reach up to the counter at Waterfoot railway station, but the man in the ticket office was persuaded by the winning smile, dark flashing eyes and the explanation that 'my auntie is waiting for me there'. Later that

3

day Bob Camb found his son kicking a ball around on the sands. 'Oh, his father would beat him mercilessly when he did something really bad,' recalls Betty Bursnell, 'but you can beat the Devil into a child, not out.'

A few hundred yards up the road from the Cambs' old home in Lench Street was the Bacup and Rawtenstall Grammar School, a fine institution attended by the children of the middle classes and those others who managed, by dint of hard work and natural ability, to climb to the open deck. Jim was a bright child worthy of a better education, but his undisciplined behaviour ruled out that golden opportunity. Already evident were contradictory aspects of his personality that would be with him for the rest of his days – his charm and courtesy, quick wit and the self-esteem that saw him always neat and clean, were counterbalanced by a knowing superiority that rubbed men up the wrong way, a capacity for misdemeanour, a restless search for something beyond the horizon. The world had deprived Jim of a mother and this seems to have brought on feelings of both anger at, and contempt for, the opposite sex. 'He didn't bother with Waterfoot girlfriends,' his cousin Florrie Stone recalls. 'He wanted something better than that.' His father was increasingly unable to cope with this firecracker in his midst, the aunts doted, the neighbours shook their heads at the latest escapade of the 'beautiful lad'. From an early age Jim's mind was set on running away to sea, which he attempted regularly. In the meantime he went to Lea Bank secondary school at Cloughfold, a short bus-ride from Waterfoot. Here, in the old mansion of the Ashworth cotton family, he bided his time. Once he left school he seemed destined, as a man of Waterfoot, to spend his working life in the slipper works.

The humble slipper had been the staple product of Waterfoot since the 1870s. 'The Ganges in India and the Nile of Egypt are sacred rivers,' a Waterfoot historian wrote in 1922, 'but if King Midas had resided in this district during the last century, he would certainly have worshipped the Irwell, which did so much towards earning for the district the title of "the Golden Valley", the hardest-worked river in the world.'

Once, the banks of the Irwell and its tributaries, Whitewell

Brook and Limy Water, two miles downstream at Rawtenstall, were lined with the mills and warehouses of the cotton industry. When a depression threw the men out of work, the Irwell's pure water was discovered to be excellent for the dyeing of felt and the warehouses became workshops where waste was turned into slippers. By the turn of the century, 3,000 men and women were employed in thirteen Rossendale Valley slipper firms. According to the 1901 census, nearly all the working men in Waterfoot were making slippers. In that year, Henry Trickett's Gaghill factory, the largest in town, produced 72,000 pairs of slippers and canvas shoes a month. There were Trickett depots not only in London, Northampton and Leicester, but also in Paris, Hamburg, Bucharest, Cape Town, Johannesburg, Cairo and Kingston, Jamaica.

The money wasn't bad, certainly better than in the cotton trade. Here was a cosy atmosphere of church and chapel, pub and working men's club, choir and the annual outing to the seaside, with extra perks like Trickett's life insurance and the company's holiday savings scheme. But by the time the fourteen-year-old James Camb left Lea Bank school in 1932 the future was bleak. The postwar boom had been followed by hard times, with lay-offs and threats of strikes. Unable to find work at Trickett's, Jim entered J. H. Hirst's Whitewell plant in the middle of the Great Recession, first as 'the odd lad knocking about', then putting protective paper over the white canvas slippers. If he showed promise he would graduate to inserting the toe puffs which stiffened the slipper-tops. But the slipper treadmill and the local girls were not what Jim had in mind.

At last, in September 1933, he went to sea, signing on to the *Roturua* at Victoria Docks in London as a galley boy bound for New Zealand. For the next fourteen years, ships would be his main source of employment; he travelled to Australia, Africa, the Mediterranean, Brazil and the River Plate, all the while moving up through scullery boy, waiter, assistant cook to assistant steward. The family in Waterfoot were proud of their exotic adventurer, secretly pleased, perhaps, that that boundless energy was being worked off somewhere else. When his cousin, Jenny Haslam, came home to find a pineapple on the kitchen table, she knew Jim was back once again from his travels. The Cambs were hit by a second tragedy when, in 1937, Jim's brother Tom, a quiet, devout Christian, died of tuberculosis. He had worked with his father as a slipper clicker at Trickett's, and his death in his mid-twenties drove Bob deeper into isolation in his frugal retreat on the River Irwell.

The little lad with the cheeky eyes was now a handsome young man. It was not by chance that Jim preferred passenger ships to the slow cargo steamers which carried neither passengers nor stewards. 'He wasn't ambitious,' his cousin Florrie says. 'They wanted to promote him to a better position, but he was happy to be where the pretty girls and the five-pound tips were.' It might have been at this period in his travels that Jim recounted the story of the rating who paid an afternoon call on a widow travelling with her small son. At a loss as to how to occupy the child's attention, they gave him some paper to cut up. While the adults were otherwise engaged, the little boy sliced the visitor's breeches to the knee. Jim told the story with relish. Whether he was the victim or not, the shipping company didn't hear of it. The discharge book, which is the merchant seaman's passport and curriculum vitae, has two 'character report' columns that must be signed by the chief officer at the completion of each voyage. Camb invariably received a 'VG' (very good) for both ability and general conduct.

In February 1938 he signed off the *Port Adelaide* at Melbourne with the intention of settling in Australia. He found work as a steward on a coaster, then as a docker, then – no doubt more to his liking – as 'house steward' to David Smyth, secretary to the late Earl Beauchamp, but again he left after a few months. This was undoubtedly the situation later described in an English newspaper: ' . . . he took a job as house steward with a wealthy man in Melbourne . . . (who had a) young and attractive wife. There was trouble and Camb left after seven months.' His home address listed in the discharge book was now care of Miss Lyda Misseiko, Moonee Ponds, Victoria. Half a century later Miss Misseiko, now Mrs Surjenko, recalls Jim as working in one of Melbourne's first hamburger houses. 'He lost his job and must have slept out for a while. I helped him pay for a room somewhere near the city for two or three weeks. One day he called at work to say he had a job and was off and that was the last I saw or heard of him.'

At the outbreak of war Jim signed on as a 'fireman' (stoker) on the armed merchant cruiser HMS *Arawa*, patrolling Australian coastal waters. The *Arawa* moved to Hong Kong in November 1939, making sorties into the South China Sea on the lookout for German blockade runners. Looking back on this period, Jim would talk wistfully of coming 'home' to his Chinese girlfriend . . . the hot bath, his whites laid out on the bed. It was not to last. In the autumn of 1940 the *Arawa* returned, via Simonstown and Freetown, to Belfast where Camb was paid off, again with two 'VGs' to his name. There had, of course, been no women on board. In July 1941 Camb sailed to India in the *Manela*, a passenger steamer attached to Coastal Command during the hostilities. He was one of thirty assistant stewards, and the records show that while he was quickly promoted to head waiter, he was soon demoted to third steward and, ultimately, to assistant steward. Here was an early sign that James Camb was not behaving himself, though the exact reason for his fall from grace – women, drink, cheeking an officer, petty theft, perhaps – is not stated. The voyage ended in Bombay, but Camb was one of ten crewmen discharged a month earlier in Karachi 'on ground of mutual consent'. The Master, in other words, was glad to see the back of him, yet his behaviour, according to the discharge book, was 'Very Good'.

These end-of-voyage judgments need an explanation. Under the 1894 Merchant Shipping Act, which for decades regulated the seagoing life of officers and ratings, the Master recorded in the logbook and in the discharge books of all seamen and officers up to chief engineer, his opinion of their ability and conduct. There were three levels of goodness: 'VG', plain 'G', and 'DR', Decline to Report. (The Mercantile Marine Act of 1850 had listed four categories: Very Good, Good, Middling, Indifferent.) Anything less than 'VG' was recognised as a bad discharge and was rarely given without the full approval of the shipping master who attended when the ship paid off, and sometimes after consultation with a trade union official. Often a seaman given a bad discharge would simply lose his book and apply for a replacement. So a shipmaster signing on a hardened old salt with a brand-new book might be excused for fearing the worst.

During the *Manela*'s stopover on the Clyde Jim walked into a tobacconist's shop in Glasgow and was attracted by the pretty shop assistant. He dated her several times in the fortnight before sailing, and wrote to her regularly during the next two-year absence. Now, within a fortnight of his return from India, on 11 September 1943, he married Margaret Clark McCombie in the Blythwood registry office. He was twenty-six, she twenty-two. Her late father was listed on the marriage certificate as 'Captain Gordon Highlanders', so she was certainly a cut above the Cambs in social standing. When Margaret was brought to Waterfoot to meet Bob Camb she might have been surprised at the house in Glen Terrace, with the inside stone staircase and the toilet 'a penny car ride away'. A family friend, Hilda Howorth, remembers seeing Jim in his naval uniform: 'He was so debonair, everyone gasped. He could really carry it well.'

Whatever the exploits of Jim Camb before his marriage, and his later philandering, Margaret was to be his only love. She wrote of those first two months as the happiest of her life, one of the rare occasions when she could have her husband to herself for any length of time. They honeymooned in Aberdeen, 'then he was gone again for almost a year, while I returned to live with my mother in Glasgow. This time he was on the Murmansk run on the *Empire Bard*, though I did not know it until he returned [in September 1944] six weeks after our little girl was born. Tootsie, he called her – we had one of our few differences over her name. I named her Evelyn, while he was away. He was rather cross about it because he wanted her to be Margaret, after me.'

The perilous runs to Russia were without incident for Jim. Having avoided the U-boats, however, he was caught out by his own captain. In a log entry dated 6 June 1944, the day of the Normandy landings, the Master of the *Empire Bard* wrote that Camb had 'absented himself from ship from 0700 hours to 0630

7th June 1944 and hereby forfeits one day's pay (8/8d) and is fined ten shillings for disobeying a ship's general order. His shore leave has been stopped for one day on first offence and he has been warned that, if he repeats the offence, his shore pass will be removed for good. He had no reply to make on above entry being read out to him.' Camb was no doubt over-staying his homecoming with Margaret. Nevertheless, two 'VGs' marked his signing-off six weeks later. Soon afterwards he joined the *Wave Monarch* as assistant steward, and was soon promoted to second steward. In January 1945 he deserted at Greenock, perhaps in a hurry to see his wife and daughter. This time, in place of the usual 'VGs' the Master wrote: 'Voyage not completed, MC (medical certificate) produced'.

Next, he was an assistant steward on the troop carrier *Dunnottar Castle* which, in peacetime, plied for the Union-Castle Line, whose larger ships sailed weekly on the Cape mail run. The remainder of Camb's seagoing life would be with Union-Castle. Now, on 23 March, the Master wrote in his log: 'Although leave expired at Midnight on the 23 inst., the undermentioned seamen were not on board at the time of sailing (from Belfast). They have been written off the articles and reported to the Mercantile Marine Office.' Camb's fellow deserters were a kitchen porter, a pantryman and a scullion. Within four days, however, he had rejoined the *Dunnottar Castle* before she left Southampton to ferry troops in the North Sea and the Mediterranean. Two more 'Very Goods'.

In November 1945, Camb returned to civilian life on his release from the Merchant Navy Reserve. Now was the time, if ever it was going to happen, to give up the sea, settle down in Glasgow, or emigrate to Australia, as tens of thousands of Britons were preparing to do. He found a shore job in Clyde-bank, but after three months selling sewing machines Margaret reported: 'He yearned for the more attractive life on a liner, and back to sea he went.' In May 1946 he signed on at Southampton as assistant cook on the *Durban Castle*, a Union-Castle mailship sailing to Cape Town and Durban on a six-week turn-around. By the next trip he was a steward again. 'He would come in loaded with presents for Tootsie and me,' his wife recalled, 'toys and sweets for her; foodstuffs, dress materials and nylons for me. They were happy times. He was a good husband and father . . . '

The impression Camb gave his wife – of being a true and faithful husband – suggests that he felt no guilt about his behaviour. He was a good actor, he understood the role expected of him, slid seamlessly from Romeo to uxorious husband. Years later, he reminisced about 'a game I enjoyed playing . . . I had, like so many other stewards, remarkable success with women passengers – especially unaccompanied girls on the first-class deck. Many women told me they pre-ferred to have affairs with stewards than with other passengers. "You're much more fun and you know the meaning of discretion," a South American millionairess once told me. On the Mediterranean cruises women used to ask me, "Meet me ashore tonight. You know the right place. I'll look after the expenses." I was spoiled for women at a very early age. Love came too easily and I never had a chance to learn its real value.'

A cousin once compared him to his 'granddad Camb, a dandy, all dressed up, and it didn't matter whether the wife and kids had a meal as long as there was a flower in his buttonhole. Poor Jimmy, he couldn't help it, it was bred in him . . . ' Self-centred, unable to function within conventional structures, he seems to have understood his limitations by choosing not to live ashore. At sea he could create a fantasy world in which he starred as the great lover, mixing with men and women otherwise beyond his social range. Here life was manageable, ordered, and if it became too tedious, you could still break the rules and get away with it.

It was not illegal to enter a passenger's cabin. Section 287 of the 1894 Act listed a series of shipboard offences punishable by the Master, but only one of these had the vaguest reference to cabin amours: 'If any person on board the steamer, after warning by the Master or other officer thereof, molests or continues to molest any passenger . . . ' During half a century at sea, Joe Chidgey, smoking-room steward on the *Durban Castle*, could not recall a single case of a seaman sacked for visiting a woman passenger in her cabin.

Camb was an excellent steward, recognised as such by admiring passengers. On his penultimate cruise, starting on 27 June 1947, he at last joined the elite, becoming a deck steward in the first class. Together with the men working the smoking room, the lounge and the bar, he was now a 'topside' steward. You ran your own show, and though the work was hard, tips regularly added up to more than the basic wage. At the end of a trip a passenger might vouchsafe ten bob or a pound, or even a fiver if someone as generous as the Rand mining magnate, Sir Abe Bailey, was on board. The snooker player Joe Davis was on that cruise with his wife, Jane. Suffering from seasickness, Mrs Davis spent much time on deck. She remembers Camb as 'very charming, a very good steward. He showed me a picture of his little girl. I was just married and better looking then. But he never made one single play for me. Obviously he was a bit over-sexed, but there was no harm in him. Joe hated him. When Camb saw me in my deckchair he would come and ask, "Is father asleep in his cabin?"'

Another passenger, Norah van Reenen, recalls him 'always smiling, excellent at his work, very good-looking and extremely popular with men and women alike'. Others saw in him a resemblance to the matinée film idol Tyrone Power. Not everyone was entranced by Camb, however. Fellow crewmen, possibly officers annoyed at this upstart muscling in on their upper-deck *droit de seigneur*, were jealous. Newspapers would later dub him 'Romeo of the Decks' – 'in the early hours he would be found, freshly washed and shaved, passing along a corridor to knock at the door of someone who had fallen under his spell'. Now, on his eighth consecutive mailship run, Camb knew the ropes inside out. On the *Durban Castle*'s outward journey from Southampton in September 1947, he was at his most predatory. He described it in offhand terms: 'a young girl invited me down to her cabin and exasperated me by her teenage behaviour. I put her over my knee and gave her a good spanking.' Another teenager, said to be a French maid, received a black eye while defending her virtue, but her employers would not report the incident for fear of jeopardising the girl's access to South Africa.

Camb was said to have a girl in every port. Sightings were reported with a girl – in some cases, 'girls' – on his arm, in Durban, Port Elizabeth and Cape Town. The myth grew like a penicillin culture.

On the afternoon of Friday 10 October 1947, the *Durban Castle* was loading in Cape Town's Duncan Dock, ready for the four o'clock departure for home. James Camb waited at the top of the first-class gangway. The few passengers returning for the European autumn were middle-aged to elderly, leavened by half-a-dozen family groups, so the young woman amongst them stood out like a movie star at a sing-song in an old people's home. Whether Camb, on seeing Gay Gibson for the first time, really did say, 'She's mine!' cannot be proven. But he certainly marked her down for early attention.

2

On to the Stage

Eileen Isabella Ronnie Gibson was the young actress who drew the eye of James Camb on that African spring day. 'Gay' – the nickname came later – was born, as she would die, in a time of intense heat. In mid-June 1926 the monsoon was gathering over Jamalpur, where the Ganges loops north to Monghyr and where Eileen's father, Joseph Basnett Gibson, was employed as assistant foreman on the East India Railway. Jamalpur was a workshop town, with perhaps 15,000 men in the pay of the company which operated the river-route line from Calcutta to Delhi. There were hundreds of these craftsmen known as 'domiciled Europeans', the only group of white men in India who worked with their hands. It was one of the perks of the Empire, to go abroad and be paid greatly in excess of what could be earned at home.

The Gibsons lived north of the railway line in the European quarter of Jamalpur, a gridiron of bungalowed streets, well-tended gardens, churches, and the 'Institute', the railway-men's club, where Anglo-Indians, but not pure-blooded Asians, were admitted to social evenings. The likes of the Gibsons were not, however, to be seen in the Indian Civil Service club up the road in Monghyr. Probably they were not interested in being there. Joe Gibson was a staunch Baptist, devoting his spare time to church work and preaching. Baptists viewed the province of Bihar and Orissa, indeed the whole of north India, as a 'fruitful vineyard' for their missionaries; they would one day number 400,000 in the sub-continent, to become, after the Soviet Union, the second-largest community outside the United States. The name is derived from the insistence that baptism should be administered only to adult believers. There is no record of Gay's baptism, but the religious beliefs of her parents must have left their mark.

When she was four months old, Gay returned with her mother and two brothers, Joe junior and Paul, to their 'semi' in Seymour Street, Higher Tranmere, on the Mersey. If the young men of Waterfoot were destined for slippers, in Birkenhead they left school at fourteen and built ships. In the mornings the Gibson children could listen to the marching feet of hundreds of men going to work at Cammell Laird's. Here, in the boiler shop, Mr Gibson had qualified as a blacksmith. His wife, 'Daisy' Ellen Victoria, was a nurse, and they had met during World War I, when Joe was doing voluntary work at Birkenhead General Hospital. It was then that old Joe experienced the first of his maritime tragedies when his brother Larry's merchant ship was torpedoed.

Joe's good deeds began in Birkenhead, as a Sunday-school superintendent and preacher at the Grange Road Baptist Church. Nobody who remembers him has a bad word to say about Joe. A big fellow, a typical blacksmith, he was as honest as the words he preached. But Daisy was the heart of the family. She managed well enough when her husband was overseas. One visitor talked of her as a 'very strong-minded lady, (but) kind, generous-hearted'. The daughter was 'dumpy and fat, rather plain, only pretty later'.

Early in 1940, before Italy entered the war, and France was overrun, Gay and her mother made a remarkable journey to join Mr Gibson in the Persian Gulf. They travelled by train to Venice, in the SS *Marco Polo* to Beirut, by car to Damascus, in Nairn Transport's sealed coach across the desert to Baghdad, by train to Basrah, and finally by plane to the oilfields of Masjid-i-Suleiman in Khuzestan. In a letter home she advised a school friend to 'get a book called *Murder on the Orient Express* by Agatha Christie, it's awfully good'.

The Anglo-Iranian Oil Company (later British Petroleum) oilfields, where Joe Gibson earned £570 a year as a blacksmith, fuelled the Royal Navy's war in the eastern Mediterranean and the Far East, and would supply the southern Russian front after Hitler's invasion. Gay's letters, still signed 'Eileen', give a flavour of life in an isolated expatriate outpost. She was fourteen, and she was reading intelligently. Writing to a friend, she mentioned *Rebecca* and *Gone with the Wind* and was midway through Galsworthy's *The White Monkey*, of which she said, 'Highbrow, isn't it?

'By the way,' she added 'I gave up golf, as transport to the golf-course is very difficult. I have been riding these last two months and have only come off once so far.' She had an Armenian girlfriend, Seda, who 'speaks perfect English and really is just like ourselves. She rides, swims, plays tennis, and loves the pictures. I miss her now that she has gone to Tehran for the hot weather.' There was no school, no wireless, the newspapers from home were three months old. In the summer, protected by mosquito nets, they slept out-of-doors under the date palms. We don't know whether she was in the audience for the MIS dramatic society production of Ivor Novello's *Fresh Fields*, described in the company magazine as 'a winner'.

But without her friends, perhaps missing the excitement of a Merseyside being blasted by the Luftwaffe, Gay sounds homesick. A year into her stay she writes that 'the days here are long and boring. I just potter about in the mornings, tidying the bungalow, the servants are a nuisance, they have no idea of cleanliness. In the afternoon I always have a bath and then I sew or read till Daddy comes in at four o'clock. Sometimes we go for walks or pay a visit to another bungalow, here we have a cup of tea and have a good old gossip. In the evening we often go to the club, there is badminton twice a week, pictures twice a week and Scottish country dancing every Saturday evening at eight o'clock. I rarely go to the country dancing however . . . ' Mrs Gibson would later claim that Gay was 'a brilliant linguist . . . spoke Hindustani and Persian', but there is no sign of an interest in languages in her letters home.

In August 1941, with Britain now at war with Japan, the company wives and children were evacuated to Bombay, then by troopship via Durban to England. When Gay's friend Mildred Jones saw her on her return for the first time for over a year, 'she was coming down the road, greatly to my amazement, with a fur coat her parents had given her to keep warm, despite the coupons. But she'd been ill. My memory may be playing tricks but I think she'd had malaria. She was not highly-strung (but) a very assured young lady.' Her old school, Tranmere Higher Grade, was now closed, and she went to Birkenhead girls' secondary. At fifteen Gay had lost the tubbiness of adolescence. Norman Foster, a friend of her father's, remembers Gay as 'very charming, but she wasn't a painted doll. She was sophisticated, and had very good conversation, had done all sorts of things, like horse-riding . . . she looked as though she knew where she was going, though the Gibsons never let on what they were going to do, they just did it . . . '

Foster claims responsibility for Gay's name-change. He and Joe organised dances in aid of the mayor of Birkenhead's Red Cross and St John Ambulance Brigade prisoner-of-war fund. They called their committee 'The Top Hats Gay Dancing Company', and Norman would refer to Eileen as 'a gay young thing, after which the name seems to have stuck'. Still, Joe did not encourage Eileen to go out with boys. By now Gay's mind was made up. A family friend, May Petterson, recalls meeting her at the Co-op butcher in Old Chester Road in Rock Ferry. 'She must have been about seventeen. "Have you got a young man?" I asked her. "Oh no, Mrs Petterson, all I want to do is go on the stage and be an actress."' The Gibsons' living room with its grand piano was the focus for serious music-making. Norman Foster recalls her singing 'Ave Maria' in 'a marvellous soprano voice . . . but she was more or less isolated and if I called and Eileen was singing they would not open the door till she was finished'.

After the years abroad, Mr Gibson's expatriate salary was enough to buy a large house in Bebington Road, something unusual in an area of council houses and rented accommodation. A contemporary and near neighbour of Gay's, Flora Green, remembers Mrs Gibson as old, small and dowdy, fairly shapeless, though quite good-looking. 'They were middle class, yet mother and daughter would go to the local and have a drink together, which in my day only the lower orders did. The mother was probably lonely, with her husband abroad.'

Gay was 'a very theatrical person, attractive, but not beautiful. She wasn't very academic, but she was very sensible, and not flighty. She used to come to our house and I played the piano and she sang Noël Coward and Ivor Novello. She had a nice speaking voice, rather throaty, and not a Merseyside accent, because she did not go to a state school. I still believe to this day that she was not promiscuous. She never ever made fellows a topic of conversation, like some of my friends. She was never boy-mad.'

Later, Mrs Gibson wrote that her daughter's 'beauty and demonstrative nature found its natural outlet in the stage. As she was so young I was not too happy about it. Nor was her father, a staunch churchman . . . but we let her take part in the children's pantomime.' This first public sign of Gay's penchant for acting was in the chorus of *Babes in the Wood* at the Liverpool Empire. She was offered more stage work, but, pressed by her mother, enrolled at a secretarial college, and even taught shorthand for a while. But her heart was not in the work. At the age of eighteen Gay was called up for National Service and, once again influenced by her mother, became a probationer nurse at Walton Hospital in Liverpool. Three months was enough for her to realise that nursing was not for her, either. She joined the ATS, the Auxiliary Territorial Service, the female wing of the British Army with the motto 'Suaviter in modo fortiter in re' (Gentle in manner, strong in deed). 'I was in Persia with my husband when Eileen joined the Army,' Daisy Gibson said later, 'but my brother had a serious conversation with her, warning her that during military service she would meet men who would try to take advantage of her.'

Gay was posted to 'I' Corps, the Intelligence Corps, with a billet in a house in Fitzjohn's Avenue, Hampstead, north London. The corps had a fair sprinkling of flighty young girls from the shires. One of these, a former private, has written that though 'social snobbery was practically non-existent . . . intellectual snobbery ran riot. Accents, background and financial position were of little importance, provided a certain intellectual and cultural standard was attained.' Gay was given a basic training in signals and coding, there were lectures on the

King's Regulations, army organisation, personal hygiene, they
went on route marches and cross-country runs, and, having
spent time in the Gulf, Gay might have studied some Farsi and
Hindustani. A colleague from those days, Brenda Rainford
(now Sadat) remembers her as 'a warm, sweet girl with a Bette
Davis mouth and eyes, a lovely skin and a delightful singing
voice . . . Because I sang too we became friends.' The privates
put on a much-applauded cabaret, with Gay doing the singing.
Their unit was due to be sent to India, but after embarkation
leave and a short stay in a transit camp it became apparent that
the war in the Far East would soon be over. The sailing was
cancelled, the unit disbanded, the corporals dispersed to
camps around the country. Gay was sent to Chester for a few
months, where she could see her mother at weekends.

During this period Brenda bumped into Gay outside
Leicester Square tube station, full of the fact that she had got
herself into 'Stars in Battledress', an army theatre unit. 'She
suggested I ought to do the same thing and gave me the details
of how to go about it . . . She was so kind, not at all selfish –
she needn't have bothered to tell me about "Stars", but she
pointed me in the right direction. I never heard her say anything nasty about anybody.'

'Stars in Battledress' began as a central pool of male artistes
who, after completing their basic military training, went out to
entertain the troops, though they could be recalled to regimen-
tal duties in the event of the war taking a turn for the worse.
The comedians Charlie Chester and Terry-Thomas, and George
Melachrino's string orchestra, were therefore on show to the
humblest Tommy in the remotest outpost. Variety was the
most popular wartime live entertainment, but in 1943 the military decided there would be no harm in catering for more
serious tastes. The 'Stars' theatre unit was for a while an 'all-
male go-anywhere unit', again consisting of players who received nothing more than their army pay – very different from
ENSA, whose members were professional actors in civilian
clothing playing in comfortable locations. Yet 'Stars' theatre
troupes attracted actors of the calibre of the young Peter
Ustinov, Wilfred Hyde-White and Faith Brook, the first woman

to break into the masculine preserve. They toured with modern, realistic productions, sometimes, as in Terence Rattigan's *Flare Path*, with the war itself as the theme. They played in Nissen huts, in aircraft hangars, under the stars if there was nowhere else to perform. But they were also soldiers, and had to report to the local barracks promptly at 8.30 a.m. the next day, even after returning from a performance in the early hours of the morning. Faith Brook recalls the women officers doing their level best to make life unpleasant for the actresses, the more so when they 'fell in' bearing traces of make-up and with their hair less than the regulation two inches above the collar.

By the time Gay joined 'Stars', the fighting was over, so that touring troupes were billeted out. In January 1946 she was cast as the leading lady in *The Man with a Load of Mischief* by Ashley Dukes, a period piece popular between the wars, when Fay Compton played the opera singer-turned-courtesan of the Prince Regent. She sees the error of her ways, uttering the lines; 'I have known too many men. Too many arms have held me. I am tired of those arms outstretched, asking much and giving little,' and runs off with a nobleman's manservant who once ogled her on-stage at Covent Garden. The play was performed for the forces in Britain, France and Germany from May to August. In October, Gay landed a small part in *Jane Steps Out*, touring England and Wales for several more months.

Gay had been right about her true vocation and quickly found her stage feet. Once released from the non-conformist carapace, the vivacious teenager blossomed into an extrovert young woman. There were distinct signs of a reaction to the dominance of her mother and to the evangelising creed of old Joe – whom she had anyway seen for only three months since leaving Persia. Mrs Gibson had rejoined her husband in the Gulf soon after Gay began touring and it was then that she wrote the intriguing words to her mother: 'I work in a sink of iniquity, but I will never change.'

Her uncle's cautionary words seem to have been forgotten for, increasingly, Gay displayed a reckless side to her nature. Some of her colleagues described her as 'hysterical', an 'excitable neurotic'. In Germany, she was 'quite infatuated' with

Pierre, who drove the scenery van, an affair starting three or four days after they had met. A burn on the palm of her hand was said to have been inflicted with a lighted cigarette, either by herself or by Pierre in some sort of amorous ritual. There were reports of heavy drinking after curtain-fall. A 'hilarious party' in the officers' mess followed a performance at the Trawsfynydd ammunition depot in North Wales. On the long ride back to her lodgings Gay passed out and lay unconscious on the floor of the coach for half an hour, her breathing heavy and laboured. It was a hectic existence and Gay, who put everything into her acting, was no shirker. But there were sure signs of ill-health. An ATS officer, Evelyn Armour, was called into her room in London late one evening in the summer of 1946. She found Private Gibson lying on the bed face upwards, resting on the back of her head and her heels, with her back arched. 'As I went through the door I could hear her breathing very, very heavily,' she recounted. 'Her tongue was well back in her throat and she appeared to be choking.' Armour straightened her tongue and Gay mumbled the word 'pain', clutching at her chest. 'She was sweating profusely. She had great difficulty in breathing at all.' The condition was 'very bad' for ten to fifteen minutes, and Gay was then taken to the Casualty Receiving Station where she appeared to be exhausted. By the morning she had got over it. When she next met Evelyn Armour, a few months later, Gay admitted to having had 'another one of these turns'. Her mother, still abroad, remained ignorant of these events, though she did know that her daughter had been in the Alder Hey military hospital with an ear infection.

By the spring of 1947 demobilisation had reduced the scope of both 'Stars in Battle Dress' and ENSA. Daisy was back in Birkenhead and Joe Gibson was now living in Durban, about to try his luck in South Africa. Gay, it was decided, would travel there with her mother. Whether she went voluntarily, or, since she was still a minor, whether the strong-willed Daisy laid down the law is not known, but it is likely that the undesirable influence of 'Stars' had something to do with it.

On 19 February, Gay underwent a medical check-up preparatory to her 'demob'. She was graded 'AW/1/non-tropical', which meant that she was fit but, because of the ear infection, precluded from serving in the tropics.

Within days Gay and her mother had embarked on the immigrant ship *Carnarvon Castle*. The Union of South Africa, as it was called, was still governed by Britain's favourite Afrikaner, General Jan Smuts, and that very month King George VI, Queen Elizabeth, and the two princesses had sailed into Cape Town to begin a lengthy tour. 'Apartheid' was not yet the official dogma and it was still respectable to go there – the Salvation Army commissioner, David Lamb, lauded Smuts as 'a consistent advocate of the introduction of "fresh blood" to maintain a white civilisation'. Not many of the 20,000 immigrants who had arrived in South Africa from Britain since the war would have had the plight of Blacks at the forefront of their minds. In the words of John Havers, a purser on one of these immigrant ships: 'Most people did not know where they were going. You'd get into Biscay and be asked when we would reach "Cape Fred Astaire".' The *Carnarvon*, still to be refitted after war service, carried 1,300 passengers, most on assisted passage schemes. One passenger recalls with a shudder the sound of two hundred children running riot on the uncarpeted decks. Gay and her mother arrived in Durban in mid-March.

Durban in the forties was a sub-tropical outpost like none other in southern Africa. The White third of the city remained British down to its gin-and-tonic and talk of 'home', with appropriate attitudes to Afrikaners, whom the Whites despised, to Zulus, who did the rough work downwind, and to the Indian merchant under-class from whom they bought bananas and 'nigger balls' at a corner shop. Africa's busiest port was a cultural backwater, not the sort of place where a vivacious actress lingered overlong, the more so when she had to live with her watchful parents. Two weeks in Durban was more than enough. The mother took the daughter up to Johannesburg, the Golden City, they checked in at the YWCA, Gay found a job with an electrical firm, and Daisy went home more or less satisfied.

Gay earned £25 a month, but it was never enough. During her six months in Johannesburg, Joseph sent her £175, which must have been a real hardship to a man working as a dispatch clerk. But at least she was free to pursue her priorities, singing and acting. She was said to have had an introduction to one of the country's leading actresses, Marda Vanne, who was setting up a new national theatre with her friend Gwen Ffrangcon-Davies. Armed with proof of her ability to hold down good parts, with her 'English' accent and her comely features, success on stage and off seemed assured. All things English still exercised considerable influence over White South African tastes. Dame Edith Evans, visiting the Pretoria Women's Club, thanked the people of South Africa for the food parcels they were sending to Britain – adding: 'We are not starving in England, we are only poor because of the shortage of money.' The upcoming actor, Noel Willman, was appearing in Rattigan's *The Winslow Boy* at Her Majesty's Theatre, while the British ballroom dancing champions, John Wells and Renée Sissons, showed off their steps at the Benoni town hall.

Gay landed a part in the Johannesburg Repertory Company's production of *The Silver Cord*, and did radio work for the South African Broadcasting Corporation at three guineas a time. In the recording studios one Saturday night she met Henry Gilbert, a British actor-manager who had recently played Mr Doolittle in a local *Pygmalion*. He was casting Clifford Odets' Broadway success, *Golden Boy*, and asked Gay to play the part of Lorna Moon, the 'blonde prostitute with a heart of gold' immortalised in Hollywood by Barbara Stanwyck. Gilbert, a keen amateur boxer in his younger days, had found a real-life boxer for the leading role, the 'Golden Boy' Joe Bonaparte torn between a career as a violinist and a prize fighter. In town on the comeback trail after losing his British lightweight crown was Eric Boon, handsome face unscathed, brain by no means befuddled, and very keen on acting.

They rehearsed for six weeks. Gay, one of the two women in a large cast, bowled the local actors over. Eric Boon talked of 'a pretty red-head . . . a very excitable girl'. The other actress, Doreen Mantle, recalls the impression she made on the cast.

'She was attractive enough for all the men to go round her like bees round a honeycomb. Her response was very, very flirtatious, as any pretty girl's would be, and perhaps the more so as she was sexually experienced. South African girls in those days were either good or bad . . . we didn't know anything. She was crazy about fellows. She was always throwing her arms round men, or talking to them, or propositioning them. It could have been the English sort of "Dahling", the thirties, actressy syndrome that South Africans weren't used to. She was a lovely looking girl. If I have to think what she was like the nearest physical type I can come to was Meryl Streep . . . she seemed to suit the Lorna Moon character very well.'

The blackguard of the play is a gangster, Eddie Fuseli, a character created by Elia Kazan on the New York and London stages before the war. Here Fuseli was played by Mike Abel, stationery salesman and keen amateur actor. He was a Runyonesque fellow, a Jewish wideboy in the mould of Sid James, the 'cockney' actor from Johannesburg. After meeting Gay for the first time, Abel was heard to say, 'I'll bet you a dollar I'll have her by the end of the week.' Soon they were leaving together after rehearsals and the whole cast was sure they were having an affair. Doreen Mantle recalls a cast party at a house with a round pond in the garden, where 'Gay accused Mike Abel of making her pregnant. There was a terrible row . . . I can remember them screaming at one another.' Parties seemed to be held almost as regularly as rehearsals. Burning the candle at both ends, Gay was under tremendous strain. Once, at rehearsal, she kicked and mauled Mike Abel for no apparent reason. The pattern of fainting fits, established during her army days, began again. She passed out while crossing Commissioner Street after an evening rehearsal. There are two versions of what happened, though they might relate to different occasions. One member of the cast, John Baron, recalls Mike Abel shouting at Gay, 'Come on, you bitch, you are acting!', and she got up and laughed and walked away. Another actor, David Lander, says that when she came out of her faint it turned out that she had not eaten for three days, 'So we had a whip-round for her'. She was not paid during rehearsals, but would earn seven pounds a week once the show started.

Did Gay come to South Africa for reasons of health? Her army discharge and the evidence of her mother suggest not, but as with those who knew her in 'Stars in Battledress', so her *Golden Boy* associates took a different view. There was talk of a heart condition, presumably the reason for the fainting fits. Forty years later those who knew her still talk of her 'alabaster skin'. Doreen Mantle: 'I thought she was a sick girl. She didn't look healthy. She had a beautiful skin, rather delicate . . . a marvellous transparency to her face . . . it was too fragile . . . I do remember she had blue in her nails.' Henry Gilbert thought Gay was too plump for Lorna Moon and sent her to gym classes with his wife, Dr Ina Schoub. Gay herself told the doctor that she had come to Johannesburg because she suffered from asthma.

We get another glimpse of Gay in Johannesburg from Mrs Franton Taylor, one of the town's most experienced singing teachers. In a statement to her attorneys (made six months after the events described) she said that Gay had been her student for three months, 'during which period I found her to be very absent-minded, so much so that her mind was always on something other than her work. It appeared to me that there was something worrying her . . . I found her a very strange girl.' According to Mrs Taylor, 'She could not sing as she could not get out certain notes due to chest and throat trouble. Her voice was never clear but was husky and she repeatedly had to clear her throat and spit phlegm into her handkerchief. I was convinced . . . that she had throat trouble and when I asked her how long she had suffered from this complaint, she told me, for the past four years, (and) that she could not get certain notes out and that she had a lump in her throat. I asked her to let me have a look and I distinctly saw a lump the size of a cherry in the back of her throat behind her tonsils just behind the uvula . . . this lump had a touch of yellow on the top of it . . . I was convinced she suffered from TB. I advised her to go and see a doctor and, in fact, discussed the matter with my own doctor, but Gay never took my advice . . . she often

24

cleared her throat and always brought up a lot of phlegm.' Mrs Taylor was pleased when Gay left 'because I feared that with her trouble she might contaminate my other pupils and even myself'. She had another reason for being pleased – Gay, pleading poverty, had not paid for a single singing lesson. 'Gay did not confide in me,' the teacher concluded, 'and I did not know anything about her private life. She did come to my flat one day with a gentleman, who wrote music for her, but I do not know his name.'

Golden Boy was Odets' first big commercial success. Despite his radical views, it was not a political piece. Today it seems dated, sentimental, but the message of self-betrayal, selling your better self for the quick buck, has a sincere ring. Lorna is sent by her boyfriend, the fight manager, to lure Joe Bonaparte from his first vocation, the fiddle. She succeeds only too well and they fall in love. Joe Fuseli, the hoodlum who muscles in on the big fight, has been called 'a Machiavel from a dark Elizabethan drama', though the model was only too common in the landscape of 1930s Chicago. Mike Abel played the part well, though at rehearsal he once failed to dodge a slow-motion version of Boon's celebrated left hook. On-stage, Boon wins his fight, but breaks his fiddler's hand. The lovers drive into the moonlight, the car crashes . . .

Opening night at the Standard Theatre on Wednesday 10 September attracted a piquant mix of the worlds of ring and stage. *The Star* newspaper conceded that Gay was 'adequately cast as the "femme fatale"', but other critics thought more highly of her performance. The *Rand Daily Mail* talked of her making 'an admirable job of the part of Lorna Moon. There was hardly a false note in her conception of the personality of the easy-going girlfriend', while the *Sunday Times* considered that Gay Gibson came out of the arduous part with flying colours – 'a harsh, metallic, but convincing portrayal'. The *Sunday Express* was not happy about Boon's performance: 'his second Waterloo' in one week after a ring defeat two nights earlier at the hands of the Dutchman, Giel de Roode. Apart from 'sharp delineations by Gay Gibson, Doreen Mantle and Michael Abel, this crisp little play had a ragged stamp and descended into melodrama'. *The Star*'s columnist predicted that the play would run for several weeks.

These were heartening notices. Eric Boon recalled that Gay 'seemed to be pleased and excited'. The play had a three-week booking, but after ten days the Johannesburg City Council condemned the Standard Theatre as a fire hazard and the show was forced to close. Gilbert decided to take *Golden Boy* to Pretoria, an hour's drive to the north. Having agreed to go on tour, indeed, according to Boon, having been eager to do so, Gay suddenly asked Gilbert to release her. She said she was going back to England to study at the experimental Gate Theatre in London. 'But it does not exist at the moment,' he told her. Gilbert tore up her contract and called off the tour. There was no time to find a new leading lady. Gay booked a third-class passage at £45 on the *Oranjefontein*, then she cancelled the ticket and reserved a first-class cabin on the *Durban Castle*. The cost, £150, with £350 pocket money thrown in, suggested that she had a new admirer.

Daisy Gibson would later say that in Johannesburg her daughter was friendly with lawyers and, by implication, with other professional people. Apart from the first month of filial supervision, Daisy's only other visit to Johannesburg was in March 1947 to see her daughter in *The Silver Cord* (she seems to have been in the audience every night before taking Gay back to Durban for a brief stay). Further visits were difficult for Daisy once she began work as a night sister in a Durban nursing home. She might have been impressed by the professional men her daughter talked about, or perhaps introduced her to. But really Gay's social life revolved around the world of entertainment which, in the booming city of gold in those carefree postwar days, was fast and furious. She seemed to be living on a permanent 'high', but she had no great opinion of South African men, writing to a friend in England: 'God forbid I should ever have to resign myself to the companionship of a South African male. They don't give a damn for music or the theatre in its artistic aspect.' Her known boyfriends, apart from Mike Abel, included fur dealer, Charles Brown, and a commercial broadcasting agent, Michael Silver.

Then, a week before the first night, Gay introduced Gilbert to 'Charles, my boyfriend'.

Charles Schwentafsky was everything her Baptist parents would have been wary of . . . Polish Jew, night-club owner, legendary seducer of women. The legend was born in Kenya, where his father had gone at the turn of the century to catch animals for the Berlin Zoo. Now, four decades on, Charles's best friend Donald Vincent recalls 'a life spent, to put it crudely, screwing. It wasn't his fault, because the girls literally threw themselves at him. He wasn't particularly handsome, but he was a charming man with a becoming smile, very sexy, penetrating eyes, blond hair, standing five foot ten inches, and a rather large nose, bent over to one side as a result of the recoil from a rifle when downing a bull buffalo.' Apart from seduction, Charles's great loves were hunting, shooting and fishing. He and Donald were once commissioned to capture a pair of colobus monkeys for presentation to the visiting Duke and Duchess of Gloucester, receiving the enormous sum of £15, though the animals died of pneumonia on the way to England. After the war the two men owned the Flamingo, Nairobi's most popular ballroom-restaurant. They ran other businesses as well, and as new cars were hard to get in Kenya, they would go down to South Africa and drive back with their purchases. During one of these visits Charley bought a dry-cleaning firm in Durban. Here he met Daisy, who was bowled over by the charming colonial, and must have suggested that he look up her daughter in Johannesburg.

It seems inconceivable that Gay and Charles were not lovers, but Donald Vincent thinks otherwise. 'Charley was very selective, he didn't just take anything that came along. I am convinced in my own mind that he did not sleep with Gay Gibson.' After her death, when news of the financial assistance became known, Vincent asked his friend, 'You mean to tell me you didn't jump into bed with her?' and Charles replied, 'Donald, I promise you she didn't appeal to me one little bit sexually. I just gave her the money voluntarily.' He is still well remembered in Kenya. Mrs Errol Trzebinski laughs at the mention of 'Porthole Charley, always up to nefarious deeds with women

. . . he was not philanthropic, he didn't pay for Gay's passage for nothing.' And there were the flowers. Eric Boon spoke of 'one particular admirer – a middle-aged man in business in the city – who came to the theatre practically every night and brought her flowers and generally lavished attention on her.' Again, Vincent was not convinced. Flowers after every performance was not his friend's style. 'He would wine and dine them, yes, as an invitation to the waltz, and if they were really good and keeping him warm he might have given them a bit of jewellery. But Charles was not a say-it-with-flowers type.'

So why did Gay Gibson take this precipitate decision to drop out of *Golden Boy*? Her mother spoke of three offers: the Abbey Theatre in Dublin, 'training ground of some of the world's great actresses' [the Gate Theatre was no longer mentioned]; a film job in Hollywood; and a chance in the projected South African National Theatre. Daisy was more than likely embroidering her daughter's film prospects, while the Abbey opening seemed to amount to no more than a letter of introduction from Charley, who had never left Africa and had no known connections with the theatre other than Gay Gibson. There was also a letter of introduction from an early escort, Michael Silver, while Gay's friend Violet Brady wrote 'a reference for her theatrical career' to Mervyn Johns, the Welsh actor whose daughter Glynis was born in South Africa. Had he met Gay, Johns, then playing Shaw's Doolittle at the Lyric Hammersmith in London, might have opened a door by passing her on to his agent. But none of these offers appears to have been firm. Even if they were, they do not explain why she should quit a role which had found favour with the critics. Gay does not seem to have got on well with the play's producer. 'Henry Gilbert has turned out to be a rotter,' Mrs Gibson reported her as saying. 'The way he mauls my back on the stage is most embarrassing.' But she had worked with Gilbert for two months. Perhaps she was exaggerating here to convince her mother that she really needed to get away.

The most likely reason for her sudden departure is that she was pregnant. Friends in Johannesburg could certainly have arranged an abortion, but it would still have meant pulling out

of *Golden Boy*. And there was the danger of her mother hearing
of it. In England, army friends would know the ropes. Evidence of her condition can never be more than circumstantial,
but it is compelling for all that. There is the excitable accusation, levelled in front of the party guests, that Mike Abel had
put her in the family way. Dr Schoub heard more about Gay's
personal fears: 'She discussed sex with me rather intimately.'
One day at the gym class, where Gay was trying to reduce the
size of her hips to Lorna Moon dimensions, she 'told me that
she had had sexual experience and that she was expecting a
period within the next week. That was at the end of July, just
after I had met her. The following week she said that the
expected period had not arrived . . . the next time she spoke
about it she was two weeks overdue.' Dr Schoub asked Gay if
she had used a contraceptive. 'She looked very blankly at me.
She didn't seem to know anything about it and asked me to
explain things to her . . . I advised that she should be fitted
with a Dutch cap.' So Charles Schwentafsky's beneficence
might have been to get her out of the country and back to
England armed with money for an abortion. But if she was
pregnant, was he the father? Gilbert had met him on 29
August, when Gay, not being one to keep her affairs to herself,
had probably not known him for very long. This was several
weeks after the missed period and the hullabaloo over Mike
Abel. She might, in the meantime, have persuaded Charley
that he was the father and he, coining money at that stage of
his life, had perhaps agreed to accept the responsibility.

Gay, on the other hand, could have been genuinely mistaken
about her condition. Dr Schoub did suggest to her that the
strain of rehearsals might be to blame for the missing periods.
Her frantic behaviour, heavy drinking, exhausting life-style at
an altitude of 6,000 feet, combined with the traces of ill-health
somewhere in the system, could have caused menstrual irregularity. Or, she might not have missed her period at all. Gay was
recognised as a line-shooter, telling members of the *Golden Boy*
cast that her parents had been killed by a V-2 bomb and her
brother had died in the navy.

She left for Durban to spend a few days with her family.

There, she visited a doctor and was fitted with a Dutch cap. She was now twenty-one years of age, an adult in law. After the appointment, Gay, as we shall see, continued to spread the word that she was pregnant.

Then she flew to Cape Town to board the *Durban Castle* . . .

3

On the Durban Castle

In 1947, passenger liners were still the most popular way of crossing the ocean. Air travel was in its infancy and, besides, the cost of flying was astronomical. The price of a Pan Am Clipper return flight from London to Johannesburg via Lisbon was £254. The British Overseas Aircraft Corporation's flying boat took off from the Solent on a romantic journey to the Vaal Dam, but several days were needed, and smooth take-offs not guaranteed. So South Africans travelled to Europe on the tried and trusted route, departing on a Union-Castle mailship every Friday afternoon on the fifteen-day voyage from Cape Town to Southampton.

The company's ships carried all the mail and most of the passengers. Northwards went the gold, grapes, oranges and cold chamber lamb; back came mining and agricultural machinery, pedigree cattle, luxury goods for the White bourgeoisie, plus settlers, prospectors, soldiers, sportsmen, and legendary figures like Rider Haggard, Baden-Powell, the big-game hunter F. C. Selous, Cecil Rhodes, Henry Morton Stanley, George Bernard Shaw, Mahatma Gandhi on the *Briton*, Paderewski, in 1912, playing Chopin in the domed saloon of the *Armadale Castle*.

There were other, less welcome travellers. In 1893, a company ship was the scene of an Irish republican settling of scores. The victim, a bricklayer James Carey, had been the ringleader in the assassination of two prominent British officials, Lord Frederick Cavendish and Thomas Burke, in Phoenix Park, Dublin. Carey turned Queen's evidence, and as a result five of his former associates were executed. He was thus a seriously marked man. Under the assumed name of 'Power' the government shipped him to the colonies on the *Kinfauns Castle*, with his wife and seven children. Carey was an incorrigible talker and the secret slipped out in the course of a boozy card-game. But a fellow passenger, Patrick O'Donnell, a Fenian from Donegal, only learned of Carey's real identity from an article in the Cape *Argus* the day the ship docked in Cape Town. The Carey family was immediately transferred to the *Melrose*, bound for Durban. O'Donnell and his wife also bought onward tickets. The following afternoon, in the second-class lounge, O'Donnell shot Carey three times. Fearing that a Cape court would refuse to convict him for an act that many regarded as just vengeance, O'Donnell was shipped back to England on a company steamer, tried and executed at Newgate Prison.

For half a century Union-Castle and South Africa had been almost synonymous, the one contributing to the prosperity of the other. The shipping line's headquarters in Fenchurch Street in the City served as an unofficial embassy for the Union of South Africa, offering a news service, guidebooks, information about emigration. Its Board was littered with former Cabinet Ministers, dukes, peers and knights of the realm.

With the end of the war in view, Sir Vernon Thomson, Union-Castle chairman and managing director, negotiated new, favourable mail and ocean freight agreements with the South African government. Thomson had put the company back on an even keel after the financial ructions of the thirties, but the 'elegant hauteur' of this 'inflexible and notoriously autocratic' Scot did not go down well in South Africa. Afrikaner nationalists complained that General Smuts had been duped by 'clever British shipping magnates'. Still, for Union-Castle the future looked rosy, and it could now embark on the expensive task of replacing the mailship tonnage lost in the war. As a sweetener, one of the new ships would be called *Pretoria Castle*.

Smuts insisted that three large mailships which had done wartime service, as troop carriers, be temporarily converted to immigrant ships. Sensing that the tide of Afrikaner nationalism was running against him, Smuts hoped to flood the country with people of British stock, give them citizenship after two years, and so bolster his electoral prospects. There was little profit in the scheme and Thomson resisted. Smuts then cabled the British Prime Minister Clement Attlee, and the company was persuaded to give way. Daisy and Gay Gibson might have stayed at home had they not been aided by a subsidised passage.

The *Durban Castle* had a proud war record. She was built, like many of the company's craft, by Harland and Wolff in Belfast, length 594 feet, breadth 76 feet, weighing in at over 17,000 tons. Her maiden voyage began on the last day of 1938, an inauspicious time for the intended role of round-Africa milk-run. War came and she was requisitioned as a troopship, with a brief interruption to bring the Greek royal family to Britain from Durban, where they had fled the Germans. Fitted out as an infantry landing ship, in 1942 she led a convoy into Arzeu Bay, Algeria, dropping off the British commandos who secured a beachhead on the eve of the landings in North Africa. In the Sicilian invasion a year later, she was first in again, putting ashore the 41st Marine Commandos. Then followed the beach landings on the Italian mainland. At Pozzuoli she dropped off 2000 Americans, including, it is said, twenty chaplains, and at Anzio she was almost cornered by Italian torpedo boats. Too large for the Normandy landings, she transported troops from Egypt for a wartime invasion of the French Riviera. The toughest assignment was yet to come: repatriating antipodeans. Senior officers who had banned liquor were threatened with their lives. The New Zealanders were a calming influence, one of the ship's officers, Alec Hort, recalls, but 'the Aussies were hardly human, swinging on service pipes in the alleyways and flooding the ship'.

Now, however, the company could at last start thinking about a return to the mailship timetable. James Camb was a steward on the *Capetown Castle* when it sailed out of the Solent in January 1947, 'the first of the mailships to be restored to pre-war standards of elegance and comfort, reviving (almost) forgotten memories of luxurious ocean travel'. Three trips later Camb switched to the *Durban Castle*, which had been refurbished and attached to the mail run for the time being.

The second round trip on the *Durban Castle* sailed from Southampton on 10 September 1947, with a full complement of 180 passengers in the first class. Among them were the Springbok cricket tourists, relieved to be seeing the end of an English summer of humiliation at the hands of Edrich and Compton. The ship's regular Master, Gorringe, was absent for some reason. Having signed the completed 'agreement and list of crew' that very day, he must have pulled out at the last moment. So the man who piloted the liner on its most fateful peacetime voyage was the company's relieving Master, Arthur Patey, a conscientious Scot, tall, aloof, respected by his underlings. He ran a strict ship, according to Alec Hort, then the ship's first officer, and was not the sort of man one got familiar with. He was a 'bit of a martinet', in fact, with his own private standing orders for senior officers over and above the company rules. The aloofness masked a shy nature. Another friend, Frank Marriott, describes Patey as 'a nervous fellow, a terrible host, for whom it was purgatory to be on a passenger liner, but all right on a small ship'.

Patey, indeed any Master of a modern passenger ship, needed to be more wary of his crew than of his senior officers. The war had altered on-board attitudes and behaviour. In the high unemployment of the thirties, men and women were grateful to find work on ships. Then 30,000 merchant seamen (and 50,000 in the Royal Navy) died at sea during the war and the pendulum swung to a buyer's market. Shipping companies could no longer be choosy. On occasion they were faced with taking on men and women they knew little about, although they continued to employ only British personnel. Just one foreigner, a Spanish cook who had lived in Britain for many years, figures on the *Durban Castle* crew list. The mailships did not even take on South Africans, although the Coloured people living in the coastal towns had an established seagoing tradition. British men of colour were rarely employed either, out of respect for South African racial practice: Union-Castle had no wish to jeopardise business contracts when they came up for renewal. (Change was on the way, however. The 'News about Ships' section of the Cape *Argus* reported on a 'socialist' liner, the Blue Funnel's *Antenor*, whose European and Coloured seamen enjoyed practically the same standard of accommodation, with crew, officers and passengers eating the same food, although Chinese and European crew members would continue to have separate quarters and galleys.)

Under the terms of their agreement, the crew agreed to 'conduct themselves in an orderly, faithful, honest and sober manner, and to be at all times diligent in their respective Duties and to be obedient . . . to the lawful commands of the Master . . . ' But many signatories had recently come out of the other side of hell. They were up to all kinds of tricks, broaching cargo, drunkenness ashore, answering out of turn. A crafty steward could buy liquor in port, sell it to passengers after closing-time, and pocket the cash. Penalties for misdemeanours had not increased since the Shipping Act of 1894. Enforcement of discipline was not helped by the fact that Camb and other seamen were not company servants, but 'unestablished seafarers', casual employees flitting from ship to ship, company to company, with no reason to acquire corporate allegiance. Standards, however, had not disappeared altogether. In 1947, dining-room staff were still made to assemble in the bureau square outside the purser's office and hold out hands and nails for a cleanliness check.

Passenger discipline had slipped as well. As late as 1914 a company rule required 'unaccompanied ladies' to go inside once the deck lights were subdued at half past ten in the evening. Murray, the Union-Castle historian, noted that this meant, in effect, female passengers having to retire to their cabins, for lounge lights were extinguished at the same time, and ladies were not permitted to enter the smoking room. 'After the war, there began a gradual encroachment on the smoking room, until by the middle twenties ladies could no longer be barred from this one-time sanctuary of males.'

Signs of tension and unruliness on the *Durban Castle* were by now bubbling up below decks, though passengers would not have been aware of it. John Havers, purser on a sister ship, recalls that she was known to have 'a bad crew'. The outward log gives an idea of the Master's problems, though we know from the absence of any mention of Camb's alleged misbehaviour that not everything was reported. Edward Riordan, a third assistant cook, was fined ten shillings for bringing intoxicating liquor on board in Madeira, and another ten shillings for drunkenness. This is run-of-the-mill stuff, but behind the scenes, an assistant purser, John Coulton, was giving every sign of having a nervous breakdown. Another assistant, a 'bit of a tearaway' on his first trip, was on the run from police. The chief purser, Ollie Middleton, a fussy soul remembered by Hort for his habit of ironing one-pound notes, was slow in coping. As a result, the pursers were behind on the staff's wage packets, an omission calculated to cause consternation as the crew readied themselves for the next round of shebeens and bordellos. Coulton was hospitalised in Cape Town, and replaced by Steward Downing, a purser on the immigrant ship *Carnarvon Castle*, about to sail northwards with few passengers.

There was more tension aboard as the ship sailed round the coast, making further demands on the Master's correctional duties. In Port Elizabeth a dining steward, Daniel Fortune, insulted the chief steward, Mr Holfert-Knight, in the first-class dining saloon, followed him into his office and 'started shouting at him whilst there. Being ordered by the Chief Steward to leave the office on account of his insolent attitude, Fortune refused to go.' Patey fined him the usual ten shillings for insolence and the same again 'for refusal to obey a lawful command'. When this charge was read out to him by the Master, Fortune was argumentative, failed to admit to the offence and disputed the fines. But he did pay up. And received two 'VGs' at Southampton. In Durban, more banal minitrials took place, as fights broke out or crew members went AWOL. Once the ship left Cape Town, with only one port of call remaining, and a small passenger list, all should have been well.

The southern tip of Africa in early spring, temperature 68°F. General Albert Orsborn of the Salvation Army, returning from a tour of Kenya, Rhodesia and South Africa, was being serenaded from the quayside by the local Sally Ally band. Camb was not alone in noticing Gay Gibson's arrival. The crime writer Benjamin Bennett was in the first-class lounge seeing off a friend. 'Nearby, centre of a small group, was a dark, attractive woman with a startlingly white skin and creamy complexion, unlike that of the average South African woman, who spoke vivaciously and laughed easily. Her vivacity, however, seemed a trifle strained and her laugh, though it came readily enough, seemed as though it might be turned off and on to order.' Bennett later caught sight of her walking along 'B' Deck, 'with gifts of flowers from friends . . . ' Wendy Noakes, a fellow passenger, talks of 'Gay wearing an obviously imitation white fur coat, very ostentatious, flung over her shoulders'.

At four o'clock prompt on 10 October 1947 the first-class gangway was lowered, the *Durban Castle* and its cargo of mail and fresh fruit nosed out of Duncan Dock into Table Bay, the harbour pilot climbed into his launch, and aided by a fresh-to-strong south-easterly, she opened her engines for the journey northward. Gay Gibson went down to cabin 126 to unpack . . .

Her cabin was on the Shade or 'B' Deck, on the port or left-hand side. Below her, on 'A' Deck, crew cabins were forward and cabin-class accommodation aft. The better first-class cabins were on 'C' Deck, while 'D' or Promenade Deck comprised the lounges and public rooms. Above was the Boat Deck and then the small Sun Deck, for the exclusive enjoyment of first-class passengers.

With only fifty-seven people travelling in the first class, every passenger, single men and women too, enjoyed the luxury of a portholed cabin. The wind was up and the nights were cool, and portholes would remain closed until the tropics. At dinner on the Friday evening the chief steward placed the young Wendy Noakes and her husband, Bindy, together with an elderly lady, at the captain's table. Gay was seated in a threesome with Frank Hopwood, the Union-Castle catering manager in Cape Town, and Wing Commander William Bray, RAF. Bandmaster Innocent offered tunes from *The Pirates of Penzance* and a medley of waltzes from the 'Vienna Woods'. Most passengers retired early that first evening, but a few sipped a nightcap in the austere smoking room, bottles of spirits hidden from view and the patrons served at tables. Sir Vernon Thomson, the company boss, was a total abstainer with decided views on other people's drinking habits, if not on the profits accruing from the sale of liquor. The ship creaked gently to the motion of the Cape rollers. During the night the clocks were put back one hour.

The passengers settled smartly into the routine. By mid-morning a hardy huddle of deck quoiters was in evidence, along with geriatric shuffleboarding and rare sightings of ping pong. Bridge fiends were busy seeking each other out. There was a well-stocked library for the bookish and the daily news-sheet kept informed those anxious about the chill in Soviet-Western friendship or the worsening turn of events in Palestine. You watched the sprightly middleagers from your steamer chair or leaned across the rails screwing your eyes to the horizon. At eleven, Camb served cups of consommé or ice-cream, weather depending, on the poolside veranda. After lunch, the elderly lay down, the few children were dispatched to the nursery. Captain Patey popped in to Mandy Noakes' second birthday party with a present of a toy dog. Evenings were devoted to housey-housey (yet to be called bingo), a film, or that hallowed institution, the Ocean Derby, where the 'jockey' cutting a tape fastest won 'The Capricorn Canter', 'The Naughtical Oaks' or 'The Scissorawitch'. The dividing-line between 'First' and 'Cabin' blurred over the equator, as King Neptune classlessly dumped first-time line-crossers into the swimming pool.

Eating, and preparing for eating, were the waymarks which guided the travellers through the day. Though the Durban Castle was a British ship, the severe rules of food rationing at home did not apply. A first-class diner might choose from an hors d'oeuvres of Mousse de Foie-Gras sur Canapé, Mixed Olives, Smoked Trout, Sardines in Oil, Anchovies Norvégienne or Légumes Orientale, followed by consommé or velouté, then turbot, ox tongue, Braised Chicken with Bath Chaps or Roast Haunch of Lamb Boulangère, with vegetables and salads to match, sweets like Pudding au Malaga and Almond Sauce, Pêche Melba, friandises, followed, with a savoury flourish, by Curried Prawns with Rice.

Belowdecks the crew tucked into their minimal entitlement under the 1945 Merchant Shipping (Seamen's Provisions) Order, a meticulously detailed weekly allowance of 4lb 11oz of fresh meat (including fresh offal or fresh sausage); 8oz of smoked ham or bacon; 20oz of fresh fish; two eggs; 7lb of potatoes; 6oz of rice (if not procurable, semolina would do); 7lb of soft bread, though if rough weather, illness, the absence of the cook or force majeure rendered the making of bread impracticable, an equivalent amount of biscuit stored in sealed tins could be issued instead; plus curry powder (¼oz), pickles, cheese, suet, coffee (containing not more than 25 per cent chicory), etc., etc. There was a page in the logbook for the Master to record the 'refusal or neglect of any seaman or apprentice to take lime or lemon juice', although this admirable anti-scurvy precaution would by then have been unnecessary.

The first-class passengers had an occupation even more amusing than deck games. They itched, in a discreet way, to find out more about the youngest adult in their midst, this arresting woman so out of character with the middle-aged-to-elderly couples, the family groups, tobacco farmers and war veterans. 'Everyone had their eye on her,' says Wendy Noakes, 'and if anyone talked to her, you would hear the whisper, "Look who's talking to her now."'

The chief purser, Ollie Middleton, invited a selection of passengers for cocktails, and Gay and her table companions were there. It was the only time Wendy Noakes met Gay. 'I found her completely dumb . . . she had little to say for herself and sat humming tunes from the shows she had acted in.' She told Mrs Noakes, who was from Birkenhead, that she came from Rock Ferry in Cheshire, 'and she certainly had a marked Merseyside accent, though not in the Beatles category . . . her appearance was fairly striking, small, slightly plump, with deep auburn hair and the alabaster skin that accompanies it. Somewhat flashily dressed, she was what I always describe as "a bit tarty", though I mean no ill by that and must admit that she and her constant companions behaved quietly. I don't think they drank excessively and I don't remember them partaking in shipboard activities except for dancing.' Mrs Noakes admits that the passengers were 'not frightfully illuminating people, so two unattached beaux were glad to find each other and her'.

William Bray, dark, good-looking, from Plymouth, was forty years old. He had been in the Royal Air Force before the war and rose through the ranks to become a wing commander. After contracting tuberculosis in Burma, he was brought back to the British Army's Baragwanath Hospital outside Johannesburg – now the leading hospital for Blacks in South Africa – for the prolonged treatment. When the royal couple visited the hospital, Queen Elizabeth (now the Queen Mother) singled Bray out for a chat; by then, according to a fellow patient, Bill Bray was 'fully recovered and left hospital in good health, anxious to get home and start life again, probably as a civilian'. Now he was returning to join his wife and family in Chichester. The other 'beau' was Frank Hopwood, in his late forties, who, as a company man, merited a cabin on the prized Promenade Deck. A family friend has described him as 'not a charmer, just a lovable family man . . . there was nothing special about Uncle Frank, but he was of the old school'.

If Wendy Noakes was unimpressed by Gay Gibson, her view of Camb the steward was uncomplicatedly laudatory: 'A very personable young man, and quite the best steward on the ship . . . efficient and always cheerful . . . delightful with the children, and as a deck steward was much in contact with them.' A minor incident on the Promenade Deck came back to her forty years afterwards. When she ordered a drink for her daughter Mandy, who was playing with a friend, 'and what will your boyfriend have' Camb asked her. This easy-going charm in the presence of his social superiors, the mixture of deference and cheek, marked him out from the flock. Belowdecks, though, he was mostly on his own, either because he wanted it that way or because the crewmen did not much care for him. Joe Chidgey, steward in the smoking room and a faithful friend, admitted that Jim 'could get belligerent if he didn't get his own way'. The work was not hard, but the hours were long. You turned to at 5.45 a.m. and though there were rest periods during the day, four hours of compulsory overtime meant getting to your bunk well after midnight. When downing a pint of Allsop's in the Pig, the crew's bar, James Camb was a man with other things on his mind. Back in his cramped 'A' Deck cabin, the extrovert loner from Waterfoot would be polishing his shoes, ironing his whites, showering regularly, readying himself fastidiously for the next on-deck performance.

James Camb's patch on the *Durban Castle* was the spacious Promenade Deck and the Long Gallery running off it, a quiet place lined with tables and chairs, giving a bird's-eye view of the sea. Here was the first-class leisure area: swimming pool, smoking room, library, lounge. Camb's 'office' on the Promenade Deck was the pantry, and there was a locker big enough to house perhaps a hundred deckchairs. It was a plum job, complete with a subordinate 'deckman' performing the more menial tasks of putting out games and quoits. The deck steward served tea and drinks, distributed deckchairs, comforted the seasick, made the elderly cosy, legs warm and rheumatism protected beneath the rug. Here Gay and Jim made their first informal contact.

After breakfast on the first morning out, Gay seated herself in a bay window in the Long Gallery. How her world had changed! She had travelled south in an overcrowded immigrant ship, the chaperone's eye of her mother constantly upon her, with little chance to exercise her natural exuberance. Now, a bare six months later, on her own in the unheard-of luxury of a first-class cabin, two reliable married men were promising to stand the rounds, and there was Charley's windfall to fall back on when they didn't. We cannot be sure of her state of mind as she sat there, but sailors know that once a liner moves away from the harbour, passengers may leave behind their normal constraints. For some, anything goes. Alec Hort, one of the company's most experienced sailors, noticed this change particularly in women, observed them relaxing, becoming their natural self: 'People put on a severe face ashore and two days after the ship gets to sea they not only change health and appearance but pour out their hearts in a way they would

41

never do at home.'

Gay called Camb over and ordered a drink. When he returned they indulged in idle chatter, at first about the quality and types of drink carried on the ship. Then Gay, her garrulousness perhaps set off by the morning alcohol, started talking about her acting career, about Eric Boon, and finally about 'Charles'. She told Camb 'she was very fond of this man, but possible complications may have set in'. The steward was not slow to pick up the cue, asking jokingly, 'You don't mean to tell me you are going to have a baby?' It was rather too soon to know, Gay replied. Camb: 'Well, if that is the position, why don't you marry the man?' It wasn't that easy, Gay told him; Charles was already married.

As Camb made a move to serve other passengers, the discussion took a more surprising turn. Was it possible, Gay asked, to have tea served in her cabin, where she would be having her afternoon rest. Here was a dilemma for a lusting deck steward, for whom cabins, corridors leading to them, even passages off which the corridors ran, were out of bounds, the strict preserve of the cabin staff. Camb explained that she should ring the bedroom steward, who would collect the tea-tray which he (Camb) would prepare on the deck. That afternoon, Walter Matthews, the bedroom steward, came up to tell Camb that the passenger in cabin 126 had requested him (Camb) to take it down. Camb: 'I then pointed out the undesirability . . . we compromised . . . he took the tray and I went with him.' So, to Gay's surprise, two stewards appeared with the one tea-tray. Camb repeated the rules to her, and anyway, he said, at four o'clock he was very busy serving tea on deck. Perhaps she wanted some other service in her cabin at some other time of the day? 'She asked if it would be possible to have a tray at supper-time.' 'Supper-time' was at 11.00 p.m., and Camb now arranged for the nightwatchman, who came on duty at ten, to pick up the tray prepared by him and take it to her cabin. So, early on in the voyage, Camb was responsible for standing orders for afternoon and late-evening trays in Gay's cabin. On the Thursday, she added a third order – after the bar had closed for the night, he should leave a large glass of rum for her on the bottle locker outside his pantry.

The sole 'official' version of these events is Camb's evidence at the trial. Eleven years later, in a lengthy debriefing with the *Sunday Pictorial* on leaving prison, he gave a more elaborate account of that first encounter. It was clearly not Camb's style, but what shines through is his rampant conceit: 'Perhaps it was an unlucky chance for both of us that she was the only attractive young woman on my deck . . . She asked for another drink – but in such a way that I felt instinctively that I need not be lonely on the fourteen-day voyage back to Southampton.' Again: 'She had the trick of tucking her long legs under the chair, clasping her knees with her hands and throwing back her head as she spoke . . . I found myself watching her sitting in this quiet corner of the gallery as I was serving drinks to other passengers. Even when the gallery filled just before dinner we would steal glances across the crowded table. When she was chatting to friends she had made on board, I felt her eyes following me.' There is no way of knowing whether this account of unspoken communications with a woman long dead was to be believed. Had Camb offered it as evidence, it might have backfired on him.

'Every morning,' the *Pictorial* version continued, 'she would be at her usual table, sitting alone. I would bring her a drink without waiting for her order. One morning she said, "Have one for yourself, later." She began to talk about her life in Johannesburg, her gay, show-business friends, her ambition to be a top actress.' But for Camb her request to bring a tray to her cabin 'meant only one thing – she wanted me to visit her. So I waited my opportunity . . . '

A day or two after the outpourings in the Long Gallery, Eileen Field, a stewardess who worked with Camb, had the first of her contretemps with the deck steward. She was returning Gay's afternoon tea-tray to his pantry and Camb asked her if she knew that Miss Gibson was three months' pregnant. The stewardess, who was also a trained nurse, seemed surprised, irritated perhaps, at this intimate titbit from the life of a first-class passenger. If it was true, she thought, it was a dangerous thing to say.

Apart from the glass or two of morning spirits, afternoon siestas and the constant companionship of Bray and Hopwood in the dining saloon and smoking room, little is known of Gay's shipboard activities. There is no evidence even of the after-breakfast deck circumnavigation considered mandatory by the sedentary voyager. Mr Noakes heard rumours that the trio had been 'slumming' in cabin class one evening, but not even that less than earth-shattering piece of intelligence could be sub-stantiated. Later there would be rumours of sexual activity – with officers, passengers – but if they were true, those involved kept their own counsel. Nightwatchman Murray saw Gay and Jim talking 'on two or three occasions' after he had come on duty, which was at 10.30 p.m. Every night at around eleven-thirty Hopwood took her down 'to see her to her cabin . . . UUturned the lights on, said good-night and then went back to my cabin'. There were no daytime cabin visits, he said – though Miss Field mentioned that it was Hopwood who ordered Gay's afternoon tray of tea. Indeed, Camb seemed jealous of the Union-Castle man, telling Gay that 'he was taking a fatherly interest in her'.

It is to Hopwood that we are indebted for an idea of the state of Gay's health. One morning, she drew his attention to her fingernails, which had changed to a 'muddy colour'. Some-times their colour was normal, he said, sometimes they changed. Do you remember, he was asked at the trial, an occasion when the girl was wheezy and said she would have to have an injection? Hopwood: 'That is correct.' Did you ask her anything about these injections? 'No,' Hopwood replied, 'but she said they were something to do with her vocal cords.' Gay, he observed, was rather depressed at times and appeared tired and worried. Was that her normal condition, he was asked, or did she appear worried some days and not on others? Hopwood: 'She was more or less like that all the time, with the exception of one evening when she seemed to brighten up.' Did she have drinks occasionally to cheer her up? – 'Yes, but she did not drink much.' Judging from this account, Gay Gibson would seem to have had something more worrying on her mind than the prospect of a London stage breakthrough.

The signs of bodily ill-health might have been a delayed reaction to the hectic months on and off stage in the high veld. Perhaps she no longer merited an 'A1' army medical clearance.

Number 126 was one of four cabins giving on to a small passage which led into the main port-side corridor. It was octagonal, one wall being the ship's side, with the porthole over the bed, while four bulkheads made up the division with cabin 124, occupied by an elderly lady. The head of Gay's bed rested against the partition with cabin 128, which was empty. Otherwise, the sleeping passenger's head would have been inches away from Gay's. You left the cabin to go to the toilet and bathroom. Baths were conveniently placed at the end of the corridor, but Gay had to cross to the starboard side for the ladies' lavatory. Passengers were discouraged from bolting cabin doors at night, but when Miss Field brought the tea-tray in the morning she always had to wait for Gay to unlock hers. She was nervous because there were so few passengers in her section, she explained to the stewardess. What did she do in there? Rehearse her songs in front of the mirror, sip her rum, climb on the bed to peer out of the porthole at the flying fish? We do know that she tied Charley's love-letters in pink ribbon. She opened them from time to time, wrote on them 'How I love you', imprinted lipsticked kisses. If James Camb could think of little else but Gay Gibson, she seems to have had room for alternative erotic fantasies. The letters were not seen in court.

So the first seven days of the *Durban Castle*'s homeward cruise were peaceful enough. The equator was crossed, the nights were warm and still, and – as if reflecting the tranquil mood of the ship – the noise of the sea was barely discernible through the open portholes.

4

Death on the Shade Deck

A week at sea, halfway home. The *Durban Castle* steamed off Sierra Leone, making a comfortable eighteen knots. There had not been much in the way of lively entertainment in the first class, but on the second Friday night out passengers were togging up in their finest regalia for the dinner dance. At a quarter to seven Miss Field called at cabin 126 to find the incumbent in a 'very happy and very cheerful' mood, dressed in a sleek black evening frock with complementing silver shoes. The stewardess folded the bedspread and turned down the top sheet. If, by a quirk of the tropical climate, a storm lowered the temperature, there were blankets in the wardrobe.

Miss Field certainly had the cocky deck steward, Camb, uppermost in her mind. Earlier that afternoon there had been another exchange over the question of the tea-tray. Miss Gibson told the stewardess that she had not received the tray, and when the information was passed on to Camb he had seemed put out. He must have made a move to discover the facts for himself, from the cabin, for the stewardess had to warn him that if he did go down she would report him to the chief steward. 'I said it more or less jocularly. I had no idea that he would attempt to go to the cabin, and it was said in a friendly tone.' Whatever her recollection of the interchange, her tone of voice must have sounded resolute enough, for the warning stopped Camb in his tracks, suggesting that by now Camb had an easy-going relationship with Gay, or at least believed he had. Indeed, his claim to be 'on extremely friendly terms' with her may have been justified by the series of chats on the Promenade Deck which followed their initial open-hearted meeting. Was he now suspicious of her, thinking she might have someone in her cabin or be in someone else's? A deck steward was well placed to monitor the activities of passengers and officers.

Dinner was taken as usual with her two escorts, followed by coffee in the Long Gallery. At eight, Mr Innocent and his musicians struck up a slow waltz on the Promenade Deck, hoping to lure the unpromising patrons on to the dance floor. There was a 'Paul Jones', but the groups kept demurely to themselves. The Noakeses shared a table with a Rhodesian tobacco farmer, John Butler, a retiring sort who was seriously embarrassed when the orchestra burst into a 'Happy Birthday' for him. Hopwood was not a dancer, but Gay did a turn with Wing Commander Bray, and with the elderly 'Sport' Pienaar, president of the South African Rugby Union, who was travelling to a meeting in London. According to Hopwood, she had 'only two or three drinks' and smoked 'very little'. She was the belle of the ball, and her infrequent appearances on the floor may have been due simply to a paucity of partners willing or able to dance with her. At eleven the music stopped, and Gay and friends sat for a while, sipping their drinks and chatting.

Darkness and the faint breeze had cooled the air hardly at all. There was talk of a midnight swim. Gay left to change into her bathing costume. In the Long Gallery she was hailed by Camb. 'I say,' he boomed, 'I have a bone to pick with you, and a big one at that.' The ship's senior nightwatchman, Jim Murray, on his first patrol of the evening, was taken aback at the frankness of the approach. But the first-class passenger did not seem to take offence. 'Why?' she asked. Neither the supper tray he had prepared the previous night nor the tea-tray had been touched. The night had been so hot, she told him, rum was all she wanted, and at tea-time that afternoon she was still asleep.

She ordered another rum, a double, in all probability, and paid for it. He arranged to leave the glass on the bottle box on the Promenade Deck. Gay continued down to her cabin, but Camb followed her there, presumably having assured himself that the nightwatchman was not about. Never short of a ready pretext for his behaviour, Camb 'asked her, did she require her supper tray or lemonade (for the rum) and she said neither. I said had she found her swimming costume, and she said, no, it must have been in one of the other trunks. I said to her in a half-joking fashion, "I have a good mind to bring a drink down and join you."' Her reply? 'I am not sure of the exact words, but I think she said, "Please yourself, it's up to you."' He slipped back to the bar to attend to his thirsty customers.

Gay returned to her companions in the smoking room and the idea of the late-night dip, if it ever had been serious, was dropped. The three sat and chatted until around midnight, then adjourned to the deck where they perched over the rail for another forty minutes. Now Hopwood accompanied her to her cabin, switched on the light and bade her goodnight. And left. Within minutes, however, Gay was up on the Promenade Deck once again. It was one o'clock by now. Bill Conway, the bosun's mate and ship's maintenance man, was in charge of a working party washing down the port-side deck. He saw Gay, still in black dress and silver shoes, leaning on the rail smoking a cigarette. 'She would have got wet if she had remained there, so I directed her to the midships on the port side . . . She said she found it rather warm down below and I advised her to sit in one of the deckchairs . . . She bade me goodnight and carried on.' As we shall see, Conway's version of this conversation was not quite as he first recounted it.

Towards 12.45, Bill Pott, assistant steward in the smoking room, saw Camb washing glasses in the pantry. Pott offered to give him a hand, but Jim had other plans. Because they shared a cabin, Jim would have had to go down with him when they finished, if he were not to arouse suspicion. Pott: ' . . . he said it was all right, he could manage. I then went away.'

The tumbler of rum had been left for Gay on the bottle box. While stacking the chairs, soon after 12.45 a.m., Camb noticed that it had gone. In its place was an alarm clock, which he supposed was hers. The clock was normally to be found on the chest of drawers in her cabin. Within seconds, there she was, standing on the deck, rum in one hand, cigarette in the other. Was it her clock? he inquired. Yes, and he handed it to her, and returned to the pantry. What did this interlude signify? Was the placement of the hands a signal for the hour of an assignation, to Camb, or to someone else? By now, several members of the crew had remarked on the frequent chats between passenger and deck steward. In private, he seems to have been on equal terms with her, comfortably joky, chiding at times. Now she had drunk her fair share – two or three at the dance, a double rum from Camb. The dreamy music and the boredom of the evening might have set her off. For the deck steward, the flirtation of the tea-trays, the double rums, the alarm clock, the 'please yourself', could now move to a conclusion. Soon after one, he locked the pantry and slipped down to the Shade Deck.

The cabin was empty – door unlocked, light on, but no sign of Gay. Perhaps he went up to the Promenade Deck for a scout-around, ever watchful for nightwatchman Murray. Frustrated, he returned to the crew area, there to bide his time on the Well Deck. Camb's lawyer Joshua Casswell would point out that 'when a steward courts a first-class passenger he has to wait upon her time; class distinctions are sometimes valid even in sexual matters.'

An hour later, at two o'clock, Camb returned to the cabin, tapped lightly on the door and found it unbolted. She was there. But where had she been before? She might, of course, have returned within moments of Camb's departure, after a visit to the toilet or bathroom. Having already spoken to bosun's mate Conway about the heat, she might have climbed to the Boat Deck, the highest point on the ship open to passengers, in search of a breath of air, perhaps on the port side where any breeze heading towards the coast crossed the ship. But so striking a figure would more than likely have been observed by one of the ubiquitous nightwatchmen or by an officer or seaman on the early watch. It has to be asked whether, in that missing hour, or half- or quarter-hour, she was to be found in someone else's cabin? Officers have a rule – avoid encounters with ladies in your own quarters; entertain preferably on their patch. A passenger, then? Camb never asked for – nor did she offer – an explanation for keeping him waiting.

Gay was wearing a yellow quilted dressing gown and

slippers. She settled herself back on the pillow; her visitor sat on the edge of the bed. The cabin was lit by the small cylindrical light on the bulkhead above her head. He had brought her more rum, and she sipped it as they chatted desultorily about how dull the dance had been. After a while, she put her glass on the chest of drawers and the yearnings slid into love-play. She unzipped the gown right down the front to reveal her nakedness beneath. Camb fondled her breasts . . . (Other versions were heard in court: that there was 'a certain amount of preliminary love-play' and 'he made love to her and finally got on to the bed with her and intercourse took place'.)

Years later, again, perhaps, with the benefit of imaginative hindsight, Camb related how, ' . . . as I pulled her towards me and kissed the nape of her neck, I had second thoughts about the (unlocked) cabin door. She smiled and said: "It doesn't matter, nobody will come in. We will be quite safe." Those were the last words she ever spoke.'

Did they get 'into' bed or 'on to' it? Camb did say in court that there was no folded blanket at the foot of the bed, and, more to the point, that the top sheet was folded back halfway. Gay was certainly not lying 'in' the bed, that is, between the sheets, during the early stages. She was known to be feeling the heat, and when the going was about to become more physical it is inconceivable that they would have arranged themselves under the top sheet in the style of Victorian suburbanites. Yet, had the lawyers been more aware of the exigencies of tropical love-making, the question of the sheets might just, as we shall see in a later chapter, have influenced the final verdict.

Intercourse took place 'missionary style'. Camb unloosened his belt and unfastened his trousers; we are left to decide whether he took them off altogether or allowed them to hang round his ankles. He lay 'on top of Miss Gibson; I was face down . . . her head was in the crook of my left arm, my right arm resting on her hip. Her right hand was around my neck; and her left hand holding my right arm . . . ' He provided two versions of what followed. At the trial: 'Just as intercourse would normally have come to an end she suddenly heaved under me as though she was gasping for breath, as though she was taking a deep breath . . . (her body) stiffened for a fraction of a second and then relaxed completely limp . . . her right arm was still round my neck when she heaved against me. That arm automatically tightened, and the left arm, holding my right forearm, gripped tightly. All this happened in a matter of seconds.' The *Sunday Pictorial* post-prison account was briefer: ' . . . time came to a stop. Gay began to moan as I clasped her to me. She gripped my arms; her nails dug into my flesh. But I felt no pain . . . suddenly, her whole body stiffened in my arms, her back arched in a violent spasm . . . she heaved a long, tired sigh and her head lolled awkwardly to one side . . . her eyes opened wide and fixed me with a sightless stare . . . '

The 'pain factor' was a perplexing hole in his story, yet he would persist in denying that the deep scratches on his right hand above the wrist were made by Gay's pointed nails. What was it that caused her to drive her fingers so deeply into his forearm – the ecstasy of an approaching orgasm, a frantic attempt to lift the hands of a strangler from the throat, or a death spasm?

He must have held her for several seconds, wondering at her complete surrender to his charms. Then it dawned on him that she had passed out, or worse. He jumped off the bed. Her body lay crooked across the bunk like a broken doll. She looked completely relaxed, as in a dead faint, one eye slightly open. Her mouth was also open, 'with a faint line of bubbles, which I assumed to be froth, just on the edges of her lips . . . a muddy colour . . . slightly blood-flecked.' He could find no pulse. He put his ear to her chest, listening for a heartbeat. There was none. He massaged the stomach towards the heart in an effort to restore circulation. No change, not surprisingly, for he had no experience in artificial respiration. He thought of smelling salts, but that drawing-room remedy was not to hand. For twenty, possibly twenty-five minutes, he worked feverishly on her inert body. A doctor was close by, literally seconds away, but if the idea of calling him crossed Camb's mind, he banished it instantly; he had broken company rules, and this time the consequences must be handled by him alone.

By now it was three o'clock in the morning, the deadest hour. The only sound in the cabin was the slow, rhythmic creaking of the ship as she ploughed through the waves. Not even the curtain over the porthole fluttered. Suddenly, a light tap on the door, and someone was opening it. Camb stepped across smartly, pushed up against the door so that it opened no more than a couple of inches. 'It's all right,' he said, ramming the door closed and switching the bolt. The position of the curtain over the aperture lulled Camb into thinking he had not been identified, but he knew that an immediate report would be made to the duty officer on the bridge. He was seized by a feeling of 'complete panic'. Afterwards, he would not be able to recall the thought processes which invaded his mind, nor how much time elapsed as he moved towards his awful solution. There is no doubt that he did agonise, but over his own predicament, not over the woman lying immobile before him. 'I knew that in the circumstances of being found in a lady passenger's cabin I should lose my job, and forfeit any chance of employment in any shipping company for that matter.' The cosy, convenient Glasgow nook, the loving wife and daughter, offering him the only real home he had ever known . . . the humiliation of his wife Margaret, learning of his philanderings . . . worse, an end to those philanderings! As he wrote later, 'I thought of my fifteen years at sea. The war years, the riotous days and nights ashore, the laughing, half-forgotten girls from Hong Kong to Sydney. The happy years as a first-class deck steward with the Union-Castle line.'

Despite his panic at the realisation that the incident would be reported, Camb claims to have tried resuscitation for a further quarter of an hour. Then it seemed that 'the touch of her body was slightly cooler', and he concluded that she was dead. The solution, he decided, was to push her through the porthole. 'I confess it sounds very foolish,' he was to explain, 'but I hoped to give the impression that she had fallen overboard, and deny all knowledge of having been in that cabin, in the hope that the captain's further inquiries would not be too severe.'

It has to be assumed that the cool, calculating feel of this witness-box explanation belied a rather more turbulent course of decision-making. However, if he was trying to feign a suicide, there were some things in its favour. Hopwood and Bray had noted Gay's depression and other signs that all was not well with her health; there was the talk of pregnancy and the sudden departure from South Africa, which was known to Camb. That evening he had observed her appearance on deck with a glass in her hand, and then her absence for an hour when she might plausibly have thrown herself overboard in a moment of rum-induced hysteria.

On the other hand, stage-managing a faked suicide was out of the question once it was known that a man had been in her cabin. That man would soon enough be narrowed down to deck steward Camb, thanks to their widely-observed chats, his altercations with stewardess Field, and richly-deserved reputation of 'tomming'. Besides, his palm-prints were firmly implanted on the inside of the door.

It was no easy matter to pass a fully-grown woman through a porthole of the *Durban Castle*. Freddy Banham, later a steward on the same ship, considered that 'you needed precision, strength and dexterity. If she was resisting, she only had to move her head slightly, up, down, or sideways . . . ' Even if she was dead, the diameter of 16¾ inches allowed little room for limp limbs and lolling head. The porthole, 4 feet 7⅝ inches from the floor, was handily placed above the bed. Camb 'lifted her up to a sitting position, and then lifted her with my hands just above her hips, to the porthole . . . pushed her arms through and then her head'. With the body now halfway out, her stomach rested on the foot-wide recess, her legs, partly covered by the open yellow dressing gown, dangled in the cabin. He lifted the legs and shot the body out. Gay Gibson dropped twenty-five feet and the man heard the splash as she entered the water. The nearest land, the Portuguese colony of Guinea, was ninety miles away.

Camb was sure the noise was not heard on the bridge. The motion of the ship, he explained, 'gives a certain amount of backwash and the initial wave of the bow cutting through the sea washes back past the ship and creates a suction noise'.

Now Camb switched off the light. He would have listened

for a sign of movement outside, opened the door tentatively, looked down the short corridor, peered out again into the main passageway, then slunk through the ship, to his cabin on the deck below, where Pott, Chidgey and the others slept peacefully. It was half past three, and though desperate for a cigarette, he might have thought it best to forego the last luxury of his day.

But even as Camb fell into what should have been a fitful sleep, his latest escapade had set off a significant chain of events. It was the days before the master-at-arms patrolled Union-Castle ships, though this practice had already been introduced on Cunard's transatlantic liners. Surveillance was performed by the nightwatchman, who saw that crewmen kept out of mischief with passengers. Early on Saturday 18 October, Jim Murray and his deputy, Fred Steer, were idling away the dog hours in their 'pantry' on 'A' Deck. You had difficulty keeping your head off the table, while waiting for the next security tramp round the decks. So quiet a passage was it that the Master had made no entry in the log since leaving Cape Town. At 2.58 a.m. the silence was shattered by the ringing of the buzzer above their heads. It cut off after a second-and-a-half. Calls from cabins were unusual at this hour, but with several doddery passengers on board it might have been a distress signal. Steer responded briskly, hurrying up the two flights of stairs to the first-class entrance hall on 'B' Deck where the indicator board showed that two bells had been rung in the port-side alleyway. He hurried there to find red and green lights illuminated, which meant that both 'steward' and 'stewardess' buttons had been pushed in 126. Matters looked all the more urgent.

Steer was at the door of cabin 126 within a minute of the call. The light was on inside. He knocked, then pushed it open a couple of inches until it was held firm and then slammed in his face by a man. 'All I saw was a man's face and his right hand; he faced towards me as he shut the door . . . (he wore) a singlet, a brown belt and a pair of blue trousers . . . he just simply said "All right" and closed the door.' Even if the door had opened wider, the curtain obscured his view of what was happening on the bed. Steer went back to Murray and told him. 'Camb's in there'. They returned to the cabin. Murray put his ear to the door and listened a while, then tiptoed back to the end of the corridor. There was disagreement about whether the light was on or off – Murray, the more reliable witness, said he could see it through the grille over the door, but Steer thought it was dark inside. Another contradiction: Steer said Murray tried the door, but Murray, for his part, was certain that he did not. They hung around for ten minutes, then Murray left to make a report to the officer on the bridge, while Steer went off on patrol (he said, wrongly, that he waited for Murray to come back). The man who was to prosecute Camb, Khaki Roberts, afterwards said that Steer and Murray 'gave honest testimony; but such is the fallibility of human observation and memory'.

The fourth-ranking sailor on board, Arthur White, was on the bridge. We have only Murray's version of the exchange, but he does not appear to have told White that the man in the cabin was Camb, or even made clear that he was a seaman, and certainly there was no mention of his reputation as a Romeo. Yet only hours before, Murray had overheard the 'I've got a bone to pick with you' interchange. White, in the belief that Gay Gibson was entertaining a guest from her first-class peer group, replied that it was not for him to interfere with passengers' morals.

Murray was worried. He returned to the cabin. Ten minutes had passed and it was now 3.20 a.m. The light was still on, but inside all was silent. He returned to his pantry after another four minutes or so, once again, apparently, without trying the door. When Steer, on his rounds, reached the cabin some ten minutes later it was in darkness. The time would have been about 3.40 a.m. By then Camb had been back in his own bunk for ten minutes.

The lawyer Geoffrey Clark, who wrote up the Porthole case in the 'Notable British Trials' series, was to say that in the last analysis, the case against Camb did not rest on the medical evidence, or on testimony about the character of the dead girl. Rather, it depended on the answer to the questions: Who rang both bells and why? In a way, the 'bells' question is a convenient prosecution shortcut; if you find the answer you want, you are halfway to filling in all the other unknowns. If it doesn't help the case, then there are other pieces of circumstantial evidence to be seized upon. It certainly should not have become the litmus test of the Crown's case, but the medical evidence was too complicated for the jury to fathom. We cannot know what aspect of the case worried the jury most, but if it was the bells, then we must inquire whether they fully appreciated all aspects – and flaws – of the argument?

Camb's problem was that he made no effort to offer a convincing explanation as to how the bells were set off. The ringing was not caused by an electrical fault, for the circuit was tested and found to be in good working order. And the court ruled out the hand of the girl falling on the buttons in her death agony, for a certain amount of pressure was required – though, as we shall see, even this hypothesis is open to question. 'What explanation was there,' Geoffrey Clark asked, 'other than that of the prosecution, that Gay Gibson rang them to summon help to save her from Camb's unwanted advances?'

This argument has two serious flaws. Nobody asked Camb whether he might have pushed the bells by accident. When the tap on the door came, he was 'standing by the side of the bed attempting artificial respiration'. The diagram of the cabin shows a space of ten to eleven inches separating the bed from the chest of drawers. The button panel is in this gap, perhaps four feet up the wall. There is enough room for someone to squeeze in between the head of the bed and the chest. A man working feverishly to revive a dying woman might well push up against the buttons, unwittingly exerting sufficient pressure to set them off. In the moments leading up to the knock on the door he would not have stayed in one position, but must have moved about, seeking the best resuscitation position.

John Addis, a Southampton police detective who investigated the case, was asked by Camb's barrister, Casswell: 'The bellpush in a private house on shore is very often flush with the woodwork but these bellpushes project, do they not?' – 'Yes.'

'If one were to lean against these pushes they would be liable to ring?' – 'They would.'

Later, Casswell asked Miss Field: 'If you lean against these bellpushes that would put them on – there is no rim round the push to prevent that, is there?' and without waiting for a reply: 'Have you known them to be put on by accident?' – Miss Field: 'I don't remember.'

'Anyone in the cabin who got between that dressing table and the bed might lean against those two bellpushes without knowing it?' 'Yes.'

Questioned by the judge, she agreed that there was 'sufficient space for you to stand between the chest of drawers and the head of the bed'.

Casswell might have been inhibited by the rules of procedure from asking leading questions of his client, and perhaps found no way of getting Camb to admit that he could have been the inadvertent cause of the bellringing. Defence counsel did argue the point strongly in his closing speech, but by then the jury had made up its mind.

So the jurors ignored the 'accidental lean-against theory', and seized on the argument that Gay rang the bells as a desperate last throw to save herself from a man who would not tolerate the rejection of his advances. But Camb had arrived in her cabin at 2.00 a.m. and had been there for almost an hour when she allegedly called for help. You have to assume a high degree of innocence, not to mention naïveté, on Gay's part to accept such an explanation. For the two of them do not appear to have had much in common to talk about except for the dance and the other passengers. Camb was unlikely to expatiate on his wife and daughter, or his romantic exploits on water and land, nor she on army concert parties or her father's mission work. In the early hours of the morning the sole mutual reason for being in each other's company was to make love. But just supposing that, after an hour of getting to know each other better, she became terrified of a violent side to Camb which had suddenly become apparent, and wanted him out, and he refused, and she rang the bells . . . If, as the prosecution alleged, he committed the murder after seeing her summon help, one minute was an all too brief space of time in which to render her unconscious and be able to answer the door in the knowledge that she would not cry out. Gay's health might not have been A1, but she was hardly wasting away and was capable of putting up a spirited defence, certainly for the short interval before help arrived. Yet no cry was heard in the early hours of that morning, when her voice would have easily penetrated the cabin wall to the woman in cabin 124.

Besides, as Casswell suggested, if Camb knew the bells had been rung, he had only to step outside and press the bulbs by the door to put out the indicator lights, and Steer would irretrievably have lost the scent.

Through the night the *Durban Castle* continued at a steady eighteen knots, drawing further and further away from the young woman in her 'dark and watery grave'.

5

Lies, Glorious Lies

That morning at 7.30, Eileen Field, a glass of orange juice in one hand, knocked with the other on the door of cabin 126, and waited for the passenger to open up. No one answered. She tried the handle and, unusually, the door opened. A light breeze rustled the curtain over the porthole, but otherwise there was no movement in the cabin. Miss Gibson was not there. As was her habit, she had hung her black dance frock at the foot of the bunk, for later transfer to the wardrobe. The dressing gown and pyjamas were not to be seen, and the stewardess presumed Gay was in the toilet. Perhaps she didn't notice the slippers on the floor. The cabin was shaded from the sun at that early hour, but she could see that 'apart from the bed being a little more disarranged (than usual) the cabin did not look any different'. The bed linen had been pulled right back. Someone had slept in the bed that night, and somebody's head had been on the pillow. The sheet and pillow had 'one or two stains', but she took little notice of them. There were no grounds for suspicious thoughts. Certainly, it did not seem as if any sort of violence had been going on. She made the bed.

Miss Field did the rounds of her other passengers, while listening out for the young woman in cabin 126. The bathroom steward said she was not taking a bath. The stewardess returned to the cabin at ten to eight. The orange juice was untouched. She continued making beds and cleaning up in her cabins on 'B' Deck. At 8.40 she asked the head waiter to let her know when Miss Gibson appeared for breakfast. By now she was very anxious. She also asked the stewards in the public rooms, including Camb, if they had seen her. She looked around the decks. By 9.30 the dining saloon was empty of breakfasters. She reported the matter to Mr Thompson, the second steward, who in turn searched the passenger decks and accommodation. Moving inexorably up the chain of command, he went to see Mr Holfert-Knight, the chief steward. It was now 9.45 a.m.

Two minutes later – we know from the log – the captain was informed. A message was broadcast throughout the ship on the loudspeaker: 'A first-class lady passenger, Miss Eileen Gibson, cannot be found. Any person who knows where she is or can give any information concerning her, please report at once to the purser.' Crewmen searched the nooks and crannies of the vessel: empty cabins, cold storage rooms, crews' quarters. Negative. At 10.30 a.m., seven hours after the event, Patey gave the order for the *Durban Castle* to reverse course. Passengers and crew leaned over the rail peering into the waves, or climbed to look-out points for a view of the horizon. The captain and his men knew how fruitless a task it was in the wide ocean, but they had to go through the motions of steaming back to the spot where the girl was last seen alive. Only one person on board knew that Gay Gibson was all of 150 miles away.

In the captain's cabin, Patey, his number two Alec Hort, purser Middleton and chief steward Holfert-Knight, discussed the likely reasons for her disappearance. Foul play was not at first suspected. Ollie Middleton thought of suicide, and Patey seemed to concur. For a fleeting moment, without his knowledge of it, Camb's solution was working. But Hort had heard Gay's story in occasional chats on deck and had talked to her late the previous evening in the company of Bray and Hopwood, and he thought it unlikely 'for a girl like that, who was looking forward to her career, to take her own life'. Then nightwatchman Steer arrived to report the incident of the bells. The man behind the door, he said, 'resembled Deck Steward J. Camb'. From that moment, Camb would be the sole suspect.

As the ship went back on its tracks, Patey interviewed half-a-dozen key people, piecing together something of the contacts between Gay Gibson and James Camb. In not much more than an hour he saw Hopwood, Bray, Conway, Steer, Miss Field, Camb, Murray, Thompson, and the *laissez faire* officer on the bridge, Mr White. The log reads: 'At 11.40 a.m., after hearing the statements of the aforementioned persons, it was assumed that Miss Gibson disappeared some time between 3.00 a.m. and 7.30 a.m. today and that no reasonable hope could be entertained of recovering her by retracing ship's course any further. To confirm this assumption the ship's doctor was consulted and he agreed . . . the Master then gave orders to resume the ship's normal course.'

Patey received a message from Union-Castle: 'Padlock and seal cabin. Disturb nothing. CID officers will come aboard at Cowes Road.' He found cabin 126 'in an immaculate condition', with nothing touched or removed, apart from its incumbent and items of night attire. The porthole window was lowered and closed. The carpenter padlocked the door. Later, Gay's luggage in the baggage room – large buff-coloured cabin trunk, leather camel-coloured suitcase, brown leather hat-box – were 'taped, sealed and labelled for safekeeping', and placed in an unused cabin, which was locked and its key given to the purser.

A 'Radio Urgency Message' went out to ships in the area: 'From Durban Castle stop Missing on board believe that lost overboard one lady passenger between 0400 GMT position 09 53 N, 16 22 W on a course 323 and 0900 position 11 19 N, 17 27 W stop Will all ships in this vicinity please keep a good lookout.' The SS *Reventazon* radioed at 12.30 p.m. that it was 'covering the route to search'. Later a 'body alert' message would be sent by Interpol (International Criminal Police Commission) in Paris, and Scotland Yard would seek the help of the British colony of Sierra Leone, perhaps providing descriptions of a yellow zip-up dressing gown and black silk pyjamas. After which, according to Sidney Birch of the Metropolitan Police, the missing actress would become a topic of conversation 'in a babel of tongues from Helsingfors to the Sandwich Isles'. Though there were no reports of sightings, we might assume that policemen in Portuguese Guinea, Senegal, Liberia and Sierra Leone did in fact ask fishermen to keep an eye out for the body of a white lady with long dark hair.

Patey had time to obtain only the briefest statements, but these revealed inconsistencies which might have shown up in the later court hearings. Bray and Hopwood appear to have seen the captain together. The Master noted that Hopwood (cabin 33 on 'C' Deck above Gay's) and Bray (in 105 on 'B' Deck), stated that 'they both accompanied Miss Eileen Gibson from the first-class Promenade Deck at about 00.35 hours and left her outside cabin 126'. There will be two further versions of this leave-taking, with variations regarding who went into the cabin and for how long. The bosun's mate, Conway, whose men were washing down the port side Promenade Deck when Gay appeared for her late-night stroll, would give the impression in the trial that she obligingly followed his request to move along. But the captain wrote: 'He (Conway) advised her to go across to the starboard side to avoid getting her feet wet. She, however, chose to disregard this advice.' Camb's counsel would not have a chance to see the log, which, unaccountably was not an exhibit at the trial.

If Steer and Murray could offer valuable information about events in the middle of the night, Mrs Henrietta Stevens, a 69-year-old Londoner in cabin 124, adjacent to Gay's, thought that she too had heard a sound as of some article, perhaps a tea-tray, being dropped, perhaps by a nightwatchman or a steward on early-morning duty. Nothing came of her offering, though tea-trays did play a symbolic part in the affair.

All the while, as the circle narrowed, Camb kept his head down, acting the part of the industrious deck steward. Joe Chidgey recalls that the morning after Gay's disappearance, his cabin mate was up as usual at six o'clock cleaning the Long Gallery. But he was uncharacteristically subdued. Camb said in his *Sunday Pictorial* version of events that he was serving a round of drinks when the captain's announcement boomed through the decks. 'Stewards exchanged glances. Officers hurried past us without speaking . . . then I felt the ship turning. We were going back to search. I went down to my quarters for a smoke, to calm my tense nerves. I must not crack . . . I wondered whether I was suspected of having anything to do with Gay's disappearance. I was soon to know the answer. The chief steward told me that Captain Patey wanted to see me in his cabin immediately.'

Camb now made the first of a succession of lying statements which would hover above his head like an albatross. The log: ' . . . on being informed by the Master that a person resembling him was seen in cabin 126 at about 0300 hours today, Camb replied, "I was not in that cabin at that time and I was not in any passenger accommodation or on passenger decks after 00.45 a.m. at which time I got to bed."' But early that morning, when Camb was sweeping out the Promenade Deck before breakfast, Bill Pott noticed that he was wearing a white coat with sleeves. This was unusual, for in the tropics, Camb, like everyone else, worked in a singlet or short-sleeved shirt. Later in the day, as tongues began to wag, Pott went to the captain's cabin. Patey summoned Camb once again and told him that in view of the suspicion that he had played a part in the disappearance of Miss Gibson, it would be in his own interests for him to have a medical examination. Camb could have refused, but the refusal would have been written into the log. Grudgingly, he agreed, blurting out as he left, 'Why all this suspicion? Let's get down to bedrock' – a word association which Freud might have found significant.

The next morning, Sunday, Patey received via chief steward Holfert-Knight a letter from Camb which enlarged on, but did not vary, his earlier explanation:

'Sir, with reference to your question of yesterday, i.e. my whereabouts at approx 0300 a.m. on the 18th, I respectfully beg to state that after locking my deck pantry at approx 0100 a.m. I went forward to the Well Deck where I sat and smoked. I felt myself dozing off to sleep, so first visited the toilet and then retired. After getting into bed, I carried out my usual practice of smoking one cigarette. My last act was to wind my clock and the time then was a little after 0200 a.m. I did not leave the cabin again until we were called at 5.45 a.m. I am, sir, yours faithfully, J. Camb, Deck Steward.'

So if he had been spotted skulking around the decks at two in the morning when on the way to Gay's cabin, he could plead that he was simply going to bed. The reference to the cigarette was surely meant to indicate innocence, but would he have been so foolish as to light up and exhale in the stuffy cabin when the last thing he wanted was for his mates to wake up and notice the time?

Dr Anthony Griffiths had been qualified as a doctor for five years. The description 'ship's surgeon' is misleading, for he was a general practitioner and not, as the term might suggest, a consultant and Fellow of the Royal College of Surgeons. Seasickness, a deckhand's arm stuck through a windowpane, the occasional appendectomy, heart failure in the geriatric wing of the first class, quite a lot of Dhobi's Itch (of which more later) are a ship's doctor's meat and drink. Griffiths found three groups of injuries on the body of James Camb. The first were recent: scratches over the back of the right shoulder, as if by a cat's claw – or a lady's finely-pointed fingernail? Next were some older scratches on the left collar bone, which Camb would claim were the result of rubbing himself too energetically with a towel.

Finally, the doctor noted scratches above the right wrist which the pathologist Denis Hocking would describe as 'of intriguing interest'. There were twelve of these, he said, 'some linear, some crescentic, running more or less horizontally across the inside of the right lower arm, commencing four to five inches above the wrist'. Griffiths thought they were caused by nails digging into the flesh, an interpretation which seems beyond dispute. The Crown said these scratches proved that the victim had dug her nails into her strangler's forearm in a desperate attempt to pull his hands away from her throat. Hocking, in the light of Camb's 'completely reasonable account' of Gay's final moment – 'she suddenly clutched at me' – thought they could equally have been the result of a 'death spasm'. Camb complicated matters by denying that Gay had caused them, but he must have realised that the scratches needed some explanation. After the medical examination he sent Patey a second letter. The 'slight scratches on my left shoulder and wrist, also a few on my right wrist' were, he said, 'self-inflicted three or four nights ago whilst in bed. I was feeling terribly hot and itchy, and I must have scratched myself during sleep. I remarked during the following morning that I'd "damned near scratched myself to death", though at the time of writing these marks are fast healing. Also early last week I broke a small patch of skin on my neck by a too-vigorous rubbing with a very rough towel. With the friction of the neckband on my white jackets this is still a little irritant.'

Sid Birch of Scotland Yard was told by Camb that the irritation was Dhobi's Itch, 'a tropical spore picked up from infected native launderers through shirt cuff and collar'. The complaint, if it was this, mostly infects the groin and is relieved by the application of Whitfield's ointment. Whatever the explanation of the scratches, to the layman they seemed like a loose plank in Camb's story. Eleven years later he would at last admit that the telltale marks were the product of 'our last embrace'.

The *Durban Castle* ploughed on, rounding Dakar, the continent's westernmost landfall. If there was dismay in the first-class, it was not apparent, though primmer, pre-war souls might have shaken their heads knowingly at the fate of the young actress. And made doubly sure they locked their cabin doors. Wendy Noakes does not recall Gay's disappearance changing the atmosphere greatly. 'She had been seen on deck late at night by a member of the crew and many people reckoned she had committed suicide and just jumped overboard. As far as we were concerned, there was no indication to passengers that Camb was under suspicion.' Afterwards, says Mrs Noakes, the two men friends, Bray and Hopwood, 'absolutely clammed up . . . did not appear to talk to anyone. There was some speculation about passengers, but not that a member of the crew was involved or that she had gone through the porthole.' In such circumstances it is the duty of the Master of a passenger liner to reassure the anxious customers and return the ship as quickly as possible to quotidian normality. When, after two days' absence, Patey resumed his seat in the dining saloon, he breathed not a word about the affair.

Belowdecks the crew were better informed. A steward told

Mrs Noakes that they were sure of Camb's guilt and were all for locking him up. The ship had a brig, which would have held him in tight security. But though Camb was considered the likeliest, indeed the only, candidate, he was not taken off his job. Hort recalls that 'we just kept an eye on him. He wasn't put ashore at Funchal, in Madeira, because we had no real proof.' The Southampton police, who were advising Patey via Union-Castle headquarters in Fenchurch Street, recommended leaving things as they were, to allay the fears of passengers who had grown attached to their charming deck steward.

Instead, Holfert-Knight ordered his stewards to put the word about that Camb should be watched and any suspicious behaviour reported back. Not everyone on board, it has to be said, appreciated the serious turn of events. At two o'clock on the morning after Gay's disappearance, nightwatchman Murray came upon William Hannaford and C. Wheeler, greaser-cleaners, loitering in the working alleyway armed with hammer and file and intending to force the padlock of the bulk storeroom door 'to steal what stores they could get away with'. The Master could not have been pleased to see them that afternoon. They admitted the offence and were given a 'bad discharge' from the company's service.

But murder was in a category of its own. As the crime was committed under the British flag on the high seas, and Camb had not yet been charged, the captain had no power to put him ashore at the first port of call, the Portuguese island of Madeira. Had he been tried in Portugal, incidentally, he might have been comforted by the knowledge that, though it was a fascist state at the time, the death penalty had been abandoned. Had Gay disappeared on the outward journey, Camb would in all probability have been sent back from Cape Town for trial in an English court – at the Old Bailey, if he arrived at Northolt Airport, at Winchester Assizes, if at Southampton docks – as informal extradition existed within the British Commonwealth. If he had been tried in the Cape Town Supreme Court, an all-White jury of macho men may well have viewed Camb's story sympathetically.

When the *Durban Castle* dropped anchor off Funchal, Bray

and Hopwood, though not under suspicion, also stayed on board. They might have thrown sixpences into the sea to be retrieved by Madeiran boys diving from the Boat Deck. Other passengers caught the ferry into town for a glass of Blandy's Madeira and a horse-drawn carriage-ride. On that day Patey received a letter from nightwatchman Murray:

> Sir, last night F. Steer reminded me that I had mentioned previously to him a conversation that I had overheard in the Long Gallery by the bar service recess between Camb and Miss Gibson. I heard Camb say, "I have a bone to pick with you and a big one at that." This happened at approx. 11.20 p.m. the night before the morning she was missing. I am sorry this should have slipped my memory and hope it will not cause any trouble to all concerned.

Camb did not deny that he had spoken these words, but the delay in the recollection is worrying, especially since, again, the defence did not have access to this entry in the log.

Tongues were wagging furiously in the crew's quarters, though Steer and Murray had been instructed not to disclose what they knew. On Tuesday, Steer reported to the captain a conversation in the crew's washroom in which Camb had asked if he, Steer, had 'made the suggestion that it was him'. No, answered Steer. To which Camb replied mysteriously, certainly misleadingly: 'Thank goodness I haven't been with her this trip (homeward bound),' adding, 'I am in a right jam.'

Alec Hort was convinced of Camb's involvement because 'he kept coming to me trying to have a conversation to sound out what we were thinking'. Camb's demeanour indicates that though he might have been intelligent, he lacked imagination. Perhaps during all those years at sea, while mastering the requirements of his job to an impressive degree, he had lost the ability to cope with anything out of the ordinary. He really believed, against every obvious indication, that he had not been identified as the man in cabin 126, and could persist in mendacious denial. At his trial, he said that after the washroom conversation he 'still thought it highly improbable that I had been recognised'.

On the night of Friday 24 October, the ship arrived at Cowes Road, off the Isle of Wight. The Noakeses watched the pilot come on board. The police were rumoured to be arriving with the pilot, but when there was no sign of them, Mrs Noakes recalled, 'My husband said, "There you are, I told you nothing was wrong." So we took a ten-pound bet, which of course I won. While we were talking, Camb was behind us in his deck pantry and must have heard all we said, but when my husband turned to him to give him his tip for the trip, he was totally normal and unconcerned.' Beneath the cocky exterior Camb must have been calculating his chances of delivering his presents to Margaret and Tootsie in Glasgow later that day.

At 1.25 a.m. in thick fog, Detective Sergeant John Quinlan and Detective Constable Minden Plumley of the Southampton police boarded the *Durban Castle* from the tugboat *Paladin*. Patey gave them the key to cabin 126 and the two letters from Camb. The detectives did the rounds, pieced together the story. Chidgey met Quinlan in the smoking room and, from the way he was dressed, 'thought he was a stevedore'. Camb later described his feelings on the ship's arrival: 'I knew my first test was coming. But I went on working through the night until, at 5.30 a.m., when I was clearing up in the foredeck washhouse, I turned and saw the two men framed in the open door.' They were police officers and wished to interview him 'concerning a certain matter'.

The three men adjourned to the deserted smoking room. The fog was lifting. The ship entered the harbour, and Camb made out the massive outline of the *Queen Elizabeth*. The *Athlone Castle* was alongside as they drew up to the mailship's double berth at nos. 35 and 36. Camb also had time to notice that the *Alcantara*, one of his long-ago ships, was moored across the water, before being asked to account for the disappearance of Gay Gibson. 'Should I know anything about it?' he replied. The lying continued, but each time a little more information was extracted. He was forced to admit that he had seen her on deck and had attended her. 'Have you ever been to Miss Gibson in her cabin?' – 'Never.' 'But is it not a fact that you have delivered afternoon tea to Miss Gibson in her cabin?'

Camb recalled: 'Without looking up, Plumley said casually, "Would you mind showing me your wrists?" "Sure," I said. I rolled up my sleeves. "Have you ever been in the tropics? . . . I nearly scratched myself to death in my sleep in the night: I have got some on my shoulders; I did that with a rough towel."' Plumley observed that the marks on the right wrist appeared to be of too serious a nature to have been self-inflicted.

Quinlan then declared that he had 'reason to believe that you were in Miss Gibson's cabin at about three o'clock on the morning of the 18th of October'. Camb: 'That puts me in a tight spot.' Quinlan asked the steward, who was not yet a prisoner, to accompany him to Southampton police headquarters. By now it was six in the morning. He could leave discreetly. His deck customers were in their cabins finishing off their packing.

On hearing a BBC radio announcement that a woman passenger had disappeared from the *Durban Castle*, the snooker player Joe Davis said to his wife, 'I bet that steward Camb has been up to his tricks again.' Old Mrs Haslam, Jim's aunt in Waterfoot, also heard the announcement and cried out: 'Oh my God, it's Jim, I know it is!' Charley Schwentafsky and Donald Vincent were breakfasting at the Carlton Hotel in Johannesburg when they saw the headline in the *Rand Daily Mail*. 'I can assure you,' said Gay's benefactor, 'I had nothing whatsoever to do with it.' Mrs Willya Abel, wife of Mike Abel, later remarked that 'Gay is rather hippy, so how the devil did they get her through the porthole?'.

The detectives returned to the liner, leaving Camb to sweat it out. Now he was getting really worried. He didn't like the waiting. Police stations are empty places on Saturday afternoons. He might have heard the duty officer's radio broadcast of the local football team being thrashed 5–0 at Newcastle. The detectives returned at five-thirty and he was almost pleased to see them.

Though the knack of telling the truth still eluded him, in the jargon of a later era Camb now began to 'help the police with their inquiries'. Their opening gambit pandered to his vanity. 'Are you in the habit of visiting female passengers in their cabins?' – 'Yes, some of them like us stewards better than the passengers.' Quinlan was not amused, but Camb went on merrily, 'I have been with women passengers several times on other trips.' He was told categorically that he had been in Miss Gibson's cabin at three in the morning on the 18th. Camb: 'I want to tell you something. I did not want to tell you in front of Mr Turner [the Union-Castle special inquiry agent] this morning as I had no right to go to her cabin. But I did go at about eleven o'clock that night to ask her if she wanted some lemonade with her rum . . . ' He still refused to come clean about the later visit. But the ice was broken.

Quinlan went out to consult with his senior officer, Acting Inspector Herbert Gibbons. They decided to draw the noose tighter. Returning to the interrogation room, Gibbons went through the evidence point by point. They could prove conclusively that Camb had been in the cabin at 3.00 a.m., Gibbons told him. And that shreds of material found on the edge of the porthole showed what had happened to Miss Gibson's body. Gibbons now warned Camb that 'the time is fast approaching when a decision will have to be made regarding you . . . You may find that such a complete denial will be difficult to explain if later you are called upon to explain it.' Camb: 'Does that mean that I murdered her, and that I shall be charged with murder?' Gibbons replied, 'You may be able to give a reasonable explanation of the cause of her death and her disappearance. If you should later decide to make such an explanation, acceptance of it will not be made easier by a continuation of the denials you have made up to now.'

Camb seized on this eagerly. 'You mean that Miss Gibson might have died from some cause other than being murdered? She might have had a heart attack, or something?' His response could be interpreted in more than one way. For Denis Hocking, the forensic pathologist who acted for the defence, the remark was 'consistent with the mental attitude of a worried man who had racked his brains to find some explanation as to why a woman should suddenly die in his arms and, in a flash, it comes to him'.

Camb remained silent for a while, then he sat back in his chair and said: 'Can you take this down in shorthand; I want to make a quick and short statement.' In the end, it was done, at copper's pace, on a typewriter. He dictated his piece, the most relevant words being: 'Whilst in the act of sexual intercourse she suddenly clutched at me, foaming at the mouth. I immediately ceased the act, but she was very still. I felt for her heartbeats but could not find any . . . ' The 'foaming' episode would be important in the light of evidence from Johannesburg.

Camb had already given two written denials and a verbal one to the captain, followed by denials to the police on board and at the station, so this confession was his sixth statement. Had it been made to Patey at the time of asking, he would have been in an infinitely stronger position. Now the lying had gone on too long. But this was his definitive version and he would stick by it unwaveringly throughout the committal proceedings and trial, even when elaboration over black pyjamas, scratches or ringing of bells would be to his advantage. It is also possible that, though defence lawyers and pathologists would accept it as a basis for a defence of death by natural causes during intercourse, Camb was keeping deliberately silent over other happenings in the cabin, in particular the nature of their lovemaking.

Having got that off his chest, Camb told himself, 'Well, that's your job finished. You will never go to sea again.' As Quinlan was leaving the room, Camb asked: 'What will happen about this? My wife must not know . . . if she does I will do away with myself.' This remark, his lawyer Joshua Casswell, was to say later, provided a valuable insight into the man's mind. 'His uppermost, or at least his expressed, thought was not "make it easy for me, guv'nor", the common plea of a criminal to a police officer, but "my wife must not know about this", the usual cry of the apprehended philanderer.'

Quinlan gave him the reply the following afternoon: 'James Camb, I charge you with the wilful murder of Eileen Isabella Ronnie Gibson . . . ' 'My God,' cried the deck steward, 'is it as serious as that?' The penny had dropped.

It was still only Sunday. The police had been conscientious, but their work would be marred by the zealous Plumley. Told to get Camb's signed consent for photographs and a blood test, the detective used the occasion to persuade Camb to embellish his confession. He reported to Quinlan that Camb had said: ' . . . I can't understand why the officer of the watch did not hear something. It was a hell of a splash when she hit the water. She struggled. I had my hands around her neck and when I was trying to pull them away she scratched me. I panicked and threw her out of the porthole.' Quinlan told Plumley to put this admission in writing, which he did, but Camb refused to sign it, knowing all too well that it would prejudice his case.

The Sunday papers were heavy with speculation – not surprisingly, for here was a dramatic tale of sex and violence on the high seas. A first-class female passenger waxed lyrically about how 'on the night Gay Gibson disappeared I thought she looked lovelier than ever I had seen her before'. Another talked of 'a jolly type of girl, a favourite with everyone. She was travelling alone and some of the older passengers more or less looked after her. Her mysterious disappearance made the voyage a tragic one for us all.'

Quinlan's team, meanwhile, had returned to the locked cabin. Sid Birch, the fingerprint expert, was there to help with 'scene of the crime' work. For forty years, chief constables had been subject to a Home Office regulation that all possible clues should be protected pending the arrival of an officer from the Metropolitan Police. These days the 'forensic intelligence officer' goes to the scene of the crime and picks up every conceivable shred of evidence. But it is likely that the man who helped Birch and Quinlan was a humble 'lab liaison sergeant'. The Scotland Yard connection did not prevent its laboratory from missing the most telling material clue in the case.

Miss Field, the cabin stewardess, had already unwittingly disarranged, then rearranged, the bedclothes. Now she was asked to restore the bed to the condition in which she remembered finding it on the Saturday morning. Cameras clicked and detectives dusted for prints. To their surprise they found the imprint of a palm on the inside of the door, so clear that it could only have been planted with tremendous pressure. Birch recalls that he and Quinlan 'gazed at the enlarged photographs of Camb's hand-print . . . It was a dim outline of the flat of the right hand – but crisp and very clear was the V-shaped pressure of the hollow of his right-hand palm, just above the wrist. Under normal pressure that should have been the least distinct part of the print . . . There is only one method that will leave the bottom of the palm of your hand fully imprinted upon it – by slamming the door violently from the inside as it is being opened inwards to the room.'

The peripatetic alarm clock was on the chest. The police removed the cabin door from its hinges, as well as the bed, the bed linen, the bellpush panel, two tins of boot polish, two pairs of shoes. Hairs were found on the bed, and in the cabin suitcase a number of letters to Gay's parents to be posted on arrival in England. And a Koromex contraceptive device and tube of cream to go with it.

On the Monday, Camb appeared briefly in Southampton magistrate's court to be charged with the murder of Gay Gibson. He was dressed in a double-breasted blue suit with a white collarless shirt open at the neck. He was not asked to plead and was remanded in custody for a week. He was represented by a local solicitor, Geoffrey Wells of the firm Woodford & Ackroyd, who asked for and received legal aid for his client.

The South African newspapers, not inhibited by the sub judice rule, ran full accounts of Gay's life and the events on board the *Durban Castle*. 'According to the police,' reported the London correspondent of *The Cape Times*, 'bloodstains were found on her pillow and also on the floor, which makes it appear that she was either strangled or suffocated.' Wrong; there was no blood on the floor.

The Gibsons received the news of Gay's death very late, although the Union-Castle offices and the police in Johannesburg, Durban and Cape Town were reported to have spent several days searching for them. Daisy was told as she left a cinema in Durban on the following Saturday evening. Mr

Gibson said, 'The least the company could have done was to notify her parents – we would have kept discreetly quiet if it would have helped the police investigations.' Waiting for Gay in London was a loving letter from her parents. They advised her to 'keep warm, sleep between the sheets'.

Camb's home town of Waterfoot was stunned, though possibly not surprised, when the suspect's name was made public. Mr Dilworth, deputy head at Lea Bank school, announced in the staffroom that 'if there is one woman on the jury, Jim Camb will be acquitted'. Waterfoot's newspaper, the *Free Press*, noted that it was the first time in fifteen years that a charge of murder had been brought without the production of the body.

It is, of course, conceivable that Camb did murder Gay Gibson, and that as he pondered his next move something at the back of his mind told him he could save his skin by getting rid of the body. In all those years at sea, he must have heard anecdotes about mariners, and the legendary captains of mutinous crews, being tossed overboard and the perpetrators getting away, literally, with murder. Most laymen, and desperate defence counsel whose best legal instincts are temporarily diverted by wishful thinking, believe that there can be no charge without the 'corpus delicti'.

This has to be a misconception, otherwise, as the prosecution counsel Khaki Roberts argued, 'the logical result would be that, if the criminal was sufficiently skilful and industrious to be able wholly to do away with the body, he would for ever remain immune from conviction'. Confronted with damning evidence of his latest victim, the acid-bath killer John George Haigh boasted: 'Mrs Durand-Deacon no longer exists. I've destroyed her with acid . . . You can't prove murder without a body.' Remains of the lady were found and he was hanged.

The legal precedent was established by the seventeenth-century judge, Sir Matthew Hale. 'I would never convict any person of murder or manslaughter,' he said, 'unless the fact were proved to be done, or at least the body found dead.' This is not an absolute rule of evidence, rather a matter of caution, as Halsbury's *Laws of England* makes plain:

Where no body or part of a body has been found which is proved to be that of the person alleged to have been killed, the accused person should not be convicted either of murder or manslaughter, unless there is evidence either of the killing or of the death of the person alleged to have been killed. In the absence of such evidence there is no onus upon the prisoner to account for the disappearance or non-production of the person alleged to be killed.

If there is no body, nor evidence of criminal behaviour towards a missing person, the courts are liable to make appalling mistakes. Hale cited an example of the incaution of a judge and jury leading to the ultimate miscarriage of justice. A man, bringing up a niece who was his heir at law, had occasion to correct her. She was heard to plead, 'Good uncle, do not kill me,' and then was seen no more. The uncle was committed on suspicion of murder and ordered to produce the girl at the next Assizes. Unable to find her, and desperate to save his neck, he brought to court a child of the same age and appearance as his ward, dressed in the niece's clothes. The deception was uncovered, and he was convicted and executed. But the girl, far from being murdered, had run away and found refuge with strangers. Years later, when she came of age, she returned for her inheritance.

"Best", the standard nineteenth-century textbook on evidence, cites the case of one John Miles, executed for the murder of his friend William Ridley, who disappeared after the two had indulged too heavily in drink. Punishment being swift, Miles had already been cut down from the gibbet when the 'deceased' was located in the deep privy into which he had fallen in an alcoholic stupor.

Judges, as a result of such errors of judgment, were wary when no body could be produced. In an early Victorian infanticide trial, the court heard about Hannah Hopkins walking with her sixteen-day-old baby from Bristol to Llandogo, a village on the banks of the River Wye. She was seen near Tintern at 6.00 p.m. with the child in her arms, but arrived in Llandogo two hours later without it. She was charged with murder, by drowning or suffocation. In a coincidence reminiscent of a Thomas Hardy story, another baby was washed up on the riverbank, but it was not Hannah's. Lord Abinger ordered an acquittal on the ground that 'she cannot, by law, be called upon either to account for it, or to say where it is, unless there be evidence to shew that her child is actually dead'.

A 1935 Australian case illustrates the concern of judges to be certain that a crime has indeed been committed. A shark netted off a beach near Sydney vomited up the arm of a man with two boxers tattooed on it. A length of rope was tied round the wrist, and foul play was suspected. The tattoo was identified as belonging to an ex-boxer, James Smith. Police subsequently unravelled a murky tale of underworld intimidation and drug-running. During the course of the coroner's inquest, however, the main suspect, a man called Brady, obtained a Supreme Court order stopping the proceedings on the grounds that the severed arm did not prove that Smith was dead. Brady was later acquitted in the criminal trial for lack of evidence.

The evidence may, on the other hand, be too persuasive to allow for the Hale escape route. In a case heard in the Admiralty Court in 1792, George Hindmarsh, a mariner on a small slaving vessel anchored off the coast of West Africa, told crewmen of his intention to kill the captain. That night he was seen to 'take the captain and throw him overboard into the sea, and he was not seen or heard of afterwards'. Hindmarsh had used a blood-drenched club on the captain before his dispatch into 'shark-infested waters'. Defence counsel argued that there was no proof that the captain was dead; many ships were in the area, and the probability was that he had been rescued by one of them and was alive. The jury found that the captain had been beaten to death before being cast into the sea. Hindmarsh was hanged at Execution Dock.

Thus it was possible to consider the case against Camb in relation to Hale and other 'corpus delicti' precedents: firstly, strong circumstantial evidence, as with the palm print on the door, identification in the cabin by Steer, and Camb's earlier contacts with Gay; secondly, his confession; and thirdly, medical evidence which would be detected by, of all people, a defence pathologist.

By now Mr Turner, the Union-Castle inquirer, had submitted his report to the company boss, Sir Vernon Thompson. The shipping line had had to explain away murders before but these were either committed belowdecks or had involved one passenger killing another, for reasons alcoholic, domestic or political. A crew member charged with killing a passenger, and in the first class at that, was the most serious crime ever committed on any company ship. The *Durban Castle* would remain in Southampton for ten days before sailing for the Cape once again. Towards the end of that period, Captain Patey would go up to London for his regulation debriefing with Sir Vernon and a marine superintendent, by which time head office would have perused the log and the letters of praise, or criticism, written by passengers on the voyage. Thus did Chairman Thompson keep his eyes, ears and fingertips on his far-flung empire. It is to be presumed that the Gibson affair extended the meeting beyond the normal three-quarters of an hour. Patey would then have taken a taxi to Waterloo in time to catch the Bournemouth Belle to Southampton. The author was refused access to the company records, so is unable to report the Union-Castle Board's official reaction to the murder or to provide evidence of laxness in shipboard procedures.

At least the laxity of the company's vetting of new staff provided the police with a bonus. While detectives were chasing clues on board, purser Middleton had sent John Catterall to inquire into their progress. An alert officer recognised Catterall as a man wanted for fraud in the Midlands. He was sent northwards.

The *Durban Castle* sailed out of the Solent on Guy Fawkes Day with Captain Gorringe back in command. Mr Noakes' freight business with the company again assured the couple a place at the captain's table. One afternoon on this return voyage Wendy Noakes was lying on her bed reading a book and smoking. Stretching across to the ashtray on the chest of drawers, her hand accidentally brushed against the cabin bell-push. Without realising it, she had summoned both steward and stewardess. The call was answered in double-quick time.

With Southampton's police court destroyed by the Luft-waffe, the committal hearing on 17 November took place in the Court of Quarter Sessions. Mr W. Bulpitt, the presiding magistrate, was assisted by Mrs J. Tosh Robb, Mr E. Moat and Mr A. E. Udall. Hampshire's chief constable, Mr C. G. Box, was there, as were members of the public, who had been waiting for hours in the cold morning air and now, reported the *Southern Daily Echo*, 'filed into the gallery filling every available seat'. Prisoners had not yet acquired the right to exclude the press from preliminary court proceedings, with the result that potential jurors could read the unchallenged catalogue of events in the newspapers in advance of the main trial.

On display in the courtroom was the actual bed in question, and a scale model of cabin 126 featuring the now notorious porthole and the palm-marked door. The theatricality of the occasion was highlighted by the solicitor for the Director of Public Prosecutions who was Edward Robey, son of the music-hall comic, George Robey. The show business in Edward's blood had bubbled up in amateur performances of Gilbert and Sullivan, where his powers of mimicry had allowed him to excel as the Lord Chancellor in *Iolanthe* and the Judge in *Trial by Jury*. Born in 1900, educated at Westminster School and Jesus College, Cambridge, his working life had been as a back-room boy at the DPP, and, recently, as a member of the British legal team at the Nuremberg Nazi war-crime trials. Though Robey did not doubt Camb's guilt, he said afterwards that 'I cannot help feeling that Gibson was flattered by his admiration and probably encouraged him up to a point'.

As junior counsel for Camb, his solicitor, Geoffrey Wells, briefed Joseph Molony, son of the Lord Justice of Ireland. At forty a rising star on the Western Circuit, Molony had been an RAF squadron leader in the war and, like Robey, was a Cambridge man.

But the star of the show, whom the women occupying most of the gallery seats had come to see, was Camb himself. Casually dressed in grey checked sports jacket with grey pin-striped flannel trousers, blue woollen pullover, blue spotted tie and a white shirt and collar, he looked 'perfectly composed', making the occasional note, saying little, as was demanded of those who must reserve their best performance for the opening night.

Robey outlined the case in detail, making much of the series of denials leading, at last, to the confession. He was able to report that the blood on the bottom sheet had been analysed and belonged to 'O' group. As Camb's was 'A', the inference, suggested Robey, was that the blood was Gay's and, therefore, 'the assault was of sufficient violence to cause the woman to bleed'. Camb's alleged admission to the over-zealous police-man, Plumley, appeared in *The Times* the following day: ' . . . my hands around her neck and when I was trying to pull them away she scratched me. I panicked and threw her out of the porthole . . . helluva splash when she hit the water.' The attempts at rebuttal would have to wait for the Assizes.

Camb's shoes and plimsolls, it was revealed, were sent to the Hendon police laboratory, but apparently not his singlet or trousers, nor his underpants, if he had been wearing them on the night of 17-18 October. The lab had found a 'yellow stain' on the bottom sheet, but Robey offered no elaboration.

Mrs Helena Baker, Gay's cousin, recounted that when she had last seen Gay at her home in Southampton two years earlier she was in good health.

Molony: 'Here is a young woman who leaves this country only early this year with her parents to settle in South Africa, and yet in October she is coming back by herself to enter on dramatic training in this country?' – 'For some reason she didn't like it out there, and I suppose took the first opportunity she could to come back to England.'

When the Union-Castle representative, Hopwood, had completed his evidence-in-chief, Molony asked whether Gay had told him why she was travelling to England. Robey objected. Molony: 'I cannot justify it but it may mean that I shall have to apply, in due time, that this trial be adjourned so that witnesses from South Africa can attend who can speak on this matter.' The exchange might have referred to her 'pregnancy' and the need for an abortion, or more generally to the state of her health or the nature of her love-life.

Hopwood varied the account he had given Patey. The *Echo* reported him as saying that after the dance, 'I took her down to her cabin. Mr Bray came down with us as far as 'B' Deck (his cabin being on the port side). I saw her actually into her cabin and then went to my own cabin.' But the official note of his deposition on file at the Public Record Office gives yet another variation: 'I then took Miss Gibson into her cabin. I saw her into her cabin. I had a few words with her in her cabin and then went back to my own cabin on 'C' Deck. I left her after about three or four minutes after I took her down.' Did he linger longer than he cared to admit? Bray, presumably on grounds of ill-health, did not give evidence.

The hearing ran into a second Monday. The women of Southampton were out in force once again, except for Mrs Tosh Robb, who was ill. Molony hinted at the line the defence would be taking . . . 'endeavouring to reconstruct the background of the relationship between the dead girl and Camb'. Witnesses were coming from South Africa 'who may be useful'. Finally Camb, reading from a folded sheet of notepaper, said: 'I am not guilty. I did not kill Miss Gibson. She died in the way I have described', adding hesitantly, 'My mistake was in trying to cover up . . . to conceal what happened. Witnesses already called could, I am sure, have told much that would help in this case, and witnesses in South Africa know about the state of her health.' He ended in a whisper, 'That is all.' He was formally committed for trial at Hampshire Assizes, and granted a public defence certificate to pay for a King's Counsel and a junior barrister.

The story was now in the public domain. 'Murder on the high seas . . . Steward and actress . . . I pushed limp body through ship's porthole', ran some of the headlines, though the Rossendale *Free Press* offered a more sedate: 'Girl alleged to have been pushed through ship's porthole'. The public's imagination was caught by the juicy drama that unfolded, of life on an ocean liner, featuring predatory deck steward and beautiful actress, Eric Boon and the RAF wing commander, a black silk pyjamas whodunnit, the body – wrapped in nothing more than a flowered dressing gown – being pushed through the porthole into shark-infested waters.

During the hearing Camb was held at Winchester Prison, the Winton where Hardy's Tess of the d'Urbervilles was hanged. Now he had a stroke of good fortune. After the suicide of the legendary Sir Bernard Spilsbury a year earlier, Professor James Webster, director of the South Midlands Forensic Laboratory in Birmingham, had emerged as the new leader in the field. The DPP had sent him particulars of the case in anticipation of his appearing for the prosecution. But Webster concluded that Camb's account of the death 'could have occurred'. He wrote back to say that it might have been caused by heart disease, giving three instances of young people dying during sexual intercourse. The DPP thereupon offered their star medical witness to Geoffrey Wells.

At the same time, Wells engaged the services of the forensic pathologist Denis Hocking, then aged forty-eight, a man with a catholic experience of death in Cornwall – a place where, his colleagues elsewhere in Britain will tell you, people get murdered in the strangest of ways. Dr Hocking, now in his nineties and still working, has always made it clear that Gay Gibson could have been manually strangled, but that there was at least an equal chance that she had died in the way described by Camb. 'I would rather be inclined to believe his description because I don't think he could have made up the medical details. I don't think he could have known what to put in and what to leave out. It was a perfectly straightforward account of somebody dying during sexual intercourse. He didn't exaggerate anything. There is no doubt that medical opinion favoured that interpretation . . . What he said fitted with what Webster and I and other pathologists had seen.'

The *News of the World* now added the power of its chequebook to the limited funds available to Camb's lawyers. This practice was much in vogue at the time, providing newspapers with guaranteed returns in the form of exclusive tip-offs from lawyers and interviews with the man on trial and his family. Two years earlier the *Sunday Pictorial* had paid for the defence (unsuccessful, it turned out) of the sadistic ex-RAF killer,

George Neville Heath. While awaiting trial, Heath wrote his life-story, described by the editor, Hugh Cudlipp, as 'a dead cert circulation raiser'. The *Pictorial*'s reporter set down a series of questions which the solicitors passed to their client behind the bars, and later visited Heath posing as a solicitor's clerk. Cudlipp: 'We indulged the murderer's vanity by furnishing him with a Savile Row suit for his appearance before the Judge; we also hired his KC, assuring us of further contact with our author.' The KC was Joshua Casswell, about to become Camb's senior counsel.

In mid-December, Wells left Northolt Airport on a BOAC Skymaster on the 32-hour flight via Khartoum to Johannesburg. With him was a friend, a Southampton businessman called called Elsom, who had taken up Camb's cause. The *Echo* described him as a 'private investigator to try to trace details of Miss Gibson's life during her South African stay'.

The two men set about their task with gusto. Doreen Mantle, a former acting colleague and now a social worker in Johannesburg, returned to her office at Child Welfare one afternoon to find three men waiting for her. 'I was dealing with child abuse cases . . . were they husbands, I wondered? Three tall men, two obviously English, came into my little cubicle. It was about Gay Gibson and could I meet them later that day? I was naïve and went to the office of the third man, a Johannesburg lawyer, Ralph Mundel. It was fairly traumatic, but they were charming. I answered their questions about Gay and the play in a very open way because I was not at all versed in the ways of the world, let alone the ways of a court. They said would I prepare a statement – they never called it an affidavit – which they would send to their counsel in England. They took me for a drink and we chatted and they said "when you come to England", not "if". Now going to England in those days was every South African's dream . . . '

Miss Mantle met the lawyers again, as arranged, though her parents cautioned against it. 'They had prepared an affidavit. They said they were delighted with my evidence because I was the first person with nothing to hide. They said I was a social worker, a person of substance. But I questioned some of the things in the affidavit. I hadn't said Gay had had a heart attack, or heart trouble even. I didn't know these things for sure. They said this would not be used in court, only for their counsel. So I signed. I asked for a copy and put it under my pillow and slept on it.' The next day Doreen Mantle consulted a lawyer. You may be a disinterested party, she was told, but if you appear in the witness box the prosecution will destroy you.

After his return to Southampton, Geoffrey Wells wrote a series of letters to Miss Mantle's lawyers asking them to persuade her to come to England. 'Wells said I was the only one able to give an objective view. The last one said I could help save Camb's life. I didn't believe it . . . my evidence was circumstantial, as all the evidence was.' Her parents sent her on holiday to Durban for the duration of the trial.

Wells' interview with Sidney Cherfas, another member of the *Golden Boy* cast, provides some indication of the lines along which the defence was working. 'I insisted I had not had a physical relationship with her, but he used words like "fellatio" that I had not heard of at the time.' The interview with Mike Abel elicited a graphic account of his sexual experiences with Gay, including her collapse during intercourse in the car. He spoke of a pain in her arm and her lips turning blue. Abel would by then have read Camb's account of her death in the local papers. But would he expose himself in public as a philanderer in exchange for a European holiday? Mundel says he was sure that Abel 'only agreed to give evidence in order to get a free trip to England for purposes of his own. I cannot say whether he was intimate with Gay Gibson or not but I would not put it past him.' Cherfas was more to the point: 'Mike Abel was a bullshitter.' But even if Abel had invented the story of Gay's collapse in the car, the whole cast had heard, like Camb, of her anxieties about being pregnant.

Wells returned from Johannesburg with twenty statements. The doctors and the lawyers sifted through them and obtained financial sanction from the court to bring two men and two women from South Africa. The second woman was to have been Doreen Mantle.

The police were also gathering in their witnesses. The four Gibsons arrived on the *Athlone Castle* in mid-December. They could not be happy in South Africa at such a time, old Joe said. 'My sons gave up jobs to come home with Daisy and me. We don't know what our future plans will be.' Mrs Gibson said her daughter had come back to take up an offer from the Abbey Theatre in Dublin. Next, Quinlan was on hand to meet sixteen-year-old Anna Jarvis – one of the young women who had made allegations against Camb after the porthole story was aired – her mother and small brother from the *Durban Castle*. The *News of the World* reported that Anna was wearing a leopardskin coat and that the family left 'for a secret destination'. [Allegations by Miss Jarvis and other girls did not surface in the trial.]

Dr Ruth Haslam, who had performed Gay's army demob examination, was by now working at the Royal Marsden hospital in London. 'A policeman walked in and showed me a picture of a girl and said something like, "Well, what about this then?" I looked absolutely blank because I didn't remember her at all.'

Camb's Christmas was lightened by a parcel of foodstuffs from the top deck of the *Durban Castle*. On 29 December, prisoner number 7651 wrote to Joe Chidgey thanking him for the 'kind gesture'. The hand is neat and small, the spelling excellent. His case, he says, comes up in March, 'but I have every faith in getting my discharge', though his wife was 'determined that I shall not return to the sea, so I'll look for a job ashore'. He asked Chid to pay a call on Margaret, now living in a flat in Waterloo Road, Southampton, under her maiden name, McCombie. 'This latter bit of news I would appreciate if you would keep strictly to yourself as life for her would be hellish if it became generally known.' And for the *News of the World*, as well.

In March, with the trial only weeks away, the defence seemed to be having an attack of butterflies. Ralph Mundel and Mike Abel broke their flight to England in Nairobi, Mundel believing that 'there is evidence in Kenya which we shall be very interested to have'. Charles Schwentafsky must have agreed, since he was out of town at the time of their stopover.

Henry Gilbert, with his wife Ina Schoub and their two children, arrived on yet another Union-Castle liner, to be met by Geoffrey Wells. Dr Schoub recalls Wells' over-confidence: 'He said the case would be thrown out of court and that Camb would be fined for pushing the body through the porthole.' Mundel met Camb only once, at Winchester Prison. 'At the time I was convinced, and I am still, of the same opinion that the accused did not kill or intend to kill the deceased . . . his story and his demeanour appeared to be genuine.' A report from Cairo gave out that Eric Boon would be giving evidence, but he never did.

When the *Durban Castle* docked once again in February, Union-Castle invited the prosecution team – Khaki Roberts, Henry Elam and Edward Robey – to view the scene of the crime. Robey recalls that 'the Union-Castle did us proud. We were entertained to a splendid lunch in the first-class saloon, with the ship's orchestra playing solely for our benefit as none of the passengers had yet arrived.' They inspected cabin 126 and the decks and staircases and pantries which made up the logistics of sex and dying on the ocean waves. 'It was,' said Robey, 'certainly the best conference I have ever attended.'

6

The Great Hall

There can be no more dramatic place to stand trial for your life than the Great Hall in Winchester. Here, in 1603, Sir Walter Raleigh was sentenced to be hung, drawn and quartered for high treason. Forty years later Captain Burleigh was condemned for a foolhardy attempt to spirit Charles I from his prison in Carisbrooke Castle on the Isle of Wight.

In the same tempestuous century, in 1685, Judge Jeffreys set out on that circuit which became known as the Bloody Assizes, punishing those who had given support to the Duke of Monmouth's rebellion against James II. Winchester was the first port of call and there Dame Alice Lisle – 'being thick of hearing' – was condemned for treason after a trial remarkable for the judge's bullying of witnesses. Three times Dame Alice's jury returned with a verdict of not guilty, and each time they were sent back by the judge until they delivered the verdict he wanted. He sentenced her to burn at the stake, and the only mercy that the king showed was to allow her to be beheaded, which act was performed in Winchester's market square at a spot now marked by a cross. It was small consolation to Dame Alice that the verdict was reversed by Act of Parliament in the reign of William and Mary.

The Great Hall is 'the finest surviving aisled hall of the thirteenth century'. It has survived by the skin of its teeth. William the Conqueror made the Anglo-Saxon city of Winchester his capital, and built a castle to serve as a fortress against attempts to oust the Norman usurpers, and to house the infant government departments of the Treasury and Exchequer. After government was moved to Westminster in the twelfth century, the castle was still regularly visited by royalty. The Great Hall went up in a further burst of architectural enthusiasm in the reign of Henry III. Length 111 feet, width 55 feet, it was fourteen years in the building and cost all of £500. The nave and two aisles were divided by columns of marble from the nearby Purbeck Hills. It has long served as an Assize court. Behind the judge's seat a brick-lined channel, the 'King's lug-ear', was once believed to lead to the king's retiring room, whence he could spy on the proceedings. When investigated in Victorian times, it was found to be part of a heating duct installed only a century before. Winchester was a Royalist stronghold in the Civil War. The Roundheads besieged the castle for a week, then rained down heavy mortar and finally broke through. When Cromwell ordered the castle to be demolished, labourers were brought in from Southampton and dismantled it stone by stone. Happily Henry's Great Hall was spared.

To this day, Jeffreys' conduct in courts from Winchester to Bodmin is considered a blot on the good name of the revered Western Circuit. The Circuit goes back 800 years, to when itinerant judges rode about on horseback bringing justice and the king's punishment to the farthest reaches of the realm. Hearings then were uncomplicated and the gaols were quickly emptied. Lord Denning, the former Master of the Rolls, lauded the Circuit system. 'It has done much to bring about a respect for the law. The coming of the judges and the barristers; the dignity of the proceedings; the panoply and the pageantry, all have played their part.' In this century its great names, not all free of controversy, have numbered Travers Humphreys, Rayner Goddard and Thomas (now Lord) Denning.

The railways did not break the Circuit spirit. The judge simply switched from his horse-drawn coach to a private first-class carriage and changed into his red robe on the train. The High Sheriff was at the station to provide a ceremonial escort to the judge's lodgings. But as Circuit towns grew larger, the impact of the Assizes waned. Barristers found it easier to catch the late afternoon train back to chambers or the London suburbs. The motorcar, more especially the motorway, and the habit of solicitors in Assize towns telephoning briefs to counsel in London reduced the size of the circus that had once rolled through the cathedral towns of the land.

And with it the Circuit mess entered upon a slow decline. Denning recalls those times with nostalgia. 'Each night the members of the Bar dined in their mess. Their conversation, their exchanges, their comradeship helped to build up that spirit that has remained to this day.' Every Assize town had a hotel with an enormous cellar and an official who combined practising law with maintaining stocks of liquor. At Winchester this was, and remains, the Royal Hotel. The mess committee organised a Grand Night at each Assize stopover. Gallons of liquid and volumes of words were disbursed at these evenings. Peggy Durrant, who worked in the Winchester Jurors' Office and also served at Grand Nights, never much noticed the after-effects in court on the morrow. 'Maybe some were a bit woolly but it was surprising how they could hold their drink.' But the mess was more than a drinking club. It decided the rules of etiquette – such as whether women should be allowed to join or solicitors be invited to dinner.

Such was the social life of the Circuit that at one time, not that long ago, 'a considerable number of barristers of all ages regularly went to Circuit, not only without any business to do, but without the slightest desire of obtaining any'. If, however, they were not averse to work, and no solicitor offered a brief, there were, in the days before legal aid, two courses open to an ambitious barrister. In murder and other serious charges, the Clerk of Assize arranged for a barrister who was paid a comparatively small amount under the Poor Prisoners' Defence Act. Joshua Casswell defended Camb in this way. In cases of lesser magnitude, there were 'dockers' or dock briefs, a long-established custom by which a prisoner selected his defence from among the expectant young lawyers and old hands waiting their chance in the courtroom. The etiquette of the Bar allowed of no refusal, but the fee of £1 3s 6d had to be paid 'cash on the nail'. The choosing was not completely arbitrary. Norman Birkett, as a young barrister making his way, literally had a head start on his rivals, as the prisoner's eye fixed on 'the bloke with the red hair'.

Sir Malcolm Hilbery arrived for the 1948 Winter Assizes with two more junior High Court judges, Sir Frederick Sellers (for 'Nisi Prius' or civil hearings) and Sir Francis Hodson (for divorce hearings). They and their wives were lodged in comfortable quarters in the Cathedral Close, an easy walk, were they so disposed, to the Great Hall. There were courtesy calls from the mayor, Mrs Crompton, MBE, the deputy-mayor, Alderman Bones, and the Town Clerk, Mr Kempton, MA. On the Sunday His Majesty's Judges of Assizes attended Matins at the cathedral, where, after singing 'God Save our Lord the King', they joined in Psalm 51:

> Against thee, thee only, have I sinned,
> and done that which is evil in thy sight,
> so that thou art justified in thy sentence
> and blameless in thy judgment.

The High Sheriff preached the message and there was a collection for the Hampshire Discharged Prisoners' Aid Society. Sir Malcolm and Lady Hilbery might then have strolled through the cathedral, to view the chest containing King Canute's mortal remains or to read the commemorative plaque to Jane Austen.

There were sixty-four prisoners on the Assize list, two of them on murder charges, three common jury actions and twenty-three non-jury actions in the Civil Court, and eight defended divorce petitions. It was run-of-the-mill criminal fare – forgery, robbery with violence, possession of counterfeit half-crowns, bigamy, infanticide by a mentally defective mother. Hilbery sent down a hayrick arsonist for eighteen months and delivered a little lecture reflecting the times: 'We are hard put to feed the beasts during the winter months in our present plight and yet you could think of nothing better to do to amuse yourself than set fire to these stacks.' He was not a sentimental sentencer. Striking a policeman on the head with a revolver collected seven years' penal servitude. A curate and a retired schoolmaster were each gaoled for two years for an attempted indecent offence. A Scottish coalman, father of ten, received four years for attempted incest with his daughters.

A Bournemouth newsagent who had shot his wife before trying to take his own life, pleaded guilty, and the trial was over in five minutes. Hilbery had no choice under the law. The *Hampshire Observer* described the scene: 'The black cap was put on the Judge's head and the Court rose as he passed sentence of death. As he came to the words "hanged by the neck until you are dead" loud screams echoed through the court, and as the Judge continued speaking the cries and sobs rose above his gravely quiet voice as a woman was escorted from the Court.' He would be reprieved, thanks to a jaw injury which made hanging impractical.

Casswell was no longer an inveterate circuiteer. He had spent the early part of the week at the Court of Criminal Appeal in London. His appeal successful, he travelled to Winchester and saw James Camb for the first time on Wednesday 17 March, the day before the trial. He was impressed (he said in his memoirs) by the 'forthright way in which he answered my questions'. When they got on to the subject of pyjamas, Casswell told Camb that if he had disposed of them he might as well say so. 'But he insisted that he was telling the truth. To my mind this attitude on his part was most impressive. After all, if he had said, "No, Gay Gibson wasn't wearing pyjamas, they were lying on the bed, but in my panic I thought they would be incriminating and threw them out of the porthole", who could have contradicted him?'

According to Casswell, 'Camb had no knowledge of what Professor Webster or any other witnesses for the defence would say until they actually gave their evidence in the witness box. Mr Wells was punctilious, and very properly so, in not letting the accused man know one word of the testimony that might save him. Until the witnesses gave their evidence Camb knew nothing of Gay Gibson's previous health or medical propensities other than what the girl herself might have told him in their chats on board the liner.'

Casswell also met Geoffrey Wells for the first time on the eve of the trial. It was the solicitor's first murder defence, 'but his inexperience was in no way detrimental to his client.' Wells had sent 'a handsome cheque for my opinion of the case, which I immediately refunded, for I knew he could not hope to be reimbursed under the Poor People's rules'.

The following notice appeared in the *Hampshire Observer* of 13 March:

The High Seas Alleged Murder Trial

Admittance to the body of the Court during the hearing of the Camb case, which starts next Thursday, will be by *ticket only. Applications* should be made *to the Chief Constable.* Accommodation in the public gallery will be limited to *50-55 seats.*

This was rather more than the number of citizens who had attended the previous week's meeting of the Winchester City Council to hear the rates raised by sixpence to nineteen shillings in the pound.

Only a few spectators would have a view of the judge. 'Notable British Trials' reported that 'the plywood partitions which had been erected, beside cutting off the view of many of the spectators, gave the court a curiously makeshift appearance'. A canvas structure inside the hall kept out winter draughts. An observer recalls that as it was 'very draughty and cold, they were always knocking bits off and adding bits on, so they put in a marquee. They were subject to the whims of High Court judges, who were like demi-gods . . . '

The first member of the public outside the court on Thursday 18 March was a 27-year-old social science student who had travelled the fourteen miles from Andover overnight. Thirty seats went to the press, among them several journalists from South Africa, where interest in the trial was almost as great as in Britain. The press box of four seats was full to overflowing. Harry Proctor of the *Daily Mail* was there, Harold Percy, Press Association stringer, J. Maggs for the *Hampshire Chronicle*, Brian Pook for the *Southern Evening Echo*, which ran the story for all it was worth. Mr Lloyd Woodland Snr, as every year since 1902, was in charge of the official transcript.

Room was found for the nobs. In the well of the court was Mrs Roberts, Khaki's German-born second wife. On the judge's bench were the High Sheriff, Lieutenant Colonel E. A. Hunter-Fell, his chaplain, Canon A. B. Milner, and the Under-Sheriff, Lawrence Bowker. Next to Roberts was his junior, Henry Elam, at six foot five inches the tallest man in court. H. J. Phillimore held a watching brief for Union-Castle. The empty seat left for Margaret Camb would not be occupied.

Sir Malcolm Hilbery sat down on the uncomfortable high-backed seat. Looming over him, fixed to the wall behind, was the most venerable piece of furniture in the land, King Arthur's Round Table, eighteen feet across, weighing fourteen hundredweight, originally consisting of 121 pieces of oak. It was not authentic. If Arthur's knightly activities were out of the sixth century, scientific techniques date the table to the mid-thirteenth. By Henry VIII's time it was already a national treasure. When he brought Charles V to view it in 1522, the Hapsburg king would have noticed that the freshly-painted figure said to be the king of Camelot had the unmistakable visage of the young Tudor.

Now, King Arthur's famous table was joined by the most infamous sleeping accommodation in the land, Gay Gibson's white enamelled bedstead, and a replica of the first porthole to achieve nationwide notoriety.

It is difficult to appreciate how much has changed in the court-room since the days when a prisoner convicted of murder was automatically sentenced to death. A good, old-fashioned murder trial, with frank sexual descriptions, the black cap, a public execution and, as a bonus, a gallows confession, was the pop concert and Cup Final of the nineteenth century. If you couldn't get to Tyburn Place or your local gallows, you read all about it in the gory pamphlets peddled in the streets of the larger towns. Prosecution and defence counsel were themselves Arthurian knights in armour, where the power of life and death might depend on the deftness of a rapier thrust. Geoffrey Dorling Roberts was the last of the larger-than-life criminal lawyers, whose predecessors had included Norman

Birkett, Edward Marshall-Hall, Edward Carson and Edward Clarke, and whose flamboyance would be rendered inappropriate by the abolition of the death penalty. Roberts was large in physique as well, six foot three inches tall, weighing eighteen-and-a-half stone. The nickname 'Khaki', from his darkish complexion, was a relic of Rugby School during the Boer War. Roberts had played rugby for Oxford and England, and was adept at tennis, golf, billiards and bridge. Four years with the Devonshire Regiment on the French front won him a Military Cross and five 'Mentioned in Despatches'. Barely a year into the war, he found himself, thanks to the slaughter at Loos, in command of a battalion.

His father was a solicitor and a mayor of Exeter and, in time, Roberts became Recorder of his home town, and later, of Bristol. The appointment was made by the town authorities to try cases of lower jurisdiction than the Assizes, so that, like all the four Porthole counsel, he had seen the world from the Bench. He was more often prosecutor than defender, usually to be found in the Old Bailey or on the Western Circuit briefed as a Treasury (Crown) counsel. This was not his first appearance on behalf of the acting profession. During the war, Roberts had unsuccessfully defended Ivor Novello for driving his Rolls-Royce without a petrol licence. (The musician served four weeks in Wormwood Scrubs, and donated a piano to the prison.) Roberts was more fortunate with Noël Coward, winning him an acquittal on a currency charge.

On the death of Sir Henry Curtis-Bennett, Roberts became head of chambers at No. 1 Temple Gardens in the Inner Temple. Over the fireplace a picture of a tramp asleep on a bench on the Embankment, with the legend 'Am I my brother's keeper?', perhaps reflected his streak of generosity – and an intimation of what the future held for him. The schoolboyish sense of fun, emboldened by generous whiskies, encouraged Circuit mythology, as with the story told of him in Bristol, attired in tiny bowler and pyjamas, umbrella in hand, pursuing a chambermaid along a hotel corridor. His gallows humour was given full rein during a golf match on the day when two men sentenced to death by his partner, Mr Justice Avory, were to be executed. 'Good morning, Judge, Good *swing* this morning?' Khaki was a hanger, like many at the criminal Bar, and a flogger as well. In politics a Conservative, he twice stood without success for Parliament. He might have been a disastrous MP.

Roberts was a lawyer's lawyer, but he could behave boorishly, and was quick to take offence if a remark annoyed him. What should have been the high-water mark of his career, as leading British counsel at the trial of the Nazi war criminals in Nuremberg, ended in disaster. He behaved gauchely towards his American colleagues, and Edward Robey, who was with him, spoke of 'many incidents that occurred on the social side of the life during the course of the trial which I am sure damaged Khaki's future prospects of becoming a High Court Judge . . . what he was hoping for as a reward for the sacrifice of many months of his practice at the Bar.'

In court at Nuremberg, in the most highly-publicised proceedings ever conducted prior to the television era, Roberts found it difficult to discard the Old Bailey style. Sir Norman Birkett noted in his diary: 'British case at Tribunal. G. D. Roberts did not shine.' To Alfred Jodl, the armed forces Chief of Staff, he said: 'If an honourable German gives his word, he keeps it, does he not?' Roberts became too personally involved for his own good, losing his temper when cross-examining the Luftwaffe Field Marshal Milch about RAF prisoners who had escaped and been shot on recapture. One of them was Roger Burchell, who had been a member of Roberts' chambers. A colleague recalls the general embarrassment when Roberts asked if it were not a matter that 'reflects shame on the armed forces of Germany'. Another prisoner was asked whether he called himself 'a gentleman'. Outwitted by Hermann Goering, Roberts was replaced by the British deputy chief prosecutor, Sir David Maxwell-Fyfe, whose consummate cross-examination destroyed the cleverest of the Nazis.

Now, aged sixty-two, Khaki Roberts was back on home ground, a tough opponent with a formidable knowledge of law and tactics. 'He can stand in court, hour by hour, day by day, cross-examining, with no apparent fatigue,' an admiring

newspaper reported soon after the Porthole trial. He was the
fellow you wanted on your side if you were fighting to save
your skin; in any other circumstances, you wouldn't want him
against you. George Snow, Roberts' clerk for thirty years,
knew him as well as anybody: 'Khaki, a man of the world, will
have understood how Gay could entertain a steward in her
cabin.'

The barrister appearing for Camb was an altogether different
person, laid back but no less skilful, a member of the Royal
Wimbledon Golf Club rather than the Garrick; family man,
ballroom dancer, amateur actor, who used his fine, deep voice
to good effect in court. And, unlike Roberts, more often defender than prosecutor. His practice was mixed, criminal and
civil. Joshua David Casswell – 'Josh' – was a contemporary of
Khaki's, long-jumping for Oxford when Roberts played in the
pack. He ended his war service as a major in the Horse Transport in France, with a 'Mention in Despatches'. But before that,
his career was off to a precocious start with an appearance for
the relatives of four steerage passengers who had gone down
with the *Titanic*, winning damages for his clients and shrewdly
cross-examining some salty witnesses. It thus spanned the
thirty years separating Britain's worst peacetime maritime
disaster from Gay Gibson's micro-tragedy of the sea. The early
twenties, with the Black and Tans operating in Ireland, were an
epoch of high tension. When Casswell accepted several con-
troversial briefs to defend Sinn Fein bombers, some solicitors
supposed, erroneously, that this was where Casswell's sym-
pathies lay, refused to brief him, and his practice suffered for a
while. He turned down an offer to become Chief Justice of
Bombay. Later he would become Recorder of Salisbury, then of
Southampton.

Casswell appreciated the regional niceties when massaging a
jury. Once, in Bodmin, he defended a local man on a charge of
defrauding the Potato Marketing Board, which the jury found
difficulty believing was criminal activity. He concluded his
peroration, in which his client's good character was emphasised, with the words: 'And, what's more, he doesn't owe a
Cornishman a penny.' Verdict: Not Guilty.

One of the best known of his forty capital trials was the murder at the Villa Madeira in Bournemouth in 1935 of the elderly husband of Alma Rattenbury, who was killed by her eighteen-year-old lover-cum-handyman, George Stoner. That, at least, was the jury's finding. There has long been a belief that Alma herself was responsible, and that Stoner confessed hoping the truth would come out at the trial. Alma was acquitted, Stoner (for whom Casswell appeared) was sentenced to death, Alma committed suicide. Stoner was reprieved and served seven years, but he told his lawyers when awaiting the appeal that he did not kill the old man. Over the years there has been speculation whether Casswell fought hard enough to establish Stoner's innocence. It would have been uncharacteristic had he not done so, for in court friend and foe used to say that 'Josh was always convinced his client was innocent'.

So here were two men at the height of their profession, high enough, almost, to be stepping off the ladder. Eighteen months earlier, a paragraph in the *News of the World* had pointed out that the two previous Lord Chancellors and Lord Chief Justices had come from the Western Circuit. 'I now hear,' said the anonymous ear, 'that two of the Circuit leaders, Mr G. D. Roberts KC and Mr J. D. Casswell KC are likely to receive judicial preferment in the very near future.'

Though both men were old hands at the game of murder, the atmosphere was strained on the first morning of the Porthole trial. Khaki had a small matter to settle with Josh. The year before, at the Bristol Assizes, Casswell had appeared for Ann Cornock, whose husband had been found dead in the bath. The case against her was very strong – bruises on Mr Cornock's head, an unhappy marriage, a love-letter from Mrs Cornock to her lodger. Writing in *The People* after his retirement, Casswell said Roberts 'had the look of a barrister who already had the case in his pocket'. But Mrs Cornock was a good witness and told a good story. On finding her husband dead, she said, she had dragged him from the bath and so bruised his head. She tried artificial respiration (which, like Camb, she knew nothing about) then waited three hours before calling the doctor, by which time she had changed her clothes, cleaned out the bath and made herself a cup of tea. Casswell battled hard to show that the love-letter was not folded and could not have been sent, and that the woman was not in love with her lodger. Mr Justice Croom-Johnson displayed clear partiality during the trial, and summed up strongly against the defendant. Which might be why the jury acquitted her. Casswell recalled that 'a cloud of disappointment spread over Khaki Roberts' face. He had seen certain victory go sour on him.'

One year later, at Camb's trial in Winchester, Khaki was determined to get the best of Casswell: ' . . . from the moment Roberts rose to make his opening speech, he conducted his case with a zeal and determination which even I, accustomed to battling barristers, found remarkable . . . As the trial went on, I could see he was using all his skill to win the case and even the score with me . . . Sometimes, in this way, the cause of justice may not be quite properly served.' Stung by these remarks, Khaki Roberts used *Tit-bits*, a popular weekly of the time, to hit back. 'I bore no grudge against my worthy friend with whom,' he declared, 'I downed several large Scotches in the Royal Hotel during the four days the trial lasted . . . On the contrary, I was looking forward to the case with some relish for I enjoyed my work in court enormously. To me the greatest pleasure in life has always been to be involved in an interesting case. And this one was "a wow".'

What followed was a contest within a contest, the dispassionate professionalism of the English Bar undermined by point-scoring. Still, Casswell, as usual, could relish the 'tense feeling of total responsibility, of almost romantic endeavour, which I always experienced before entering court on the first day of my murder trials.'

His client ascended from the bowels of the Great Hall. Having waited five months to prove his innocence, Camb must have been relieved that his ordeal was about to unravel. The Clerk of Assize was already speaking: ' . . . that on the high seas, you did murder Eileen Isabella Ronnie Gibson . . . Do you plead guilty or not guilty?' In a clear voice, the prisoner replied: 'Not guilty.' He was allowed to sit.

The jury was empanelled. None was challenged, unlike the

Lisle case, where nineteen jurors were passed over by the Crown before the requisite dozen were chosen. As with that case, they were middle class. The property ownership or householder qualifications had not been increased in more than a century, so that by 1947, the actual value of the house you lived in was no longer important. But the great majority of Hampshire people were not householders anyway. Jurors were not paid for their services. It was not until 1949 that jurors were able to claim expenses and some loss of earnings.

Though the Public Record Office lists two women on the Porthole jury – Pauline Marguerite Donnell and Minnie Gertrude Hyman, all eye-witness reports talk of three. So one of the following men was not in the final dozen: James R. Anderson; Alfred Edmund Claude Andrews; George H. Browning; Frederick Athelstan Chivall; Frederick C. Cummins; John W. Funnell (possible Fennell); Walter Ernest Hulbert; Ross I. Lawless; Sylvester J. Mitton; and Arthur Moore.

The jurors were mostly ordinary folk. They included two ex-policemen, but the man presumed to have had a strong moral and intellectual influence on their thinking was Lieutenant Sylvester James Mitton, mentioned in despatches in both world wars, retired business consultant, and a leader of English Catholicism, later MBE and Supreme Knight of the Order of the Knights of St Columba, a Catholic men's society.

The jurors swore 'by Almighty God that I will well and truly try and true deliverance make between our Sovereign Lord the King and the prisoner at the Bar and true verdict give according to the evidence'.

The prosecution had the advantage of imposing its version first on the minds of the jurors: a strong case, vividly presented, was akin to a five-yard start in the short sprint. 'Magnificent and menacing', was Camb's first impression of G. D. Roberts as he levered his huge frame from the seat. 'With grave, accusing deliberation he outlined the charge against me. He did not spare me. He exposed my lies and earlier evasions with a devastating well-polished ease.'

Roberts: 'The case is that the prisoner murdered this girl and disposed of her body by casting it away into the ocean through a porthole, the liner then being ninety miles from land in a shark-infested sea, or alternatively, that he cast the body into the sea when life was still in her body, he having overcome the resistance of the girl.' He warned: 'It would be futile not to recognise that this case has aroused a great deal of public interest. You may have discussed it yourself; you may have heard other people discussing it; you may have seen press reports or articles about the case. But you will realise, sitting in that jury box, that you have sworn to try this case according to the evidence, so you will discard any impression or opinions which any of you may have formed. You will decide this case solely upon the evidence which you will hear in this court, and you will bear in mind at all times the guiding principle of our law, namely, that it is for the prosecution to prove the case beyond reasonable doubt before you find a verdict of guilty . . . '

Roberts then recounted the story of Gay Gibson's life and fateful voyage. It is very much *her* story. The jury were told of Camb's statement, and no one else's, that she might have been pregnant. 'Now in justice to the memory of the dead girl I think you will be satisfied from the mother's evidence that that statement is not true.' The prosecution case would be conducted as a matter of courtly honour, and not always as a cool presentation of the facts. Roberts catalogued the episode of the bells, the scratches, the missing pyjamas, Camb's denials and eventual confession, and his careless, damning description of her going through the porthole: ' . . . I am fairly certain that at the time she was dead.' There was Detective Plumley's 'hell of a splash', with the bloodstain left to the end.

Khaki Roberts, wig askew over tortoiseshell spectacles, milked the story in classic forensic style. All that he outlined his witnesses would of course have to prove, but even when a telling point was shot down by the defence, the impression might lurk in the back of a juror's mind. He warned: 'You will not make up your minds until you have heard both sides, but, in my submission, when you have heard all the evidence the inference that you will draw will be that this girl objected to whatever advances the prisoner was making, and that she pressed both bells for outside help, she scratched the prisoner, and that for his self-preservation he throttled her. You will hear from the medical evidence that in manual strangulation there will be a haemorrhage and blood may be discharged from the mouth, and you may think that that being the position, that body being the most vital and deadly evidence against this man that it is possible to imagine, he took the only course which he could for the preservation of himself and put that body through the porthole. You may think that you can equally draw the conclusion that this girl, having objected, as I say, to his advances, he overcame her and rendered her past the power of speech or past the power to resist, and then, living, but unconscious, unable to resist, he destroyed the witness against him, the witness who could prove the crime of rape or attempted rape; he threw her, according to this second statement, into the ocean through that porthole.'

And as to Camb's defence – 'If she had died a natural death in his arms, as he now says she did, what would have been easier for him than to have slipped unobserved from that cabin (as in fact he did) and then the next morning this girl would have been found in her bed, sleeping her last sleep, having died a natural death, a fact which any medical man could have established in two minutes?'

In three-quarters of an hour the story was told – to those who had not already heard it from the Southampton hearing. Camb later admitted: 'I could see that the jury was impressed. Two women jurors turned and stared at me curiously.' Roberts had imposed his version on the drama. He concluded: 'Anxious as you are to do justice, can you imagine any other emotion which prompted this man to cast that body through that porthole except the emotion of fear – cold fear – the fear of the murderer disposing of the body which would be deadly evidence against him, or the fear of the ravisher whose advances have been rejected, disposing of the one witness who could give evidence against him?'

Little time was wasted in those days. The judge was on a tight schedule, and the court would sit on Saturday to complete the Assize list. Five days had been set aside for the trial. After

Roberts' opening, the court would hear thirteen witnesses before the day was out.

The first witness, a Southampton police sergeant, gave a nautical send-off to the proceedings with the measurements of cabin 126 – 8 feet 4 inches abaft, 8 feet 6 inches athwartships and 8 feet 5 inches from floor to ceiling.

Captain Patey was second in the witness box. He told of Camb's statements and actions during the second half of the voyage. As usual, the more revealing evidence was elicited in cross-examination. Thus, Casswell: 'If [Nightwatchman] Steer had reported [to the officer on the bridge] that it was a deck steward in 126, I presume investigations would have been made at once?' – 'Yes.'

'If Camb had been found in that cabin would he have been dismissed?' – 'He would have been logged for that, his book endorsed and finally dismissed.'

' . . . He would never get another position in any reputable line?' – 'I would not like to say that, but I expect he would find it difficult to get another job.'

Later, when Roberts asked, 'Generally speaking, are ships' officers concerned with passengers' morals?' Patey answered carefully, 'With discretion.'

The next witness was Sid Birch of Scotland Yard, who confirmed that the impression found on the inside of the cabin door was an 'identical palm imprint of the prisoner'.

By now the British and South African witnesses and reporters were in town, staying together at the same hotel. The atmosphere was ripe with irreverent journalistic speculation. Gay was said to have had afternoon sessions with a Union-Castle official on board. The suggestion was groundless, but it tied in with the teasing matter of the missing pyjamas. Still, here was some spice to enliven Hopwood's appearance in the box, and a good reason for Phillimore to hold a watching brief for the shipping line.

Casswell's first inquiry established that Gay's other beau, Bray, would not be giving evidence because he was back in hospital. In the absence of the ship's log, Casswell was unaware of inconsistencies in Hopwood's account of how he had escorted Gay to her cabin. If Hopwood's evidence was intended to provide reassurance about Gay's fitness, his answers raised question marks about her health. He gave away more than the prosecution might have wished.

Casswell: 'You said she appeared tired?' – 'Yes, that is true.'

'Or depressed?' – 'No, I would not use that expression.'

'Fatigued' – 'Yes, it may be; worried, I would say.'

At this point, the judge made the first of his intrusions: 'Or bored?' – 'It may be. Some mornings she was not with us; she stayed in the lounge and would not come on deck.'

'Was there any reason for her to be worried?' – 'None at all as far as I can make out.'

But Casswell would not be outdone: 'Was that her normal condition, or did she appear worried some days and not on others?' – 'She was more or less like that all the time, with the exception of one evening when she seemed to brighten up.'

Point to the defence.

Next to be called was William Albert Grosvenor Pott, aged forty-six, assistant smoking-room steward from Portsmouth. He had shared a cabin with Camb, and could not have relished giving evidence about the episode of the long-sleeved jacket. Still, he it was who had opened the way to the clue of the scratches.

Next came bosun Conway. He hardly knew Camb, since they mixed in different shipboard circles. He gave a rosier account of the late-night encounter on the Promenade Deck than had been written into the log. Now he did not mention that Gay ignored his request to move updeck so that her dancing shoes would keep dry. Conway also told of a meeting with Camb on the Saturday afternoon which indicated that many of the crew suspected him. On seeing Camb, Conway had remarked that it was 'sad about the lady passenger missing. I asked him what time he saw her last, and he told me he saw her around midnight talking to two gentlemen passengers on the starboard side of the Promenade Deck.'

The story unfolded with solemn deliberation. Now night-watchman Steer told of the bells. Once again, without access to the log, Casswell had no chance of tripping him up on discrepancies of evidence which might have carried some weight with the jury. Yet Casswell sensed that here was an unreliable witness. What is missing from the contemporary reports is a sense of the interlocking social and sexual structures on that ship – the second officer's avant-garde views on passenger morals; nightwatchman Murray's unwillingness to implicate Camb, or, perhaps, to embarrass Gay; the presumption that Murray, as the guardian of the ship's security, should have known that Camb was a wild one, even if his ear had not been close enough to the deck to hear of the advances to the young women on the outward passage.

The prosecution's secondary aim, apart from convicting Camb, seemed to be to protect the shipping company. Thus . . .

Casswell: 'When you reported to the bridge, for quite an intelligible reason you did not mention Camb's name, but merely said there was a man in the cabin?' – 'Yes.'

'You led the officer to believe it was a passenger?' – 'I expect so [this ambivalent reply could not be sorted out as White was not called as a witness] . . . The officer asked if there was anything they could do about it.'

'What exactly did he say?' – 'He said that he could not interfere with the passengers' morals.'

Roberts, re-examining Murray: 'Out of the kindness of your heart, were you trying to shield a fellow member of the crew?' – 'I think I can put it that way.'

'I am not criticising you, but were you shielding Camb?' – 'Yes.'

Of course, if Murray had told White that it was Camb in the cabin, and they had suspected that all was not well in there and barged in, they would have found him with Gay either still alive, or strangled, or dead by natural causes. Everyone would have been saved an awful lot of trouble.

Eileen Elizabeth Field, aged thirty-five, the cabin stewardess on the *Durban Castle*, was a qualified nurse from Portsmouth. At the witnesses' hotel there was yet more unsubstantiated gossip, to the effect that she was in love with, and so jealous of, Camb. It was most improbable. Her evidence did not help his case. She told of reprimanding him for leaving 'D' Deck and trespassing on her patch, Gay's cabin. But she did not hide the fact that Gay had seemed to encourage this.

Casswell: 'You really cannot tell us why it crossed your mind that Camb might be going down to her cabin?' – 'By the conversation before I thought they might be a little friendly.'

The day's last witness was Helena Baker, Gay's cousin from Southampton. Her evidence, intended to reinforce the idea of good health, was briefer than at the committal proceedings. It was frankly mediocre, serving to allow the defence to score an inevitable point by questioning the need for the witness to have been called at all. This would happen in the case of certain defence witnesses as well. No, she told Casswell, she had not seen Gay since the summer of 1945.

'For how long did Miss Gibson stay with you?' – 'Only that afternoon.'

Hilbery: 'And then she did not make the least complaint about her health?' – 'No, she appeared perfectly happy, and healthy in every way.'

This intervention from the Bench concluded the first day of the Porthole trial.

Khaki Roberts removed gown and wig, and hurried to Winchester railway station in time to catch the four-fifty train to Waterloo. That night, in the company of fellow Inner Temple Benchers, he dined with King George VI.

7

A Duke Swapped in the Cradle

'Even British justice can be unequal,' Khaki Roberts, an admirer of the legal system, was once moved to admit. 'Everyone connected with the law knows that because no two human beings have the same ideas, one judge may be very severe and another may be mild. It is just one of life's little lotteries as to which accused will appear before which judge.' The chemistry which threw the phosphorescent James Camb into the fusty waters of Malcolm Hilbery's courtroom reacted only too predictably. Forty years on, Roberts' junior counsel, Henry Elam, retains a vivid recollection of that first morning in Winchester: 'Hilbery was very much against Camb.'

Our interest here is to relate the judge to the prisoner in the dock, to understand what manner of man Camb and his lawyers had to contend with. Little has been written about this Victorian figure. There is no biography of Hilbery and his sole contribution to literature, apart from learned judgments, is a slim tome, *Duty and Art in Advocacy*, which used to be presented to barristers at Gray's Inn on their being 'called'. George Malcolm Hilbery was born in 1883, the son of a solicitor. His mother, born Julia Moncaster Mitcheson, is not mentioned in the son's entry in *Who's Who*. The Hilbery home was at No. 30 Hilldrop Crescent, Camden Town, a featureless north London street which, twenty-seven years later, would achieve notoriety as the residence – at No. 39 – of the poisoner Dr Crippen. Hilbery was educated at University College School, Hampstead, and then entered Gray's Inn, where he remained, spiritually, if not physically, for the rest of his life.

Hard work allied to a good brain won him the Certificate of

Honour in the final Bar examinations, and he was awarded an Inn scholarship. He soon made a name for himself in the courts, with occasional briefs from his father's office in South Square, Gray's Inn. But his generation needed more than parental help in order to survive. The First World War cut a mighty swathe through officers and men alike. Hilbery spent the four years as a lieutenant on a minesweeper. Once over that hurdle, the way was easier. He specialised in 'running down' cases, where his skill in cross-examination appealed to insurance companies resisting the claims of accident victims. In a rare cause célèbre, he appeared for the London Passenger Transport Board, one of whose Green Line coaches had collided with a car driven by a Hungarian marquis. Hilbery's cross-examination of the front-seat passenger, the society beauty, Lady Londonderry, clinched the argument.

There was also defamation work in the Courts of Justice in the Strand, and some criminal cases in Kent and Sussex. Francis Cowper's profile of Hilbery in the Dictionary of National Biography said that, whether pleading before judges or chairmen of tribunals, he 'achieved clarity of exposition based on thorough preparation so that his points were perfectly thought out and lucidly marshalled'. Not headline-grabbing, but reliable, and viewed favourably in the right places. So the inevitable progress – Recorder of Margate, King's Counsel, Commissioner of Assize in the South-Eastern Circuit, until, in 1935, at the age of fifty-one, he became a judge of the King's Bench Division.

The English Bench in those days was akin to the priesthood, the Lord Chancellor endowed with a Pope-like infallibility, the Law Lords on a par with archbishops, and High Court judges comparable to bishops, all deemed to be above human frailty. There were, to be sure, occasional lapses from these demanding standards, when judges wandered too far from the cloister. One was espied in a brothel. Another, Mr Justice McCardie, gambler and womaniser, committed suicide.

Hilbery's was a life of unusual insularity, despite his liberal schooling and the opportunities offered by a comfortable start in his profession. 'In private and in congenial company', said

Cowper, he was 'an interesting conversationalist on a wide range of topics, well versed in English literature and with a dry, ironic wit'. We don't know whether he travelled abroad, or even on a London bus, to Clapham or anywhere else. His experience in the courts was so narrow that the first murder trial he ever attended was the one that he presided over. The round of Assizes, with its vicarious view of the seamy side of life, at least brought him into contact with a world much different from that of the Inns of Court.

For his motto, which went with his coat-of-arms, Hilbery chose 'Nosce teipsum' – 'Know thyself'. It seemed to imply that he understood his limitations, and would not venture beyond them if he could avoid it. To Francis Cowper, he was 'the last of the High Court judges in the grand manner. Tall and slender, with a long, grave, impressive face, he consciously upheld the image of judicial dignity and impassivity whether in or out of court. His height lent itself to the loftiness of manner which he cultivated in speech and demeanour.' On journeys to and from the courts he was attired in silk hat and morning dress and was observed walking to the opera in Covent Garden wearing a top hat. As barrister, and more so as judge, he was a stickler for good manners. 'Day by day,' he lamented, 'you will see barristers addressing the court as if they were engaged in a casual conversation in a club smoking room with a fellow member for whom they had little regard, hands in trouser pockets, lolling back on the desks behind, apparently weak, listless and indifferent.'

Malcolm Hilbery was wedded to the law, both in the practice of it and in his daily life. Home was Gray's Inn, a clutch of handsome buildings, walks, lawns and flowerbeds on the ramshackle Gray's Inn Road running between Holborn and King's Cross Station. In that arcane society of barristers he wielded great influence, at various times Bencher (member of the governing body), chairman and treasurer of the house committee, "Master of the Walks" and inspiration of the garden committee. He was active in the Debating Society, the golf club, the Masonic Lodge. In the Blitz, he organised the storage of the Inn's art collection, and after the war played a role in restoring the hall, chapel and library which had been destroyed by the Germans. An acknowledged expert on art, Hilbery was responsible for the acquisition of paintings for the Inn. When the widow of the Appeal Lord, Uthwatt, offered his portrait to be hung in the upstairs hall alongside other prominent sons of the Inn, Hilbery declined. The fellow, he explained, was wearing a 'country suit', not the proper apparel for such high office. No matter that the painting was the work of the Royal Academician James Manson, and that Uthwatt was a fine judge and an engaging man. All deferred to Hilbery. Years later, when he was no longer a resident of Gray's Inn, the widow offered the picture again and it hangs there today.

His real persona occasionally broke through the judicial carapace. Hilbery was rather vain. Once, when he was trying a master and servant case and counsel made a submission favourable to the servant, Hilbery broke in: 'Mr So-and-so, are you saying that if I employed a butler . . . which incidentally I do . . . ' The effect was accentuated by his London middle-class acc_nt, a form of educated cockney that was going out of fashion at the time of his elevation to the Bench. His observations sometimes bordered on self-parody. Walking through the Meads in Winchester with a fellow judge, he solemnly declared that he had never been able to take an interest in coarse fish – 'they're much too common for me'. Sir Norman Birkett, for his part, sharing Leeds Assizes with Hilbery, found him 'a most pleasant companion with crosswords and literary and Biblical talk'. However, while members of his own Inn respected him, he earned little affection. According to Francis Cowper, Hilbery 'felt in his bones that he was a duke's son who had been switched in the cradle for a lesser being'. Contemporaries speak of his often expressed regret at not having studied at Oxford or Cambridge. Lord and Lady Devlin lived beneath the Hilberys at No. 5 Gray's Inn Square. Lady Devlin talks of his pomposity: 'His wife, who liked to be called Lady Dorothy, was charming. They were very keen gardeners. But really, they were a rather faceless couple.'

In his love of gardening Hilbery might have seen himself retracing the footsteps of the Inn's most revered son, the seventeenth-century Lord Chancellor, Francis Bacon, who once wrote that 'God Almighty first planted a garden; and, indeed, it is the purest of human pleasures'. Gardening brought Hilbery closer to royalty than even a duke might have achieved, when the Duke of Gloucester, the Queen's uncle and an honorary Bencher of the Inn, became treasurer of the garden committee for a year and Hilbery stood in as his deputy. A 1954 copy of the Gray's Inn magazine, *Graya*, shows the (real) Duke and Duchess strolling through the 'walks' in the company of His Lordship and Lady Dorothy.

Graya also reported regularly on meetings of the Gray's Inn Masonic Lodge, of which Hilbery had been a founder in 1937. In those days, freemasonry enjoyed an enthusiastic following in all four London Inns. It was said that 'anybody who thought he was anybody and did not have any objection to masonry joined the Lodge'. The 'Right Worshipful Master the Hon Mr Justice Hilbery, PGW' was Master of the Lodge in 1939. The Lodge entertained visiting masons in the Connaught Rooms, Great Queen Street, the London headquarters of British freemasonry, among them privy councillors, High Court judges, KCs and MPs. The forensic pathologist, Sir Bernard Spilsbury, was a guest speaker at the 1936 Michaelmas Term dinner.

To the outsider, there are certain similarities between freemasonry and the Bar. The legal profession is not a secret society, but it can conduct its affairs in a language unintelligible to ordinary mortals. The Bar in the thirties was dominated by the products of public school and the ancient universities, a self-perpetuating elite of the English upper-middle classes. The Lodge enabled them to continue playing their games, as it were, after school. During the day, Bench and Bar donned wigs and costumes of ermine or silk and exercised their profession in public. At night, they opened another door of the wardrobe and changed into the fancy dress of imperial wizards. To someone like Hilbery, who had missed out on the great educational tradition, the Lodge offered camaraderie and a 'swear-to-secrecy' exclusiveness.

It is impossible to know how much, if at all, Masons received favourable treatment in the matter of judicial appointments.

But it is a fact that both Malcolm Hilbery and Walter Greaves-Lord, appointed judges on the same day in 1935, belonged to the Gray's Inn Lodge.

On his elevation to the High Court, Hilbery, according to custom, was knighted, which should have ironed out some of his social hang-ups. Yet his want of educational status still rankled. In 1948, the year of the Camb trial, he was one of only a handful of twenty King's Bench judges without a university degree. The majority were Oxbridge men, though three had been to Liverpool University. The great public schools also predominated, with the exception of two of the finest lawyers among them, Norman Birkett (Barrow Higher Grade School) and Tom Denning (Andover Grammar). Indeed Hilbery was not ashamed of University College School, later serving as chairman of its council.

As a judge, Hilbery was a reliable workhorse. He was considered a good criminal judge, keeping the rudder straight as behoved a man who sailed a yacht until late in life and whose one outside club, apart from the inevitable Garrick, was the Royal Thames Yacht Club. In twenty-seven years he was rarely overturned on appeal, but his cases are no longer cited as precedent. If he had hoped for an appointment as a Lord Justice of Appeal, he was by now being passed over for younger men. Still, life had much to offer. Malcolm Hilbery might have been the judge of whom a wife once said that he liked 'being prayed for in cathedrals'. Lord lieutenants flattered him and court officials were obsequious. And there was the adulation of his peers. Those at the 1935 Gray's Inn dinner to celebrate the two judicial appointments were told by the senior Bencher, Sir Miles Mattinson, that 'few positions in Britain are greater than that of a High Court Judge. But there are even in the judiciary higher flights, and I have no doubt that these two distinguished friends of ours will rise to those heights, because they are Gray's Inn men, and it is in the blood of Gray's Inn men, it is a characteristic of Gray's Inn men, that when they enter upon a race they continue until they succeed, and there is no limit to their success.'

There are sightings of Hilbery at work. George Lyttelton

heard him 'holding forth to great purpose in dismissing a claim for compensation to a man who had fallen off a perfectly sound ladder. "Nowadays, if a man chokes over a biscuit he sues the confectioner; it's all rubbish."' Other views were not so kind. 'A very tough judge. We knew him of old,' recalled Allan Woodford, partner of the late Geoffrey Wells. Before becoming an Old Bailey judge, Edward Clarke had often pleaded in Hilbery's court: 'A bloody awful judge to appear before if you were defending. Most of the judges in those days were against the defence from the start. Malcolm Hilbery was an old-fashioned judge, and most of the judges in his day, including Rayner (Lord Chief Justice) Goddard, were grossly unfair.'

Hilbery prided himself on speaking little from the Bench. He was fond of quoting the Psalmist: 'I held my tongue and kept silence, yea, even from the good words, but it was pain and grief to me.' But the retired Lord Justice of Appeal, Sir Frederick Lawton, saw him in a different light when he appeared before him as senior counsel. 'When you got up to open a case, Hilbery was exceedingly unpleasant for the first half-hour. In my years at the Bar we had a generation of rather rude judges. When my colleagues got on to the Bench in the early sixties there was a great improvement in judicial manners. Judges didn't interrupt, didn't make sarcastic comments anything like they used to.'

Some judges are able to make their feelings known in a manner which defies reporting in the official transcript. The forensic pathologist Denis Hocking recalls Hilbery in the Camb trial tapping his pencil impatiently whenever Casswell adopted a line of cross-examination not to his liking. It must not be done assertively, or the jury may respond with an acquittal. Francis Cowper has talked of 'something hard to define with Hilbery; he was persuasive but he would not be seen to be pushing the jury. He had an authoritative manner in court and people did not like to stand up to him.' The ermine and wig and the regalia of the officers of the court, the trumpets and traditions of the Assize court, all conspired to render the judge a superhuman figure in the eyes of ordinary mortal jurors. Lord Devlin, in his study of juries, found that 'in a criminal trial the judge appears to the jury to be a more imposing personage than he does in a civil case, and perhaps a little terrifying. There is much ceremony, particularly at Assizes, that invests the judge with the majesty of the law and identifies him with the enforcement of law and order.' The more so when the manner was cool and detached – another of Hilbery's aphorisms was borrowed from Robert Louis Stevenson: 'Beware of purple passages. Wed yourself to a cold "austerity".'

There is no reason to believe, however, that Hilbery was a 'hanging judge' in the sense that his chief justice, Rayner Goddard, was said to be. Judges, until the first reform of capital punishment in 1957, had no discretion in imposing the death penalty for murder, though they would have to pass on a recommendation for mercy from the jury, or perhaps suggest it to the Home Secretary themselves.

If Hilbery was thought of as impartial, that reputation risked being dented in an Old Bailey trial of 1953 in which Michael Davies, one of a gang of teddy boys, was charged with murdering a youth of seventeen on Clapham Common. In an earlier trial, two of Davies' mates had testified that it was he who wielded the knife. The first judge had warned the jury in his summing-up that the youths were Davies' accomplices in the attack and that their evidence should be treated with caution, as a result of which the jury were unable to agree. In the retrial, Hilbery failed to offer the same warning and Davies was convicted. The point was argued before the House of Lords, and though it was lost – and Hilbery's action confirmed – Davies was reprieved. When he left prison Davies gathered evidence to show that he had been framed by two of his erstwhile friends. Did Hilbery believe, like his mentor, Francis Bacon, that 'laws are like cobwebs, where the small flies are caught and the great break through'?

When Malcolm Hilbery first saw James Camb in the dock, he might, unconsciously, have recalled a tragedy in his and Lady Dorothy's life. Having no children, they adopted a son, Michael Seymour, who served in a Royal Navy Q-ship in the Second World War. He died bravely, going below in an attempt to rescue shipmates after their boat was torpedoed, demonstrating a chivalry far removed from the deck steward's treatment of Gay Gibson.

8

White as the Driven Snow

On the second morning of the trial, senior counsel for the Crown boarded the breakfast train at Waterloo. After a sober evening in the presence of the monarch, Khaki Roberts would be in the mood to open his *Times* and follow the current crises – the aftermath of the Communist coup in Czechoslovakia; Jews and Arabs killing one another in Palestine as the chaotic birth of Israel drew near; civil war in Greece; a challenge to British rule in, of all places, Singapore. On the sports pages was a reminder that the English rugby team would be at Murrayfield the following afternoon. As the Wealden forests raced by, perhaps he gazed out and remembered his own day of glory against Scotland forty-one years before. Did he glance at the brief report of the proceedings in Winchester and recall the duel of honour awaiting him in the courtroom?

Women again outnumbered men in the public gallery. Gay's brothers, Paul and Joe junior, were seated at the back of court, while outside the Gibson parents waited their turn to give evidence.

Khaki Roberts opened proceedings by calling the ship's surgeon, Anthony Griffiths, resident, when ashore, of Appledore, Devon. The jury was soon plunged into complicated medical matters. Griffiths detailed the marks he had noted on Camb's body the day after Gay Gibson went missing. He admitted to being not quite sure how some of the scratches and abrasions were caused. The disputed marks were narrowed down to two areas – the right side of the neck and the right forearm. From his demeanour, he seemed concerned to remain above the fray.

It was 'fair to say', Griffiths agreed, that the six to nine scratches on the neck could have been inflicted in the early morning of 18 October. He rejected Camb's explanation of rubbing his neck with a harsh towel. But he would go no further, offering no satisfactory explanation of their provenance. The scratches which he saw were 'fine, similar to those inflicted by a cat's claw'. The presence of a cat being unlikely, the cause must have been 'some sharp projection or object'. When Roberts moved him down to the forearm, the doctor spoke with greater certainty about the marks on the front of the right wrist, nine to twelve 'separate injuries', between one-quarter and half-an-inch in length, 'entirely consistent with scratches caused by fingernails. I put each of them at between twelve to forty-eight hours old previous to my examination at midday on the 19th.'

Roberts: 'That is consistent with them having been caused in the early morning of the 18th?' – 'Yes.'

Camb had explained to him that 'two days previous he had been woken up in the night with severe itching and had inflicted these scratches himself'. But Griffiths had seen no sign of skin disease.

Casswell then began the first serious cross-examination of the trial. He placed the witness's medical experience in perspective – Griffiths had qualified in October 1942, spent two-and-a-half years at sea, never been in private practice.

There followed an exchange on the healing process, relevant because Griffiths' contemporaneous description of the marks on Camb's body were to be compared with police photographs taken more than a week later, by which time some scratches had turned into scars, and even disappeared. Griffiths, not surprisingly, could not say whether Camb was a quick or slow healer.

Hilbery: 'Was the whole of the scab pink?' – 'No, some of it was a delicate yellow.'

Casswell: 'Does that mean that there would be some pus underneath?' – 'No; when a scab forms it begins as pale yellow and as it ages it gets darker until it is almost dark brown.'

The police photographer had taken a shot of the neck abrasions, the ones which Camb said had been caused by rubbing with a harsh towel. But these were not the ones the court wanted to see, and there was no photograph of the disputed scratches on the right side of the neck. The matter was settled when Dr Griffiths confirmed to Casswell that the 'cat's claw' scratches on the neck were not caused by finger-nails.

Relieved, Casswell could move him on to the difficult hurdle for the defence, the wrist scratches. Griffiths was more certain of himself here: ' . . . no doubt in my mind that they were caused by fingernails'. For a jury jostled along in a confusion of abrasions and scratches, pink and yellow scabs, and what the doctor saw and the camera snapped, here at last was some-thing in plain English.

Casswell was left to dispute how the girl's nails came to dig into Camb's flesh. The battle ground was being narrowed. He suggested that these 'marks' were consistent with a sudden clutching and not a dragging across of the nails. He gripped his own right wrist to make the point clear. 'Do you agree that they are more in the nature of indentations than scratch marks?' – No, Griffiths did not. 'They are much too long for mere inden-tation.'

Casswell now implied that Gibson had clutched at Camb as she died her natural death, after which her fingers were re-leased, or were pulled away by Camb. On the contrary, said the prosecution, she dug her nails into the arms that were throttling the life out of her.

Hilbery: 'Did you think a scratching motion with the nails, or a digging action with the nails?' – 'It is difficult to divorce the two.'

'Then you think these were both digging and drawing?' – 'Yes.'

Casswell: 'Are they consistent with the man's arm having been gripped tightly and then having been freed?' – 'Yes.'

'You have heard, no doubt, of Professor Webster, of the Forensic Science Laboratory, Birmingham?' – 'Yes.'

'If Professor Webster is of the opinion that these injuries were caused by convulsive gripping of the wrist, would you agree with him?' – 'I would bow to his superior knowledge.'

Above: The Cambs, Jim (left) with Bob, and brother Tom, in Sunday best, Waterfoot, *c.*1933.

Below: St Michael's Church of England mixed infants' school, Lumb, a few miles from Waterfoot, *c.*1924. Jim Camb stands next to the headmaster, Mr Baxter.

Above: The fomer Margaret Clark McCombie and James Camb, newly married, Glasgow, 1943.
Below: The *Durban Castle* sails out of Cape Town, where the fateful voyage began.

Above: Gay Gibson, at the time of *Golden Boy*, Johannesburg, 1947.

Below: Henry Gilbert at the opening night of *Golden Boy*, Johannesburg, September 1947. Gay Gibson, in fur coat, is behind him. Eric Boon is in boxing gear and Mike Abel holds a straw hat. Doreen Mantle is third from the right.

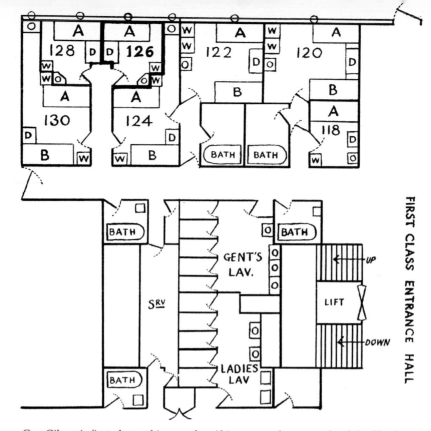

Above: Gay Gibson's first-class cabin, number 126, was on the port side of the Shade or 'B' Deck.

Below: Most first-class social activities took place on 'D' or Promenade Deck, two up from the Shade Deck. The ship's stern is on the left.

PROMENADE DECK

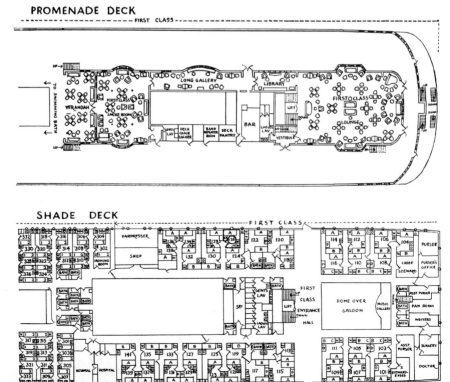

SHADE DECK

Above: Captain Arthur Patey, Master of the *Durban Castle*.

Below: Southampton Detective Constable Minden Plumley and Detective Sergeant Herbert Gibbons seek clues from *the* porthole.

Left: His Lordship, Mr Justice Hilbery.

Below: The Round Table looms over the Great Hall, Winchester, where James Camb stood trial for the murder of Gay Gibson.

Above: Joshua Casswell, Camb's counsel, on becoming a KC in 1938.

Right: G. D. 'Khaki' Roberts KC, who prosecuted Camb, in characteristic pose, refreshment at his elbow.

Above: Defence pathologists,
Dr Denis Hocking (left) and
Professor James Webster (right),
have a word with Camb's solicitor,
Geoffrey Wells, on the final day of
the trial.

Right: Mrs Daisy Gibson, Gay's
mother, in Winchester.

Before Casswell could register satisfaction, Hilbery leaned towards the witness. 'Against that, you have the advantage of having actually seen the injuries?' His Lordship turned to Casswell: 'It may be a matter of superior opinion, but it can't be a matter of superior knowledge.'

Casswell (to Griffiths): 'The knowledge of what it looked like the day after is yours, but have you ever had to deal with a case of what I understand here is alleged throttling, and scratching by the victim to release the throttling hand?' – 'No.'

'So that you would not be able to say whether it is usual to find marks, say, high up the arm in such a case?' – 'No.'

Roberts re-examined, anxious to win back ground lost on the 'fine' neck scratches. A possible explanation, said Griffiths, was a ring with a sharp projection. But he was quite sure they did not come from 'a female who wore her fingernails sharpened to a point'.

Still his witness would not give way on the arm scratches. To the 'tricoteuses' in the public seats, and the court reporters and their readers, and most importantly, to the jurors, that was the one real fact they could unscramble from the jumble of medical assertions popping up for attention like hungry goldfish in a busy bowl. Camb's own explanation would make matters worse.

Next, the coppers. Detective Sergeant John Quinlan, aged forty-two, was university educated, a policeman since 1929, with crime-busting successes in the area of fraud, rather than violence: a wartime meat racket, a NAAFI scandal, a US Army stores fraud.

He gave his account of how the statement was coaxed out of Camb. He had handed, direct to the Hendon Forensic Laboratory, three phials, containing hair from the top of Camb's head, from the side of his head, and a pubic hair, as well as the blood sample.

'What is exhibit 29?' Roberts asked Quinlan. – 'A Coronex contraceptive and a tube of Coronex contraceptive jelly which I found in a large brown suitcase by the side of the bed in cabin 126. The suitcase was shut but not locked.'

The effect of this revelation was much as if the great pacifist of the day, Bertrand Russell, had been caught with a bomb in his briefcase. Khaki Roberts had been told that a virginal girl had equipped herself with a birth control device. Hilbery tapped his desk and silenced the murmurers.

Roberts sat down. Casswell gave instructions for the contraceptive to be shown to the jury. His first question: 'Is that what is called a Dutch pessary?' – 'I believe that is the common term for it.'

The main thrust of Casswell's cross-examination was to discredit Quinlan's assistant, Minden Plumley, who had since left the Force under a cloud. He asked about Plumley's unexpected extraction of the second 'confession'.

Casswell: 'Did it occur to you that this most important statement which Plumley said he [Camb] had made to him was one which you should put to him [Camb]?' – 'No.'

'Is Mr Plumley now in the Southampton Police Force?' – 'No.'

'Why not?' – 'I do not know; I have no information on the point. I was not here when he left.'

'Do you remember an occasion when a man called Tallon was before the Southampton Quarter Sessions in July last year?' – 'No.'

'Do you remember a case in which Plumley had taken a statement which the Recorder of Southampton refused to accept?' – 'I don't remember it, I was not there.'

No ratting on former colleagues. The stage had been set for the sideshow of the rogue policeman. The defence rightly feared the potential damage of this second statement. Plumley was brief, repeating the disputed confession word for word: he had 'resigned' from the Force in January, following a catalogue of misdemeanours, though none apparently related to the Porthole investigation. Casswell seemed to know him and his unorthodox methods.

'At Southampton Quarter Sessions last July did you put in a statement which you said the prisoner, Alfred Caller, had made?' – 'I did.'

'Did the man give evidence that you had given him beer to drink before he made the statement?' – 'Yes.'

'Did you deny it?' – 'No.'

'In a public house?' – 'Yes.'

'Did you take him to police headquarters and prepare a statement?' – 'Yes.'

In his memoirs, Casswell wrote: 'Then I paused to let the full tenor of my questions seep into the jury's mind – "Were the jury directed by the Recorder not to convict?" The constable paused in the witness box. For a moment he did not answer. Then – "I do not remember the summing-up by the Recorder." I took a quick look at the jury and saw from the expression on their faces that I did not need to ask any more questions on this score. They had formed their own opinion of the value of the witness's power of recollection. For myself, I remembered very well what the Recorder had done. I happened to have been the Recorder!'

Casswell pressed on with the mauling. His solicitor must have had good contacts in the police.

'Was there another occasion when you and another officer smashed up a car together?' – 'Yes.'

'Was that something to do with your resignation?' – 'I do not think so.'

'Did the chief constable complain about it?' – 'Yes, he did.'

'That was one instance at any rate when the chief constable found fault with you?' – 'That is so.'

Casswell was enjoying himself: 'Was there another occasion when there was a scuffle and a police officer was found with two or three other men, and did that officer turn out to be you?' – 'I do not remember that . . . '

'Did you take part in a fight and get knocked about yourself shortly before Christmas . . . was there any occasion when property which had belonged to a prisoner was found in your locker, and you had not entered it in the Property Record Book . . . ?'

By destroying Plumley's credibility as a truthful witness, Casswell had cast the second 'confession' into the wastepaper basket. He cleared the decks for the battle to come over Camb's statement and the prevarications leading to it.

Dr Walter Montgomery, Fellow of the Linnean Society,

senior scientist at the Metropolitan Police Laboratory, had examined the bed linen, the hairs of Camb and Gibson, the lipstick, powder puff, boot polish, hairbrush, blood and other *trouvailles* in cabin 126. On the top pillow he had found tea stains; on the bottom one, lipstick and perspiration; on the counterpane, brown boot polish. (Casswell would suggest that 'Miss Gibson had been cleaning her shoes on it.')

On the top sheet, eighteen to thirty inches from the end (which end, we are not told) were traces of human blood group 'O', which was not Camb's, and so must have been Gay's. On the bottom sheet: 'Two small human bloodstains, but they were too small to determine the group . . . there was (also) a yellow stain, the nature of which I could not determine.'

Casswell went easy on Montgomery. 'Did you form any opinion,' he asked, 'as to whether the hair given to you as coming from the bed had come out naturally?' – 'No, the hair was incomplete and I was unable to say how it had come out.'

The most significant reply was the last, to Roberts, re-examining: 'How many spots of blood were on the top sheet?' – 'I removed two, each about the size of a sixpence.'

'And on the bottom sheet?' – 'Two, very similar to those on the top sheet.'

Which seemed clear proof that they, or Gay alone, depending on the version one accepts, were not lying between the sheets, but on top of them.

It was only after Montgomery had left the box that Dr Hocking, who was advising the defence on the scientific evidence, realised he had slipped up in not asking to see the slide preparations. 'Montgomery's examination of the fibres from the porthole was most perfunctory. He just talked of "fibres" and "contents of pillow", but a very minute examination should have been made for skin scrapings and fibres from the dressing gown and the black pyjamas. It might have solved the pyjama difficulty. If she had been wearing the pyjamas I would have expected some fibres from the legs as they went through. In which case, there might have been no skin scrapings. And there must have been a lot of fibres from the dressing gown, but they were not mentioned. It was my fault. Montgomery should have been severely cross-examined.'

The army now made its appearance, with a brief march-on performance by Senior Commander Phyl Macdonell of the ATS Medical Service. She produced Miss Gibson's file. No, there was no record of any medical treatment ever having been afforded to Eileen Gibson while she was in the service in 1946.

She was followed by the strapping figure of Lance Corporal Audrey May Puttock, medical orderly stationed at the War Office Holding and Drafting Unit, North Mimms, Hertfordshire, who confirmed the signature of Miss Gibson and Captain Haslam on a file recording the final medical examination.

Dr Ruth Haslam, who gave Gay her demob medical check-up, was examined by Roberts' junior, Henry Elam, whose tall frame towered over the courtroom. Since being notified that she was to give evidence, Dr Haslam admitted, she had not been able to recall anything of her transient patient. She had been doing as many as ten examinations a day. She confirmed the correctness of the entry on the file, that Gay was a healthy woman when she had left the army. The form which recorded that final 'medical' was a 'W/3149'. The young MO – she was twenty-eight and had joined the army after the end of the war – used it as an aide-memoire to answer questions. She laboured under the further disadvantage of not having had the customary preparatory interview with prosecution solicitors before going into the witness box.

'Was there anything at all the matter with her?' Elam asked – 'According to the form, the only thing I found wrong was an old infection of the right ear, and I noticed that the drum was scarred; it had last discharged three weeks before, and I noticed that her hearing was impaired. She had had a recent cold, but her general physical condition was good . . . she was a bit wheezy, but there was nothing of significance in that . . . When I listened to her breathing I noticed that there were slight sounds, sibilla, which indicated that she had slight bronchitis.' Dr Haslam had written 'NAD' – 'nothing abnormal discovered'.

Elam asked what conclusion she had come to on Gay's general fitness for service. Dr Haslam, still reading from the form:

'I put her down as AW/1/non-tropical; that is to say, her general condition was fit, apart from the ear condition, for which reason I made her non-tropical.'

Casswell picked up the questioning: 'Before you make such a report do you have any sort of medical history sheet before you?' – 'Usually one does, but I cannot say whether I had one in this case.'

'So if there was not one before you, you would only have her word to rely on as to her medical history in the Service?' – 'That is so.'

'Supposing you had had reported to you that at the beginning of July 1946 she had had a sort of seizure which lasted for a considerable time, would you have examined her carefully about that?' – 'Yes, but I should have examined her much in the same way as I in fact did.'

'I suggest you would have examined her still more thoroughly?' – 'That is possible.'

'And if, in addition, she had told you that in December previously she had had a seizure while travelling in Wales which lasted more than half an hour, would you have thought that something which you ought to look into?' – 'It would rather depend on what kind of a seizure it was.'

'You would have wanted to look at the full account of it?' – 'Yes.'

From her file, Casswell produced another document, a Service and Casualty Form, which showed that Gay had been admitted to Broadgreen Hospital, Liverpool, from 1–6 February 1947.

'That was a fortnight before you examined her?' – 'Yes.'

'That does not show up on this report at all?' – 'No.'

'I have got another one, "Sick at Home, w.e.f., 9th April 1945, and rejoined 14/4/45"?' – 'Yes.'

'I find from the medical sheet that at Liverpool, on 25th January 1945, there is a note of her being "scarred on the neck from poultice", on the right side of the neck?' – 'I do not remember seeing these statements at the time I examined her in February 1947.'

Mr Justice Hilbery, perhaps aware that an intervention was

overdue: 'Is there anything in those previous records which would have caused you to modify your opinion about the health of that young woman when you examined her in February 1947?' – No, Dr Haslam told him. (The question, it should be borne in mind, was related to a medical examination which the witness could not recollect without the aid of the piece of paper in front of her.)

Casswell had one more question. 'You record that she was suffering from a recent cold, and had a wheeziness. Was that something which was subjective, or was it something she told you?' – 'If I put it down it was something I discovered myself; whether she told me or not I cannot say.'

Roberts re-examined: 'When you saw her on 19th February, after her discharge on the 6th, she was suffering from the seasonal effects that we are all so well acquainted with, of an English winter, having a cold and wheeziness?' – 'Yes.'

Years later, Dr Haslam recalled her day in court. 'I remember feeling at the time that I was rather biased in my own mind against the chap . . . and I was rather horrified that I should feel that way before the evidence was there. It wasn't unnatural of me, but I thought I should have been more objective about the whole thing.'

One of Britain's most experienced army doctors, John Ewell, who ran army medical services in the south of England during the Second World War, and retired with the rank of colonel from the Territorial Army in 1970, averaged three discharges an hour in those demob days. 'In twenty minutes,' he recollected recently, 'you had a height-weight-urine test, clinical examination, a look at the joints, blood pressure, cardiovascular system. You might have missed all sorts of things. The overriding thing is, even if something was wrong with her and she was seen by a doctor the day before she died, I doubt whether he would have spotted anything.'

Lunch. The prisoner descended, escorted by two prison officers, the judge departed amidst scenes of bowing, followed by his clerk and chaplain. Mrs Casswell had driven from Wimbledon with a special meal for Josh, to placate his ulcer. Spectators – regretfully, for the promised drama had not materialised – filed out to eat sandwiches or hurry home to walk the dog. Left in the courtroom were a handful of minor officials and policemen watching over the site. Conversation moved on to the 'furnishings', to the replica of the porthole. How easy or difficult was it to pass a body through. 'Ah, there's Peg, she's a bit like Gay Gibson, let's try her,' said a Hampshire policeman. Peg Durrant of the Jurors' Office, eighteen years old, recalls: 'Two or three of them held me up and pushed me headfirst through the porthole. It was not easy. Had I struggled or just put my arms out they would never have done it. And I was much slimmer then than I am now.'

The first day-and-a-half of the trial of James Camb had been a subdued affair. There would be no blood-curdling performances in this judge's court. If there were to be drama, it would be of the restrained sort. Now, at last, the onlookers prepared to shift their emotions into a higher gear as the usher called the name of Ellen Victoria Gibson.

Gay's mother wore a mustard-coloured raincoat over her dark suit. 'A tragic figure in the witness box', said the *Echo*. 'A pleasant, round-faced, middle-aged Englishwoman, just like millions of other English mothers, with the same pride and the same loyalties,' Casswell recalled. In other words, a dangerous witness, determined at all costs to clear her dead daughter's name. She stared intently at Khaki Roberts. Her first words set the tone: 'I am very proud to be the mother of Eileen Gibson.'

Roberts turned to Gay's health. 'Generally speaking, for the whole of her life, how was her health?' – 'Excellent. She was one of the finest types of English womanhood, physically, mentally and morally.' The clipped syllables of the ward round added a note of authority.

'During her time in South Africa did you see any traces of ill health in her?' – 'None whatever; her health was excellent.'

'When did you last see her?' – 'When she came down to Durban, the day before she left on the boat for England. It would be 7th October; she went by air from Durban to Cape Town. I did not go with her.'

'When you last saw her was she a healthy young woman?' –

'Yes, perfect.'

'How was she in spirits?' – 'She was very healthy, and very happy at going home to England.'

'How did your daughter wear her nails?' – 'She let them grow rather pointed.'

'Did you notice that in South Africa?' – 'Yes, and my sons noticed that she let her nails grow longer than usual.'

And that was it. In ten minutes his examination was over. Daisy Gibson's dignity, the terrible reason for her presence in the witness box, the unfaltering manner in which she had established her daughter as a credible human being, had made a profound impression. Roberts handed her over to his learned friend and settled back to observe sparks flying.

Afterwards Casswell noted: 'There was no more unpleasant moment of the whole trial than soon after lunch on the second day when I rose to cross-examine Mrs Ellen Gibson, the dead girl's mother. She, of course, knew in advance the line that those charged with Camb's defence would have to take . . . she must have entered the witness box . . . realising full well that in a sense her dead daughter was as much on trial as the man in the dock . . . I had to do my best to tear the shreds of self-deception about her only daughter from this woman for whom one could have only sympathy.'

He began 'quietly, gently putting to her certain details about Gay's early life which could have caused no possible offence'.

Then he tried to establish just how much contact she had had with Gay after joining the army: 'I suggest that you were parted from her most of the time she was in the Service.' – 'No. In 1945 she came home from time to time.'

'Did you hear anything about her having an affair with an RASC driver?' – 'I did not know what he was, but she knew somebody by the name of Pierre.'

'She was really keen on him?' – 'I do not think she was really keen on anybody; she was not particularly interested in men or marriage; she had one interest in life, and that was a theatrical career.'

'In July 1946, did you hear of her having an illness while she was still in the corps?' – 'I know she had a septic hand, which was burnt with an electric iron; that is the only illness that I know of.'

'You did hear that she was taken ill suddenly in July when she was at Sloane Court West?' – 'No, I was in Persia then.'

'Then again in December 1946, did you hear that she had been taken ill?' – 'Never.'

'She never said anything to you about this?' – 'No, the only trouble she had was her hand and her ear. She was in the military hospital in Alder Hey with her ear.'

Moving on to her return voyage to England, Casswell inquired whether Gay had had injections. Mrs Gibson: 'As she was going to England I advised her to have injections to avert colds because she was rather susceptible to a common cold which left a little catarrh . . . I understood she would have some when she got to England. A lot of people have them when they come home from the tropics.'

When Casswell turned to the Johannesburg theatre world, Mrs Gibson braced herself. 'Was she there in a theatrical company run by a Mr Gilbert?' – 'No, there was no company run by Mr Gilbert. She was in Johannesburg, in rep, in *The Silver Cord*. Mr Gilbert ran a little show in imitation of Tommy Handley at Broadcasting House, Johannesburg, and she met him there. They were a different class of people from us.'

'You mean that Mr Gilbert and his associates were a different class of people?' – 'Yes. I advised her to take a refresher course in her shorthand, to have a regular job, and to stay in repertory as a diversion, and she said, "Yes, Mother, I will."'

'You took her to Johannesburg after about a fortnight in Durban. Did she return to Durban?' – 'No; she had a good singing teacher in a Mrs Taylor at Johannesburg and so she stayed there, but after a while she could not continue with her singing lessons.'

'Was not that because it hurt her throat?' – 'No, she said she would have to give up her singing lessons because she had not got the time to practise.'

Casswell returned to Gilbert. 'And the last play she was in was being produced by Mr Gilbert?' – 'Yes, the only play he ever produced.'

'You do not seem to be very friendly with Mr Gilbert?' – 'No. She was working for Mr Gilbert in the preparation of this play. She worked very hard. She was a very conscientious type. There was a shop in Johannesburg which supplied the dresses and costumes, and they said, "The young lady that wears these dresses can keep them", but instead of that Mr Henry Gilbert sold them; not that she wanted them, but it was just the principle of the thing which was not nice. She said to me, "Mother, Henry has turned out to be a rotter." On the stage he had put his arm around her, and she said, "The way he mauls me about on the stage; he is most embarrassing."'

And there was a Dr Schoub?' – 'Yes, she is a doctor of medicine; she is casualty officer at the Johannesburg hospital.'

'She befriended your daughter, did she not?' – 'Befriended her! Never.'

'Did you know that your daughter went to Dr Schoub for advice?' – (indignant) 'My daughter would go to a consultant for advice, not to Dr Schoub . . . My daughter would consult me if she wished for advice; she had a very poor opinion of Dr Schoub; she said, "She is a bit of a quack." She had a very poor opinion of Henry Gilbert, his wife and their associates.'

'Did you know your daughter consulted Dr Schoub on the ground of pregnancy? – 'My daughter was not pregnant.'

'Did you know your daughter was going about with several men in Johannesburg?' – 'I know my daughter was not going about Johannesburg with men, because she told me everything and I know she was not interested in men; her career was her life.'

The court listened spellbound to the parrying of punches. Though the introduction of the pregnancy allegation raised the atmosphere almost tangibly, the only sound was the regular drumming of the judge's pencil on his desk. A contemporary observer saw Khaki Roberts slumped in his seat, hands in trouser pockets, face gloomily impassive, eyes half-closed behind the tortoiseshell spectacles, his only gesture, to pluck his wig from his head by its topknot and drop it back slightly crooked.

Casswell played what he justifiably believed to be a strong

card. Could she explain the contraceptive found in her daughter's cabin? Her reply, that 'university students and others often carry them about with them; that is nothing to go by', raised brief laughter, a rare moment of light relief.

'Why do they buy them?' – 'To avoid pregnancy.'

'You would avoid pregnancy by never having intimacy with a man, would you not?' – 'My daughter was a very honourable girl, and it was not until she got in touch with this man Gilbert and his wife that anything questionable about her character could be suggested. Her friends were lawyers like yourself in Johannesburg, honourable men. Ask them about her character.'

'Did she ever tell you that she had a contraceptive in her possession?' – 'No, she told me practically everything – well – she told me everything.'

Casswell asked about Mike Abel. – 'She said to me, "Mother, I think he is a real gangster." He had to play the part of a gangster on the stage.'

'And when she kissed Abel, and then kicked him on the shins?' – 'That is just Mike Abel's talk.'

'You would not believe it, would you?' – 'Nor would you if you had known my daughter. She said that Abel was a real gangster and she said that both wives were jealous and were squabbling.'

'Why were they jealous?' – 'Because she was a good woman and they were a pack of crooks.'

'Why would that make the wives jealous?' – 'She was very attractive.'

'Do you mean that she was going about with the husbands in a way that they objected to?' – 'No, she did not go about with them; you cannot make out that my daughter was something she was not.'

So Casswell, having tried the army driver Pierre, illness in Sloane Court, pregnancy, Dr Schoub's advice, Mike Abel's shins, and the 'pessary', without making much impression on witness or jurors, turned to Charles Schwentafsky.

'Did you hear the name of Charles Sventonski?' (a phonetic rendering, presumably) – 'Yes, she knew him about a fortnight. I met him in Durban.'

'Did you know that he sent her flowers every night and took her away from the theatre every night?' – 'No, I was not there at the time.'

'Did she introduce him to you as her boyfriend?' – 'No, she introduced him to me as a man who was interested in her career.'

'She suddenly decided to go back to England?' – 'She had an introduction to the management at the Abbey Theatre and to some friends of Sventonski; a letter of introduction.'

Hilbery: 'Is he a man of the theatrical world?' – 'Yes.'

Casswell: 'Have you seen any of these introductions since she disappeared?' – 'No. I saw them in her bag before she left. I think Sergeant Quinlan has them.' (They were not produced in court.)

Schwentafsky paid for her daughter's first-class fare, she conceded, and transferred £350 into her bank account, making a total of £500. Why should he do that? Casswell inquired. Because, said Mrs Gibson, he was interested in her career.

'Did you approve of her receiving £500 from a man she had only known a short time?' – 'It was a business proposition; he was a very successful man; whatever he supported seemed to be successful; he was said to be very lucky in his business affairs. My daughter said to me, "He is very involved in his business matters, and I am very involved in my career." He was ready to back her in her career as a business proposition.'

'Had he ever been to England as far as you know?' – 'Not as far as I know.'

'What makes you think he had any influence with English theatrical circles?' – 'Because he knew a lot of people, and he gave her a letter of introduction.'

'You say you see nothing wrong with your daughter accepting £500 from a man she had only known a short time?' – 'She said she would very soon pay him back. She was a hard-working conscientious girl, and she was hoping to become successful in her career.'

Henceforward, English court records would identify Charles Schwentafsky, night-club proprietor, *roué extraordinaire*, game hunter for royalty, as a substantial man of affairs, with connections leading from his colonial outpost into the heart of the metropolis. In his absence, the prosecution used him well. Heaven help him if he had appeared as a witness for the defence. Khaki Roberts might have attempted to carve him into small pieces.

From now on, Casswell had the air of a rattled man. He repeated questions which on no account should have been aired again, having failed to get the answers he was looking for . . . Mike Abel's shins, the state of her daughter's health, her pregnancy. To this last she was able to reply: 'I am a nurse, and we were very close friends, my daughter and I; we had no secrets from one another. I said, "You are quite sure about this man?" [Schwentafsky] and she said, "Mother, you can rely on me."' You almost saw, heard, felt the good men and women in the jury box nodding in agreement.

'Was she very highly-strung, very emotional?' – 'No, she was very calm, very controlled, with dignity and poise, a lot more than I have.'

'A girl liable to create scenes without the slightest provocation?' – 'Never. That is definitely an invention, like the other invention about her being pregnant.'

'Did you know that she was drinking heavily, among other things, vodka?' – 'No, she would not drink vodka.'

'Nothing I might put against your daughter would you believe for a single moment?' – 'No, that is so.'

Casswell, almost pleading now: 'You would not accept anything I suggest?' – 'No, one's character does not change in a fortnight after twenty-one years of honourable and conscientious living.'

Eric Boon would have admired the uppercut to the chin.

Casswell assayed a last, flickering sally at the dead girl's character. 'Did you know that she told Mike Abel that you and her father had been killed by V-2 bombs?' – 'It sounds like the allegation of a gangster.'

'And that her two brothers had been killed on service with the navy?' – 'No, that looks like the invention of a gangster.'

'Do you think it is possible that in the time she was in

Johannesburg, she may have deteriorated?' – 'I do not.' (She clutched the court Bible.) 'My daughter was most truthful.'

As Casswell groped for his next question, Roberts lumbered to his feet. 'I do not want to object to anything, in a trial of this importance, which the defence reasonably do, but, in the interests of time, I submit that this attack which is being made on the character of this dead girl has not the slightest relevance to the issue which the jury have to try. I can see some possible relevance in the state of her health, but how an attempt to blacken the character of this girl who is dead and cannot answer for herself, can be relevant to any issue which the jury have to try, I fail to see, and therefore I respectfully submit (although I do it with the utmost reluctance) that these questions are not admissible, as not going to any issue before the jury.'

Roberts knew well enough what his old adversary was driving at. He would have done exactly the same thing in his position. Years later he admitted: 'The defence tried to impugn Gay Gibson's morals. This was quite a legitimate ploy, for it is the duty of defence counsel to try to get his client off, whether innocent or guilty . . . '

The judge waited for Casswell's reply. Lamely, he said: 'It is suggested that this was a rape which took place on the night of 17–18 October . . . '

To be interrupted, almost as irrelevantly, by Hilbery: 'Attempted rape was what was suggested in the opening.'

Casswell: ' . . . that this girl would not willingly have received this steward into her cabin is the suggestion, and therefore I submit that it is highly relevant to see if she was inclined to be over-friendly with men.'

Hilbery was not impressed. 'I do not know. There are cases in the books which show that a prostitute can be raped. I suppose there is a possible relevance. It must go on. In such matters I am in the hands of counsel . . . '

Mrs Gibson picked up the word 'prostitute'. 'In her dealings with men she spoke to them as man to man, but she did not go farther; she was a very honourable girl.'

Casswell sat down. Thankfully? We will never know.

Roberts rounded off with a question or two about Gay's earnings and financial help from the family while in Johannesburg, then he too sat down. Daisy Gibson's agony, and triumph, were over. The jury would carry her words and gestures with them for the rest of the trial and when they departed to consider their verdict. It was a virtuoso performance. Her daughter, the actress, could scarcely have done better. Daisy was writing an epitaph. The only way she knew how was by rebutting automatically every tittle of fact and gossip put to her about her daughter.

Dr Denis Hocking was equally impressed: 'She was very downright, very emphatic that there was no better blue-eyed girl in the whole world than her daughter. I would probably have done the same for my daughter. And the judge completely agreed with her.'

Yet it cannot be said that Mrs Gibson lived entirely in a fantasy world. In her letters home and on her brief visits to Liverpool or Durban, the budding actress must have charmed the family into believing that she lived a life as white as the driven snow. The Gibsons were a hard-working, religious couple, to whom it was inconceivable that their daughter might be drinking, having affairs with men or running up debts.

Casswell, for his part, had everything to lose by this turn of events. With hindsight, he might have been wiser to have left the mother well alone, or simply to have restricted his cross-examination to matters of her daughter's health, leaving allegations about her sex-life to the defence witnesses. Too late. Daisy had upstaged much of the defence case by impairing the credibility of the three South African witnesses before they had even entered the witness box.

How do you prove that a woman is not a virgin without producing in court a man who will swear he has had intercourse with her? The wise would stay away, out of deference to the dead, or fear of being destroyed in cross-examination. A fool or a brave man might risk it, but as the subject was dead, he might be thought to be lying. The jurors in Winchester were men and women from a background similar to Daisy's. We know little of their private lives or their secret prejudices but it is safe to assume that they found it easier to understand the picture painted by the loving mother than by the defence.

The trial had turned decisively. Casswell knew he was fighting for his client's neck.

But what of the 'pessary' in the suitcase of an unmarried woman? Was it not a damning piece of evidence? Should not the judge, as a guardian of public morality, and the prosecuting counsel and jury, have viewed it more seriously? In his retirement, Khaki Roberts threw some light on the perplexing question. 'I countered the defence allegations by setting the girl on a pedestal, for I believe she was no worse than any modern miss. Besides, she was not there to defend herself. The defence brought out the fact that a woman's contraceptive had been found in a suitcase in Gay's cabin. As a man of the world, I say this does not mean she was promiscuous.'

In his memoirs, Roberts disclosed that the day before leaving for England, Gay saw a woman doctor in Durban and 'was provided with a contraceptive'. He added that 'although the doctor did not come from South Africa to give evidence, she wrote to the prosecuting authority saying that she found no signs of pregnancy in Gay Gibson, and that the girl made no complaint of such a condition'. This was a contradiction, for if Gay did not complain, the doctor would surely not have looked. There is no way a doctor fitting a diaphragm could have guessed her patient's condition if Gay was less than two months' pregnant, if indeed she had panicked into returning to England because of missing a second period. South African laws were strict. The British Family Planning Association could only supply a diaphragm to a married woman, and then only if she had had a child or suffered a miscarriage. Durban, in those days, had no such family planning unit, so the doctor took the measurements, showed the patient how to insert the device, and sent her to the chemist to buy it.

It was an unsatisfactory aspect of the trial that the defence lawyers were not shown the Durban doctor's letter, or given a chance to contact her. They might have learned why Gay, if she were living a nun-like existence, should have to protect herself against unwanted pregnancy. All we know is that she seems to have been converted to contraception by Dr Schoub's advice on the facts of life. There is no way of telling if the device was used; was it embarrassment on the part of the detectives which caused them not to ask the Hendon police laboratory to determine whether the device was still in its wrapping case? Or whether the cream in the tube had been squeezed?

Any one of a number of conclusions may be drawn from the fact that Gay was not wearing it on the night of her death. In the prosecution's view, this showed that she was not expecting Camb. But equally persuasive is the argument that, being pregnant, or believing herself to be, she remembered the maxim about the horse and the stable door. Or, having perhaps had too much rum, she simply forgot about it. Or, having acquired the contraceptive only ten days before, she had not mastered the manoeuvring necessary to put it comfortably in place. Perhaps she had not really expected Camb to come and, when he knocked on the door, she could not be bothered to dig it out of the suitcase and follow the detailed instructions . . . squeeze a "full teaspoonful of the contraceptive jelly onto the indented dome of the cap and a little of it smeared round the rim and on to the under surface of the cap . . . "

All Casswell would have wanted to know about the 'pessary' was whether it implied that its owner was no longer a virgin. And, therefore, was the sort of person liable to welcome a visit from a man in the middle of the night. He appears to have been sparsely briefed on the subject.

What was a 'Koromex contraceptive'? Contraception entered the modern era in the 1880s when a Dutch woman physician, Aletta Jacobs, published a study of a vaginal diaphragm, which used vulcanised rubber shaped into a domed cap and attached to a circular watch-spring. This 'Dutch cap' covered the upper vagina and cervix. The arrival of the diaphragm in Victorian England advanced the emancipation of women, at last promising effective birth control on a mass scale. In the twenties and thirties women could buy these diaphragms by mail order – though they were sometimes misleadingly called 'pessaries'. By Gay Gibson's day, doctors could claim that over ninety per cent of women fitted at clinics with the diaphragm-and-chemical method were adequately protected against conception. Dutch caps were compared to motorcar tyres – look after them and they'll last for years. When Gay sought protection, the doctor's natural response was to recommend a diaphragm, plus a cream which would both lubricate and act as a spermicide. The 'Koromex' Dutch cap was recommended by the British Family Planning Association. It was an American product, shipped to South Africa via Britain.

So, the question Casswell would have liked to have asked was: 'Could the thing be fitted in a virgin?' One of America's contraceptive pioneers, Dr Hans Lehfeldt, has said that only 'in exceptional cases a virgin with a very flexible hymen could be fitted with a small-sized diaphragm'. Just how exceptional, can be gauged by people of long experience in the trade. In the view of Toni Belfield of the Family Planning Association: 'Gay Gibson most definitely would have had sexual experience, though the hymen could be stretched, by athletic activities like horse-riding.' George Tenby of Lambert's, the old Dalston firm now in Luton: 'A virgin? – unlikely. I'm not a medical man, but I do not think it is possible. Obviously she was well-prepared.' Another man in the trade, Ed Sloper (Celeg Pharmaceuticals) thinks it 'extremely unlikely' that a virgin could have been fitted. 'No doctor would have given a diaphragm to a woman with little experience . . . too painful to insert.'

We are left with the search for the real Gay Gibson. Was she, as her mother claimed, a paragon casting aside all pleasures in emulation of Gertrude Lawrence and Edith Evans? Or, as those witnesses from South Africa and Britain were preparing to say, a starry-eyed young actress not averse to the lusty pursuit of wine, men and song?

Had she been embarking on army service or a career on the stage a decade-and-a-half later, Gay would have been an obvious candidate for oral contraception. Its great advantage is to provide protection before the hymenal membrane is rent. A careful woman about to lose her virginity could rely on it . . . but not on the female diaphragm. It seems beyond dispute that when Gay paid her visit to the Durban doctor her hymen was already broken.

Meanwhile, back in the Great Hall at Winchester, the drama of day two was not yet played out . . .

9

A Musketeer of Pathology

Forensic pathologists are an independent breed of men, unusual among doctors in that they see all of the dead and not much of the dying. They will happily give up their social life to freeze in ditches and mortuaries, exhume in cemeteries, testify in coroner's and criminal courts. In a working life of forty years, some have been known to cut up 25,000 bodies.

With forensic medicine now so much a part of criminal investigation, it is difficult to appreciate that its acceptance is barely older than the century itself. The specialty suffered a setback in the 1850s in a muddled Scottish case in which Dr Thomas Smethurst was charged with poisoning. At the committal proceedings, a toxicologist, Taylor, reported finding traces of arsenic in the body. But at the trial, he admitted that the substances came from an imperfection in the apparatus used in his analysis. Worse was to come, with contradictory evidence from two other prosecution medical witnesses. A national outcry followed Smethurst's conviction, and he was granted a free pardon.

It took decades for public confidence to be restored in the 'beastly science', as the study of morbid anatomy was often called. At the turn of the century a group of doctors made St Mary's Hospital, Paddington, the centre of pathology research in England. They were joined by Bernard Spilsbury, who was to have a profound influence on the role of the pathologist in British courts, making his mark in the 'crime of the century', the Crippen case of 1910. The trial was preceded by a dramatic seaboard arrest of the American doctor fleeing England with his mistress, dressed in boy's clothes. But the more routine work was done by the doctors. Human remains dug out in the cellar at Hilldrop Crescent, Camden Town, were identified by Spilsbury as those of Mrs Crippen. He was able to prove that a scarred piece of skin was the relic of an operation on her lower abdomen. Crippen was hanged. For the next thirty-five years Spilsbury did a series of one-man shows in the English courts. He was the essential 'detective-pathologist', with the sharpness of a Sherlock Holmes and the priceless ability to see a crime through the eyes of the police. The name and the black bag were as synonymous with murder and hanging as were Charlie Chaplin's walking stick and bowler hat with comedy on the screen.

But the personality cult of Bernard Spilsbury went too far for some. J. D. Cassels, KC, later a judge, once complained bitterly when a jury accepted a version of the sole prosecution witness against eight defence medical witnesses: 'It will be a sorry day for the administration of criminal justice in this land if we are to be thrust into such a position that, because Sir Bernard Spilsbury expressed an opinion, it is of such weight that it is impossible to question it.' One present-day forensic pathologist, who wishes to remain anonymous, admits: 'Spilsbury made mistakes. They are known to myself and to his contemporaries. He was such a wonderful witness that his word was regarded as beyond reproach. But in my view, he got men hanged who shouldn't have been.'

Or, as Casswell had discovered, saved them from the gallows. This happened when he prosecuted a particularly bad egg, Harold Loughans, for the murder and robbery of a woman publican of The John Barleycorn in Portsmouth. Loughans' right hand was deformed, but the thumb was intact. The defence sprang a surprise by calling Spilsbury, who had been to Brixton Prison and told Loughans to shake his hand as firmly as he could. The grip was so limp, Spilsbury reported, that this man could not possibly have throttled the woman. Loughans was acquitted. But Spilsbury had been taken in. Writing in *The People* years later, Casswell declared baldly that Loughans had killed her. Loughans sued the newspaper and Casswell for libel, and lost. Soon afterwards, he walked into the newspaper's offices. He was dying of cancer and hadn't long to live. He had a confession to make: 'I done the job in the public house in Portsmouth.'

In the 1950s, a trio of pathologists, the 'three musketeers' Keith Simpson, Francis Camps and Donald Teare, inherited Spilsbury's medico-legal work in the metropolis. When Professor Webster expressed his contrary views about Gay's death and was handed over to the defence, Teare was given the nod by the prosecution.

Donald Teare, a Manxman, was then assistant pathologist and lecturer in forensic medicine at St George's Hospital, London. Though only thirty-six years old, he had made a name for himself by nailing an American serviceman, Hulten, for the murder of a London hire-car driver. Teare borrowed a skeleton from his medical school and put it in the car where the dead man was sitting when shot. He found a dent in the inside panelling of the front door made by the soldier's bullet. With a steel rod, he traced the path of the bullet backwards through the skeleton to the position in the back seat whence the gun had been fired. The ingenious reconstruction satisfied the jury that the shooting was in cold blood, not in the heat of the moment or in panic. The soldier was hanged, though his Welsh girlfriend, for whom Casswell was junior counsel, was reprieved.

Mid-afternoon. Teare, ruddy-complexioned, signs of stoutness apparent, stepped into a witness box still steaming from Daisy Gibson's appearance. Teare had a pleasant courtroom manner. He gave an impression of fairness in all he said; his opinions were invariably well balanced. In another time he would be said to have the right 'body language'. In short, he was a witness a jury could warm to.

Roberts went directly to his point. In death by strangulation, was any discharge of blood from the victim likely? – 'Yes. It sometimes occurs as a result of the tongue being forced against, or between, the teeth; (or) as the result of scratch marks by the victim in attempts to release herself or himself; (or) as part of the general picture of death from asphyxia which is

139

characterised by small haemorrhages in the more delicate linings of the body, the gums, the back of the throat, the lungs, the lining of the nose, and occasionally the ears.'

Roberts: 'If the throat is firmly clasped between the fingers, how long before unconsciousness supervened?' – ' . . . probably not more than fifteen seconds.'

'And how soon, if the same pressure was maintained, would the victim die from suffocation?' – 'Probably within a minute.'

Recall the 'one minute' that nightwatchman Steer said it took from the ringing of the bell to his knock on the cabin door. And that Roberts, in his opening speech, said that Camb, seeing his victim ring the bell, set about throttling her 'for his self-preservation'. If the prosecution case was correct, that she had resisted tenaciously by digging her nails into his wrist and neck, the job was no pushover. Camb would have been cutting it rather fine. Unaccountably, when Casswell cross-examined Teare, he failed to pursue the time factor.

Roberts then asked Teare if suffocation by a pillow would bring on external bleeding: 'I would not expect it, though it might occur.'

'In cases of manual strangulation, would you get froth on the mouth?' – 'Yes, I have seen it myself, either from the vomited material passing into the air passages and becoming churned up, or it may come purely from the rupture of small blood vessels in the lining of the tissues which wells up from the lungs, the bursting of these small vessels causing a blood-stained froth.'

But when Roberts turned to Camb's scratches, Teare offered little comfort. 'Were those on the right wrist caused by indentations or by the nails moving?' – 'I would find it extremely difficult merely on these descriptions to express an opinion.'

Roberts was taken aback. Teare was, after all, his witness. 'Then I am not going to ask you to do so. You are a man of great experience?' – 'I have some experience.'

'Do you think you could fairly express any opinion on that matter not having seen the hand and arm at the time, and only having seen photographs taken eight days later?' – 'I do not.'

Roberts turned to the muddy nails. Teare: 'The conclusion

which one might draw . . . is that this girl was suffering from such defective circulation that periodically her fingernails went blue; but (in that case) I should expect her to show more dramatic signs in the shape of breathlessness, or attacks of blueness of face and lips.'

'Would you have expected such a girl to have been marked AW/1 on being discharged from the ATS six or seven months previously?' – 'No, I should not.' (She was, of course, marked 'AW/1/non-tropical'.)

Mr Justice Hilbery: 'And that was after an examination by a doctor who seems to have had not only the general degrees, but also those of BM and BS of London. They are very high degrees, are they not?' Teare replied, 'Yes, they are.' He could hardly demur. Dr Haslam had stayed on to listen to the evidence. 'It amused me,' she recalled, 'because it was the lowest degree, my first.'

This ended the examination-in-chief. Teare had been curiously insubstantial. He was the expert witness for the prosecution, and yet had added nothing of significance to the mystery of how Gay died. He might have been conscious of the circumstances under which he had been brought in as a replacement for the more experienced Webster. At this stage, the prosecution case seemed in tatters. Had Casswell got up and sought one or two clarifications on the bloodstains, then sat down, the case against James Camb would have looked flimsy in the extreme. The defence would almost have had grounds for moving 'no case', arguing that there was no evidence suggesting cause of death, and so no prima-facie case for Camb to answer.

Casswell's first line of inquiry disposed of that option. Did he know of Dr Hocking, the pathologist of the Royal Cornwall Infirmary? Teare did.

'Have you heard that Dr Hocking took away some samples from these sheets?' – 'I have not heard that.'

'Did you know that from one of the sheets the sample showed quite a lot of dried urine?' – (Very surprised) 'No, I did not.'

'It is very likely to be the last act of a person before death?' –

'Yes.'

Hilbery: 'Is it, in the case of strangulation?' – 'Yes.'

In half-a-dozen swift questions and answers, the noose was back around James Camb's neck.

Casswell continued: 'Whether the patient died from strangulation or from natural causes, it is not unlikely that urine would be passed as a terminal act?' – 'Yes.'

'Is there . . . anything taken from any of these exhibits which points to rape or attempted rape?' – 'No.'

Hilbery: 'What would you expect to find?' – 'I thought that counsel was referring to the presence of semen on the sheets, and also I would expect to find more blood than was found.'

Which left the way clear for strangulation. Casswell resumed: 'In the analysis of that urine, no blood has been found at all?' – 'I did not know that.'

'But the presence of the very small cells which are usually found on the private parts of a woman would lead one to believe that here was the passing of urine from parts which were not injured?' – 'Yes.'

'I suggest that although (the bloodstains were small), they were too large to be consistent with a compression of the larynx?' – 'I do not agree, but perhaps my meaning would be better expressed if I said they are not too small to be consistent with manual strangulation.'

'I did not put it that way: compression with the thumb and finger?' – 'They are not inconsistent with compression by thumb and finger. It is possible to produce strangulation with very small pressure if it is applied in the right place.'

Casswell revealed that, according to Dr Hocking, the bloodstains on the sheet came from the mouth, and showed saliva and small flecks of lipstick. Teare agreed that would be consistent with frothing at the mouth.

Would it be possible, Casswell asked, for a person with a history of asthmatic attacks, and some sort of heart disease, 'to die under sexual excitement?' – 'I cannot exclude the possibility.'

Casswell personalised the point. 'If you had heard that this girl had had more than one attack of asthma, and if in the course of one of these attacks she had actually foamed at the mouth, would that have made it a little more probable that she might have died in that way?' – 'Well,' said Dr Teare, 'the story would not convince me that she was suffering from asthma or heart disease.'

Casswell persisted: 'If you had a person who is asthmatic, and also shows signs of heart disease, and that person passed out during sexual connection, I suggest that is equally consistent with what was found as (is) the theory of strangulation?' Dr Teare did not agree: 'I feel that what has been found is more in keeping with death from strangulation than death from heart attack. I was not aware that urine had been found on these sheets. In my experience death from asphyxia in particular, which includes death from strangulation, is frequently associated with terminal urination.'

'I suggest that death from asphyxia without strangulation will equally lead to the same result?' – 'It may, but you ask me if equally, and I say the chances are not equal.'

Roberts re-examined, rubbing it in. 'When you were asked to approach this case, one of the first questions you asked was whether urine had been found?' – 'I did.'

'Now that you know that the defence have ascertained the presence of urine on one of the sheets of this bed, does that strengthen your view as to whether death in this case was from strangulation?' – 'It does.'

Hilbery: 'Considerably?' – 'It does, My Lord.'

Of all the expert medical opinions heard and still to be expressed, the jury understood this one most clearly.

Donald Teare's widow, Kathleen, remembers the day. 'The urine stain took my husband by surprise. It was the one missing thing. That night he said, "Now, it's virtually sewn it up."'

Terminal urination is a function of the body's involuntary muscles, which include the muscle cells in the bladder wall. But the muscles which close the urethra (the passage from bladder to exterior) are voluntary. At death, then, the urethra muscles immediately relax, while those of the bladder wall carry on working, so that urine is expelled. The action takes place whether death is violent or natural. No one can say with any certainty how much urine Gay Gibson passed or with what pressure she voided her bladder, except that the discharge would have happened at the point of death.

There were good reasons why the defence should play this urine-stain card when it might have been safer for their client to have tucked it back into the pack. Hocking and Casswell were honourable men, for whom it was unethical to withhold vital information from a court of law. Dr Hocking says, 'The prosecution is always scrupulously fair. If they have a point to give away, they give it away – don't try to hide it at all.' And yet, as far as barristers and the Bench were concerned, there was no duty to disclose the finding. When defending, the most eminent judge will tell you, there is no obligation to produce any evidence at all.

The defence did believe, however, that the urine disclosure strengthened their hand by eliminating any lingering doubt that Gay might have been alive when thrown into the sea. To that extent, it did Camb no harm in the eyes of the jury.

Not many pathologists were equipped to detect the urine. Hocking was a chemist as well, and was called in on the suggestion of Webster to resolve the mystery. As he tested the stain in his laboratory in Truro, the urine showed up as a faint whitish fluorescence under the ultraviolet light. He examined the bottom sheet as well, but found nothing. It may have been that there was no urine, but four decades on, Hocking still has his regrets. 'The amount of urine would have been slight, some would have been mopped up by the dressing gown, so that only a smear was passed on to the underlying sheet and insufficient to affect the lower sheet. But, with hindsight, and realising that so much would be made of these stains, I should perhaps have taken samples from the lower sheet in the region of the upper sheet stain and submitted them to much more accurate chemical tests that confirm the presence of urine, notably urea and particularly uric acid.'

The irony of Hocking's discovery, as we shall see, is that it was seized upon by the other side and utilised more effectively to their advantage. But it was extraordinary that this finding should become the single most important piece of evidence against Camb. Lawyers, who demand certainty in the way they conduct their trials, were able to persuade a clever pathologist to speculate that a faint urine stain on a sheet was more likely to mean death by manual strangulation than by any other means. This, without any evidence as to whose urine it was on the sheet, or, if it was Gay's, whether she might not have leaked some of it on to the sheets when lying down in the afternoon. Nor did anyone bother to inquire how often the sheets were changed. Might it have been, even in first class, that the linen was laundered on alternate days.

If perhaps the defence, instead of surprising Dr Teare with the urine stain, had given him warning in advance, he might have mulled it over, read the references, discussed it with colleagues, and come up with a more measured judgment. For his reply was a judgment, on the life of James Camb.

Casswell, having cross-examined all ten of the second day's witnesses, rose to make the opening speech for the defence. Although in his sixties, and not in perfect health, he showed no sign of strain.

He told the jury that this case was unusual because there was no body, and 'if anybody is to blame for that it is my client'. But it must be remembered that 'we are not here to decide whether he ought to have disposed of a dead body, nor is the charge that of having concealed a dead body: what he is charged with is having murdered that girl, and it is for the prosecution to prove to your satisfaction that he did murder her before you can find a verdict of guilty. It is not a question of suspicion, it is not a question of probability; it must be a question of certainty in your minds beyond reasonable doubt; not a flimsy doubt, of course, but by bringing your minds to bear upon it as men and women of the world. That is why you are here so that you may bring common sense to your deliberations.'

This was directed at a jury still aching at the plight of Mrs Gibson. Casswell could not avoid mentioning her. He talked of the unpleasant duty of putting questions to a mother about a child whom she believed beyond reproach. 'I should not have undertaken that painful duty had I not believed that it was an essential point in this case, and may I tell you why? . . . I think that you should know something of what other people have to say about her, whether she was easy to approach, whether she was ready to go about with men and even to associate with them quite intimately, and whether or not she was a girl who spoke of private and intimate matters quite soon to comparative strangers. It is, is it not, a material point for you to know?'

Casswell disclosed that two of the British witnesses who had offered evidence to the police had been handed over, like Professor Webster, to the defence. But for good reason he would not go into the particulars of the witnesses from South Africa and Britain – Camb had not been told the result of any of the inquiries made in either country. 'And if I were to describe to you now the evidence which is going to be given, then it might be said, "Oh yes, he heard his counsel tell the jury what these people knew and that has necessarily coloured his own evidence." . . . You see, knowing practically nothing about this girl it would be highly improbable that he would make up a story and give an account which fits into the previous history of things which happened to her not only in England in 1946, but also in South Africa shortly before she left for this country; not one isolated attack, but several; not one instance of infatuation, but several.'

He outlined, at considerable length, the very story Camb was waiting to relate. The language was careful, decorous even. On the events leading up to the 'unfortunate occurrence', Casswell said: 'After a while she made it plain to him that she was not dressed underneath this dressing gown, and what happened was – wrong, as it was no doubt, but it was what one might expect in these circumstances – he made love to her and finally got on to the bed with her and sexual intercourse took place.' Afterwards, Camb having 'failed to excite a single spark of life in that motionless body', Casswell continued, 'you may be quite sure what he ought to have done. He ought to have gone to the doctor straight away . . . but, members of the jury, in moments like that sometimes human nature asserts itself and the first thing one thinks of in panic is self.'

He finished with a gentle swipe at his learned friend. 'You

have heard, and I suppose it is still in your ears, the opening speech of Mr Roberts, made with such force, and you may be quite sure he has not omitted a single fact or argument which would throw suspicion upon this man, while doing his duty with that fairness for which he is famed, but I am sure you will give as much attention to the evidence of the defence as to that of the prosecution.'

His first witness was James Camb.

10

Camb's Story

Five o'clock came and went, and Sir Malcolm Hilbery's court pressed on. Newsmen reported that 'When Camb was called to the witness box he walked smartly from the dock and stood erect while taking the oath.'

Casswell took a breather. Camb, who sported a white handkerchief in his breast pocket, was handed over to Joe Molony for examination. As a prelude, the clerk of the court faced the spectators and solemnly warned that 'some of the testimony to come is of an intimate and personal nature. If any of the women present wish to leave the court, they may do so now.' No one budged.

'I am thirty-one years of age, married and live at Clover Street, Thornliebank, Glasgow. I have a little girl of three. I have been at sea since 1933, always on the catering side except for a short period during the war when I served on the armed merchant cruiser *Arawa*, returning to the merchant service in 1941. I have been with the Union-Castle Line off and on since 1935, and have served with them continuously since early in 1945.' The first words were out; jury, judge, spectators, and the lounging Khaki Roberts, could begin to assess the stocky, handsome man talking for his skin. He recounted his version of the story in considerable detail.

The first stir, a sign of tension moving up a ratchet, came with the mention of Charles Schwentafsky from Nairobi. 'She said she was crazy about him . . . but possible complications may have set in . . . I said in a joking fashion, "You don't mean to tell me you are going to have a baby?" She said, "Well, it is rather too soon to know."'

Camb was soon in the swing, retelling the events he had settled carefully in his mind during the months in prison.

Casswell, an inveterate doodler when not seeking answers in court, might have been sketching His Lordship, or his own client pressing with the upright posture of a carrier of trays against the back of the witness stand. Hilbery tapped his pencil and listened, waiting his chance. It came as Camb described his first visit to Gay's cabin in search of her bathing costume. The sexually-loaded half-joking remark, 'I have a good mind to bring a drink down and join you', peeved the judge.

Hilbery: 'What made you make that observation?' – 'It is hard to say; simply because we were so friendly by that time.'

'What was it you intended to convey?' – 'I think I intended to convey what really happened later.'

'Was any time discussed as to when you might join her?' – 'No, I simply suggested later.'

'What was her answer?' – 'I am not sure of the exact words, but I think she said, "Please yourself; it's up to you."'

Molony: 'Did she say anything to you which showed that the idea was objectionable or distasteful to her?' – 'No.'

As Camb progressed, it was clear that the story was increasingly distasteful to the judge. The formalised, almost disembodied rhythm of question and answer, far from easing the tension, mesmerised listeners in both public gallery and official seats. Whether they liked to admit it or not, this was what they had come to hear. Thus –

Molony: 'What had happened to the rum drink that Miss Gibson had had put out by you?' – 'She had been steadily sipping it until it was finished, and then she put it on the dressing table.'

'What happened after five or ten minutes?' – 'I climbed on to the bed beside her.'

'Did she raise any objection?' – 'No.'

'At what stage did you see whether she had clothing on underneath her dressing gown?' – 'Almost as soon as I laid down beside her.'

'How did you see she had none?' – 'When she unzipped her dressing gown, which fastened up the front, full length.'

'What happened after that?' – 'There was a certain amount of preliminary love-play, and then sexual intercourse took place.'

'When intercourse took place, what were your relative positions?' – 'I was lying on top of Miss Gibson; I was face down.'

Throughout the trial, one seat remained vacant. Margaret Camb would have found this distressing. She was kept informed of events by Geoffrey Wells' office.

' . . . unloosened my belt and unfastened my trousers . . . intercourse followed a normal course . . . Suddenly she heaved under me as though she was taking a deep breath . . . her body stiffened for a fraction of a second and then relaxed completely limp . . . one eye just slightly open.'

A men-and-women-of-the-world jury, mindful of the weakness of the flesh across the class divide, might have given his account a chance up to this point. Now they were about to see the arrant selfishness of the man.

Molony: 'Did you do anything to the body of Miss Gibson?' – 'First of all I listened and felt for her heartbeat. I could not find any, and I attempted by massaging the stomach towards the heart to bring back her circulation.'

No, Camb explained, he had no experience of artificial respiration, though he had seen it demonstrated. He thought of smelling salts, but not of summoning the doctor just along the passage on the same deck, fifteen seconds away. The absurd massaging continued for twenty, twenty-five minutes.

Hilbery was heavy with irony at his next intervention: 'Where was she when you were, as you say, trying to revive her?' – 'Lying face upwards on her bunk.'

'Where were you?' – 'Standing beside her.'

They moved to the ringing of the bells. The arrival of Steer, Camb said, threw him into a 'complete panic.'

Molony: 'What were you afraid of?' – 'Being found in that cabin. I knew that in the circumstances of being found in a lady passenger's cabin, I should lose my job, and forfeit any chance of employment in any shipping company for that matter.'

For the second time in a matter of minutes, the jury looked askance at the trifling nature of his reply seen against the fearsome plight of the woman.

'What did you decide to do?' – 'I confess now it sounds very foolish' (the *Echo* used the word 'selfish') 'but I hoped to give the impression that she had fallen overboard, and deny all knowledge of having been to that cabin, in the hope that the captain's further inquiries would not be too severe.'

Hilbery interposed, sharply: 'What did you decide to do, was the question.' – 'To dispose of her body.'

'In what way?' – 'By pushing it through the porthole.'

The body was slack and rather awkward, but he managed to push her through. At no stage, he assured his counsel, had he done anything violent to her.

Outside the courtroom, the equinox twilight turned to night. Hilbery brought a halt to the dramatic day. 'Tomorrow we will sit late,' he told the jury. 'There will be no half-day. I believe in killing a Saturday outright instead of merely wounding it.'

Camb had been in the witness box for an hour and ten minutes, under 'friendly' examination. Hocking recalled his feelings about him – 'confident, almost arrogant, not a nice person. I really think his attitude swayed the jury. Here is an utterly callous young man, doesn't care a damn about the girl or anyone else, as long as he gets his way.'

Camb sensed that his story was not going down well. 'I had the feeling deep in my heart that the jury did not believe me,' he admitted later. Khaki Roberts was still to get hold of him.

It was splendid box-office and too many people wanted to be present. The Porthole trial was rivalling Winchester Cathedral as the town's leading tourist attraction. Camb reminded the ladies of the film actor, Victor Mature. On the Saturday morning, as he was brought into court and taken to the witness box, 'a lush, full-bosomed young woman' broke from the spectators' seats, rushed up to him and pressed a letter into his hand. She was intercepted and ejected. The confiscated note appeared to express her belief in Camb's innocence, and contained some rather unconventional proposals for the time when he might be released.

Molony picked up the thread from the evening before, and it was, once again, the scratches. Camb denied absolutely that he had received any injury of any sort that night.

'Did no blood come from your body while you were in that cabin?' the judge asked. – 'To the best of my knowledge, no.'

Camb gave his answers in a calm, reasoned manner. He seemed intelligent, articulate, his world under control. When Molony asked him to look at the photographs of the reconstruction of the cabin, he turned over the pages of the bound volume with steady hands. Peggy Durrant of the Jurors' Office recalled 'a very debonair little fellow; always calm, too calm – he always seemed to have an answer'. His demeanour did not give the impression of someone who might have panicked, even under the extreme conditions of the woman in his arms dying without warning in the climax of love-making.

Forty-five minutes into the morning, Khaki Roberts began his cross-examination. He had been enjoying the trial. Subscribers to *Tit-bits* would later read that 'In all modesty, I have to admit that I was in sparkling form. As the evidence unfolded and the defence tried to sully the reputation of Gay Gibson . . . I formed a resolve to go all out for a conviction. My "zeal and fervour" [a reference to Casswell's complaint about him] were not lessened as I listened to Camb's story . . . He had a pretty-boy look and tried to appear cool. But he shrank under my barrage of withering questions.'

Roberts never went into court without his measure of phenobarbitone, a calmer of nerves in the days before valium, though nowadays it is used only occasionally for the treatment of epilepsy. It was a highly addictive barbiturate with nasty withdrawal symptoms. Hocking recalls writing out a prescription for Roberts during a trial in the West Country. Also on his desk was his little bottle of 'medicine', believed to be gin, from which he swigged at regular intervals.

If Camb had created a morbid excitement among the women of Hampshire, Roberts, for his part, was not favoured as a pin-up. Peggy Durrant recalled the 'massive, ugly bulldog-type man. He bulldozed his way round, but he could be very bluff, though not very charming, in cross-examination . . . '

Roberts well understood the impact of the first question. 'What may be good tactics in one case may be quite unsuitable in the next,' he once wrote. 'It is not unlike the ploy of the hands in bridge; now you must take out the trumps, next time it would be fatal.' He played the ace of trumps.

'Would you describe yourself as a truthful man?' – 'I think so, sir.'

'You do. You were the last person who saw Miss Gibson alive?' – 'Yes.'

'You put her through the porthole at three o'clock on the morning of 18th October.' – 'Yes.'

'Did you for the next eight days make untrue statements with regard to that on at least six occasions?' – 'I did that, yes.'

'How does that fit in with your description of yourself as a truthful person?' – 'I would say that that description arose from the predicament I found myself in.'

'When do you normally depart from the truth, being normally a truthful person?' – 'I had already departed from the truth for a selfish reason, I am afraid. I was thinking of myself.'

'Self-preservation, in fact. Did you intend to persist in that untrue denial on your part? – 'I think I did.'

'Did you intend to take that secret with you to your grave?' – 'That is hard to say.'

'You must have known. Cannot you answer the question?' – 'I would say, "yes".'

'No matter what unhappiness or misery caused to her relations or anybody else . . . ?'

With that devastating tirade, Roberts might have been tempted to sit down and invite the jury to view Camb's story as a ghoulish figment of his imagination. But he was merely getting into his stride. He recounted later how 'persistently and relentlessly, I forced him to admit again and again that he had lied and dissembled to save himself'.

Reading the exchanges, Roberts' attack seems unprepared, almost unstructured. But there was a plan: after capsizing Camb's already leaking veracity, to attack the dozen or so real or perceived Achilles' heels in his story. The cross-examination would be of fairly short duration, but counsel for the prosecution intended to play each trump for all it was worth.

The first flaw he exposed was a variation of the theme, 'Once a liar, always a liar'. 'When did you decide to alter your story?'

he inquired. – In the police headquarters, said Camb, when he realised he had been definitely incriminated by Steer. 'I then proceeded to tell the truth.'

'It was another account, another story; you say it was the truth?' – 'Yes.'

'You have been to sea since 1933. Have you ever before heard of such a terrible happening at sea: a member of the crew of a British ship throwing the body of a passenger through the porthole?' – 'No.'

'If the second story . . . is true, you destroyed the best evidence in your favour, did you not?' – 'I didn't think of it at the time.'

'Please apply yourself to it now and answer the question.' – 'I did, yes.'

Flaw number two showed up Camb's conceit, and that he was still lying, though in this case it was to protect his wife.

'Did you tell Sergeant Quinlan that some of the passengers preferred the stewards to their fellow passengers, and that you had occasionally gone into their cabins?' – 'Yes.'

'Had you been often before into passengers' cabins?' – 'No, these other occasions were several years previously, before the war.'

'And since the war?' – 'Only Miss Gibson's.'

The third flaw emphasised the heartless fellow he was. Asked why he did not think of going to the doctor, Camb said, 'It is possible to bring a person out of a faint without expert medical attention.'

'So you say to the jury that you would not mind how much risk to the passenger's health or life would be caused by not getting a doctor, but to save your own skin you would not get one?' – 'Putting it that way, yes.'

The bells were, in Roberts' estimation, the fourth flaw. 'Who rang those two bells?' – 'I don't know.'

'What would you expect a passenger to do who, in the night, objected to the advances of a member of the crew?' – 'Shout.'

'Not much good shouting. Is not ringing the bells a much better thing for a passenger to do?' – 'They both amount to the same thing.'

154

'That is what she did, is it not?' – 'She didn't touch the bell.'
'Who did then?' – 'I don't know.'

'Are you suggesting that the bells went off of their own accord?' – 'I cannot suggest how the bells were rung.'

'Did you have to work quickly to silence her then before the bell was answered?' – 'I didn't have to silence her at all.'

This indication of Camb's inflexible state of mind led him to the fifth flaw, the mini-saga of the pyjamas.

'You say she was not wearing a nightgown or pyjamas?' – 'No.'

'What had happened to her pyjamas?' – 'I have not the slightest idea.'

'Miss Field says that they were there the previous day and were missing the next morning: pyjamas and dressing gown both missing: can you give an explanation?' – 'I did not know she had any black pyjamas.'

'I do not think it matters whether you knew or not. The evidence is that they were in the cabin the previous day and they were missing the next morning when she went missing. If you did not know she had black pyjamas and she was wearing them, that shows you did not get access to her body, does it not?' – 'She was not wearing pyjamas.'

The sixth flaw was not strictly a flaw, but a brilliant Khaki-ism, in which he turned the embarrassment of the Dutch cap in the suitcase to his own advantage, without having to ask Camb a direct question about it.

'I suggest to you that the disappearance of these pyjamas, the non-use of the contraceptive, and the ringing of the bells entirely negates your story of sexual intercourse with her consent?' – (No answer.)

The seventh flaw was offered unnecessarily by the prisoner. It was Hilbery's turn to do the questioning: 'You want the jury to understand that that night in the cabin, when someone came to the door, you were quite satisfied that he had not had an opportunity of identifying you?' – 'Yes, My Lord.'

'If she was found dead, nobody could know if it was a passenger or a member of the crew who might have been there?' – 'Inquiries would have been made and I might have been incriminated.'

'But you said you had not been identified. You could not be incriminated if you were not identified by the person who came to the door?' – 'At that time the description was of "a dark person". There were few dark persons on the ship at that time. I was sure to be interrogated by the captain amongst the dark persons on board.'

But no 'dark person' was being sought as Camb pondered what to do with the body. And he reasoned too elaborately for a man in a panic.

The next flaw: he still denied that Gay scratched him, then almost changed his story. Roberts: 'In your association with Miss Gibson in her cabin that night you received no injuries from her at all?' – 'To the best of my knowledge, no.'

'We have heard suggestions that the marks on your right wrist and also on your forearm were indentations caused by nails digging in. You are not suggesting that they were caused by Miss Gibson?' – 'Some of them may have been. What I said was that I had caused the original scratches myself.'

'This is what you said: "I received no injury of any sort while in company of Miss Gibson." Do you want to alter that now?' – 'No.'

The ninth flaw might have been the most damaging. Roberts: 'It must have been exceedingly difficult putting that girl through the porthole, was it not?' – 'Not particularly.'

'It is quite different from what you said [in his confession] on 25th October, is it not? The jury have seen this statement. They know it was handed to you to be signed and read through, and that you corrected it in certain parts. You said, "After a struggle with the limp body . . . I managed to lift her to the porthole and pushed her through. I am fairly certain that at the time she was dead, but I was terribly frightened." "Fairly certain" is quite different from "quite sure", is it not?' – 'Yes.'

Hilbery: 'Why did you not strike out the word "fairly" and just leave the word "certain"?' – 'It had not occurred to me that one word would make such a difference.'

Roberts: 'You did not care whether she was alive or not when you put her through, did you?'

Flaw number ten involved knocking the pregnancy story, putting the working class in its place and upholding the honour of a stewardess.

'Did you tell Miss Field that she was pregnant three months?' – 'I told her she was pregnant but didn't state the time.'

'Are you saying that her evidence is not accurate?' – 'She may have misunderstood.'

'Is this another occasion where you were departing from your standard of being a truthful person yourself by romancing to Miss Field, saying that she was three months' pregnant by a married man?' – 'No, there was no point in it.'

'I suggest that you were boasting of your relations with first-class female passengers?'

By now Camb's story was so heavily besieged that even the policeman Plumley gained in stature.

'You ask the jury to say that your evidence is to be preferred to Plumley's?' – 'I don't ask them to prefer anything.'

At last it was over. 'Now, Camb' (for the first time, Roberts uttered the name) 'I put it to you that your second story, the story you have told today, is just as untrue as the story you told on the *Durban Castle* for six or seven days?' – 'No, sir.'

Khaki Roberts sat down. He skewed his wig and took a deep draught from his medicine bottle.

Casswell salvaged what he could. 'Are you proud of what you did that night, Camb?' – 'I am not, sir, I am ashamed.'

'You said it was beastly conduct not to tell people, in order to save yourself. You think that?' – 'I do.' A limp, unconvincing apology.

Camb left the witness box. Roberts recounted later that he had been 'shown up as one of the most cold-blooded men ever to face a murder charge'.

Yet Hocking remained hopeful. 'The whole of Camb's cross-examination was a testing experience, but he stood up to it perfectly, without being shaken or departing in one detail from his account of the way in which the girl died.'

That was the trouble with his testimony; it was set in concrete. So intent was Camb in sticking to his definitive version that he refused to vary or explain it, where it would have been perfectly acceptable to do so. Hocking says that in the prison cell, when questioned by Casswell on the statement before the trial, Camb would not change a word of it. 'He stuck to it straight through without making a single alteration.'

Thus, the pyjamas. Those with memories of the newspaper reports of the trial invariably recall the missing pyjamas, almost as clearly as the body going through the porthole. The reasons may be salacious, but it was also an easy measure of the inconsistency of Camb's account. It caused him inestimable damage, yet need not have done. He flatly refused to entertain any notion of using his imagination. As Hocking says: 'If she had the pyjamas on as well, why not say so? There is nothing against his having opened her pyjamas as well.'

But the question remains, where were they? In the stifling heat, Gay might have been happy to go about without them. The corridors of her deck were quiet enough after midnight. She could safely go to the toilet dressed only in the full-length dressing gown. Hocking is more explicit: 'Going to the bathroom after a session with another passenger? Not at all unlikely. And leaving the pyjamas behind? Again, not unlikely.' Hocking heard a rumour, as did others at the trial, that the pyjamas were to be found in the cabin of a distinguished passenger who promised to come forward with the missing garments if Camb was sentenced to hang.

Similarly, Roberts and the judge simply took it for granted that Gay had rung the bells, when they should have been challenged by an alternative supposition. For, instead of Camb's blank 'don't know', it would have served him better to have used his imagination, once he had declared so categorically that she was in no state to push the button. The commonsense explanation must have been that, in his frantic efforts to revive her, he rammed his hip against the bellpush. Here was a case where solicitor and barrister should have insisted on an explanation of some sort, and not left it to others to make the running.

And the scratches, an omission more damaging than most. Hocking felt that Camb 'did himself irreparable harm by denying that he suffered any injury at the hands, literally, of Gay Gibson. I must confess it is one of the major weaknesses in his story. His original statement that Gay Gibson had gripped his arm at the moment of death was certainly a kingpin as to the credibility of his statement. And yet, after his completely reasonable account of what had happened, he denied that any injury had been done, whilst it was obvious that some injury had been done, consistent with his account.

'This came as a complete surprise to Mr Casswell, his solicitor and me, and I must say left us confused. The matter does not appear to have been discussed between Camb, his solicitor and Mr Casswell. I did not see Camb myself. He obviously did not appreciate the importance of it. I feel rather certain that his denial weighed very forcibly with the jury, as it completely undermined his very good case.

'I can only think that Camb had got it fixed in his mind that somehow these marks could have been done only during an act of strangulation, and as he was denying strangulation, he had to deny these marks.'

James Camb is not likely to have been analysed at any stage by a psychiatrist. So assessments forty years later of what made him act as he did must be less perfect than if he were sitting in front of us today, providing answers to our questions. But his three hours as a witness did offer some meat for a psychiatrist to work on.

Since Camb was a self-evident liar, how can anything he says be believed? Dr David Somekh, forensic psychiatrist, prefaces his remarks with a warning that Camb is 'a very dim figure'. In general, he says, 'this is a common issue which comes up in trials. It is standard for the prosecution to say that because a defendant lied at different stages of the investigation, then anything he says in court must be suspect. It has probably been standard practice for centuries. But it doesn't actually mean anything. We know people lie to defend themselves. That's normal behaviour.

'But,' Somekh adds, 'if someone does lie, then it means that whatever he does tell you can't be accepted as the truth. If people are functioning under stress, they tend to behave like six-year-olds, which means they are more likely to lie when they have difficulty in describing reality . . . When a chap changes his story three times, it may well contain ingredients that are true. But we must accept that there are other things he feels he must conceal.'

Asked how this man, so cool and reasonable as a witness, could be the same man who panicked in the cabin, Dr Somekh replied: 'A court is a theatre. Even people used to going to court have butterflies, or stage fright, before going into the box. All are affected by the theatrical atmosphere. And people, when they have a part to play, will compose themselves. It seems to me there is very little comparison between that formal and intense atmosphere and the atmosphere in somebody's first-class cabin when you are in your underpants (with a dead body on your hands). So I give no credence to his coolness in court. Few psychiatrists would. A red herring.'

Dr Arthur Hyatt Williams, one of the country's most eminent prison psychotherapists, now retired, squares Camb's performance in the dock 'with the fact that I think he had rehearsed and rehearsed it. He composed himself. He also had the idea that the more calm and collected he was, the more they would believe him. His solicitor had told him he would get off, and he probably believed it. That also militates towards the fact that he probably didn't do it, that he had some belief in justice . . . "If I didn't do it, they can't hang me." Hence his performance.'

Another forensic psychiatrist, Dr Mervyn Glasser, also cautions that when 'you look at an account of a person's life and start analysing it, you need to spend a great deal of time with the man himself'. So his comments on Camb are careful: ' . . . this man with a turbulent and disturbed underside but with a presentation which is all very controlled, hence his panic in the cabin and the perfect performance in court. There's an impression of a lack of concern for the other person. To take Gay Gibson, the woman he had just been making love to, and throw her out of the porthole, that takes a lot of doing. He has a capacity to be uninvolved with that person. And it sounds like that's how he related to people in general. Which, paradoxically, enables him to be very manipulative. Because you don't get caught up with a person. You can think what to do to get the right effect.'

As to Camb's well-dressed appearance, in the dock and at all times, all three psychiatrists fixed on the term 'narcissist'. Dr Hyatt Williams found he could sympathise with the judge: 'When reading the [author's] report and documents I found I didn't like Camb and it is very easy to be unfair to people you don't like. Camb, I think, was a narcissistic man with some definite psychopathic trends, but all subordinated to the narcissism, as a result of which he thought he was God's gift to women, and women were God's gift to him. Everybody would fall like a ripe plum in his hands. There is evidence that he was quite kind when he went home to his wife and child, loaded with presents. In other words, this philandering could have stemmed from a large split-off area of himself, a Mr Hyde, where Dr Jekyll who surfaced occasionally could go home and deal appropriately with his wife.

'The fact that his mother died early would have affected him, given him something which would get woven into an elaborate fantasy system about death. It would also, out of loyalty to the idea of his mother, make him perhaps devalue other women as whole people. But what he might do then, out of the part of him which was angry with his mother for dying – which sounds illogical but it's true – is punish these other women instead of being able to punish his mother. So he must have had an aggressive component to his sexuality. But if it was fairly muted, it may have been very acceptable and been mistaken for sexual ardour.

'If one had as bad a conscience as he and if the "target for the night" died, he would feel sufficiently persecuted, because however suave he could be in court, when he had to think about it, I think he would have panicked. If somebody died in the course of a rather promiscuous kind of intercourse, I reckon he would have felt immediately a flash of guilt from which he would abdicate later. But his panic reaction could well have been to shove her out of the porthole, evacuate the cause of his embarrassment, which was the dead body. This is a likely reaction, quite compatible with a non-murder by an unscrupulous man who could have had murder in his heart, who could be quite aggressive, quite callous, and very self-centered, but who would want to go on leading his self-centered, philandering life.

'Then, with bold composure, he would pull himself together and think, "I'm not going to suffer for this." He is a little bit of a megalomaniac sort of bloke . . . "They'll believe me for this." What the judge called callous. Lying would be quite on the cards, though usually it would tie him in knots. He told one story, then another. I think the last story is quite plausible and it is also quite plausible that he didn't kill her either.'

Whether the jury would have agreed with these comments is much in doubt. The forensic psychiatrist, or alienist, had long been part of the American judicial scene, but doctors who blamed mothers for their children's crimes were not yet allowed to darken the doorways of British courts.

Now the temperature cooled as the world of theatre moved on-stage centre to offer its view of Miss Gibson, actress.

11

Out of Africa

While journalists from the Sunday newspapers transposed the 'Khaki and Camb' show from notebook into a 'Winchester, Saturday' piece, they could have missed the relevance of the next witnesses. For now, having presented Camb's version of events in cabin 126, the defence offered two further categories of evidence to back up Camb's case – the health and morals of the dead woman.

The army reappeared in the handsome guise of Evelyn Armour, ATS subaltern, once paymistress to the 'theatrical' soldiers of the central pool of artistes. She knew Gay from pay parades. Now she recounted the alarming incident in London that evening in July 1946 when she found Gay, back arched and resting on her head and heels, breathing, 'very, very heavily'. Miss Armour explained that she had called an ambulance and accompanied her to the Casualty Receiving Station in Lennox Gardens, Kensington. 'I assisted the VAD nurse on duty to put her to bed. By this time she appeared to be over (the) fit, but very exhausted.' Evelyn Armour saw Gay again two months later when she had come out of hospital and noticed that she had grown considerably thinner and had lost weight. Gay had since had another of 'these turns'.

In one way, Miss Armour's experience was similar to that of Professor Webster. On reading about the case she had informed the authorities that she knew the dead girl, and was then contacted by the police. What she had to say was considered more useful to the defence than to the prosecution. Now Roberts had to diminish the impact of her evidence without discrediting her as a person.

He pointed out that Gay's arrival at the casualty station was not entered on a 'Service and Casualty form'. Not surprising, said Miss Armour, 'because going at eleven o'clock that night you did not wait to write out a normal sick report; at the casualty station, if they had considered it necessary to send her to a specialist, they would have made out a document which would have gone with her normal medical hospital report.'

'Whatever the nature of her illness, it was not considered necessary to send her to a specialist?' – 'That would be on the medical officer's authority. But the type of fit was over, or nearly over, before I got there. I am not in a position to say what the medical officer thought of the case.'

'You are not by any chance making a mistake as to the girl?' – 'No, not in the slightest.'

Casswell asked only one question on re-examination. 'Look at the last photograph in exhibit 5. Do you recognise it?' – 'Yes, Private Gibson.'

Peter Arthur Dalby had also offered evidence to the police and been turned over to the defence by the Director of Public Prosecutions. Not surprising, in the light of what he had to say. He knew Gay well, having been with her in the same unit for a year. Before then, he was a private in the medical corps. He had toured with Gay, shared digs, travelled across the country doing shows. In early 1946, he said, Gay was 'very, very hysterical and a quite excitable neurotic'. The show moved to Germany, but there was no change in her 'neurotic and excitable' state. Then came the incident in Wales, when they were returning from a show at the Trawsfynydd ammunition disposal unit. 'The road was very, very rough and the weather was very, very bad. The (coach) was bumping and lurching all over the place . . . Miss Gibson fell off the seat and had some sort of hysterical fit on the floor . . . '

Casswell: 'You say she was on the floor of the vehicle. Did you notice her face?' – 'No, I could not, as the coach was very dark.'

'Did you notice anything about her breathing?' – 'Yes, it was very, very heavy; very laboured.'

'Did you see where her hands were?' – 'No.'

At this unusual question, Hilbery intervened. 'Was she a good actress?' – 'She was good – to a point.'

'Convincing?' – 'Yes, and very enthusiastic.'

'Realistic?' – 'Yes, I think that one of her faults was that she was much too realistic.'

Casswell, anxious to correct: 'Do you think she was acting on that occasion?' – 'I am quite sure she was not . . . (she remained in that position for) about twenty to thirty minutes; after that she was carried from the coach to her digs by a member of the show.'

Do you agree, Roberts asked, that 'as a class, actresses are inclined to be temperamental?' – 'Yes, but I can assure you that her hysteria was above average of the temperamentality of actresses.'

'Was Miss Gibson absent for one day from duty in 1946?' – 'No, she was not.'

Once again, Roberts' consummate skills, this time with scalpel, minimised the value of the coach incident. The effect was almost mesmeric.

'After the show, were you given a party in the officer's mess?' – 'Yes.'

'Was it a quite hilarious party?' – 'Yes.'

'Was a Scotsman there in a kilt and did he put on some eightsome reels?' – 'Yes.'

'Did everyone dance it?' – 'I believe Gay did with some of the others.'

'And Gay danced with her usual enthusiasm?' – 'Yes.'

'Without anybody getting drunk, did everybody drink a good deal?' – 'Yes.'

'Were some of the young people drinking more than was good for them?' – 'It could be said so, yes.'

'After that, did you have a twenty-mile drive over very bad roads?' – 'That is quite right.'

'And in a lorry with a cover?' – 'It was a charabanc.'

'Nothing to hang on to?' – 'Nothing.'

'It was rocking all over the place?' – 'Yes.'

'Was Gay Gibson violently sick at the back of the vehicle?' – 'I didn't know she was.'

'Did you know that she was so far recovered that night as to see to her own water bottle?' – 'I cannot say.'

In other words she was merely drunk.

The focus now shifted back to the *Durban Castle*, the next witness being a naval architect, Roland Soper, who had measured the distance from the nightwatchman's pantry to cabin 126 as 162 feet 9 inches. At ordinary walking pace it had taken 63 seconds, halting briefly at both indicators. He had tried it at other paces. The quickest was 25 seconds, implying that if Steer had walked more briskly than he thought, there would have been even less time for Camb to strangle his unresponsive hostess.

The battle over the health and character of Gay Gibson was now reaching a climax. 'The great difficulty in our way,' Casswell wrote later, 'was the clean sheet of health (apart from the ear infection) given to the dead girl at the medical examination before she left the ATS. Also the fact that there was no record of her having been medically treated for the complaint.' The witnesses were brought over from South Africa to prove two things: 'that Gay Gibson was medically liable to suffer from the kind of attack which, according to Camb, killed her . . . Furthermore, they all gave evidence that pointed to Gay's sexual promiscuity.'

All had sworn affidavits making firm allegations about Gay, so that Wells and Casswell had good reason to believe they could offer an alternative to the personality presented by the prosecution. Mike Abel's affidavit, like the dozen others from Johannesburg, is now lost, but the nub of it was a description of Gay's collapse while making love in a parked car. Dr Ina Schoub now recalls her late husband repeating Mike's words: 'She nearly died on me last night – I was screwing her in my car and she passed out. I thought she was dead; then she came round.'

The 'Golden Boy' trio were staying, with other defence witnesses and a group of reporters, at the Norman Mede hotel, fifteen minutes' walk from the courthouse. Dr Schoub, Gay's gym teacher, read Mike Abel's deposition on the third morning of the trial. It described the scene in the car, the shooting pains on the underside of her left arm (a symptom of heart disease), her lips turning blue. When witnesses had travelled so far to give evidence, spectators might have been forgiven for expecting something dramatic, if not sensational. But they were to be disappointed. As the three walked to the Great Hall along Southgate Street, Abel was 'as white as a sheet'. He told Dr Schoub and her husband: 'I'm afraid I've got to perjure myself; I can't take the risk, my wife is pregnant. But I'll still help Camb.'

An American observer described Abel as 'a heavy, swarthy man wearing Hollywood-style dark glasses, flashily dressed in the fashion of Broadway or Wilshire Boulevard rather than in the more conventional English mode.' When he came forward to give evidence, Mr Justice Hilbery regarded him with 'aloof curiosity'.

Abel told of the occasion when he took Gay home after rehearsal. He had parked outside the flat, Temple Court, for 'a little general talk on show business. She then caught my arm and said, "Mike, I love you." With that, I told her, "Look, Gay, it's late; don't be silly. I am married," and I don't know, but she just seemed – well, she got excited, I suppose, and she fainted. I called two people who were passing by to give me a hand. We laid her on the front seat; the lady undid her clothing and forced her head between her knees – that is, between her own, Miss Gibson's legs. It took a little while, and then she came round, tidied her hair, and ran upstairs.'

We must assume that this unlikely chain of events, his perjurious omission, caught Molony off-balance, standing there with Abel's deposition in front of him, the important phrases underlined in red ink as an aid to quick reading.

He persisted: 'Was there any reason for that faint that you could see?' – 'She was excited, but I cannot understand her fainting.'

'What made her excited?' – 'I may have been a little selfish when she said she was in love with me. She told me that twice, and I said, "Gay, please stop it."'

'Did you notice her eyes when she fainted?' – 'After her faint, her eyes seemed very bloodshot, very red.'

'Did you ever hear her cough?' – 'Yes, very often.'

'On any particular occasion?' – 'Well, not any particular occasion; she coughed at rehearsals. Occasionally she coughed when she was excited, a very heavy cough. I should call it a "smoker's cough".'

'Did you notice anything about her breathing at the time?' – 'Very heavy after her faint.'

'Did you notice anything about the colour of her face?' – 'She was pale, and I noticed that her lips were sometimes a bluish colour.'

'Did she ever mention pain to you?' – 'While the show was running she said, "Don't play very tough tonight; I cannot get out as much as I have to," and she complained of pains in her tummy and left arm – a sort of shooting pain coming down into her fingers. She asked me to massage her arm for her.'

Abel described other occasions when Gay had passed out. Once, in a car at the Doll House, a drive-in for coffee and snacks: 'The late Miss Gibson seemed to lurch over on to my side and I put my arms round her left shoulder, and she seemed to go back with her arm against the back of the seat . . . corners of her mouth white with saliva . . . (lips) a slight bluish colour.'

And: 'Time and again, at my house, when I gave a party for her and the cast, she went out into the garden and fainted . . . We brought her on to a couch; we brought water and she was sitting there, perspiring, and she had her teeth tightly clenched . . . but she came round all right, went inside, carried on dancing, and was her normal self again.'

At the Gilberts: 'Miss Gibson was enjoying herself very much and then she excused herself for a while. She had been drinking . . . we missed her for a while . . . I walked into the garden with a member of the cast for a cigarette, and Gay came out, threw her arms up and fainted . . . on the ground, next to a tree, or rather on the lawn.' 'How long did she remain in that condition?' Molony asked. – 'I went up to her and said, "Get up, Gay." She got up, brushed herself and said, "I am sorry".'

How the jury viewed these fallings in and out of love and consciousness we can only surmise. Here was a pearl of

English womanhood fainting at the sight of this heavily built, strangely-accented man telling exotic tales out of African gardens and stationary vehicles.'

One night, Abel continued, ten days after they had first met, Gay talked about her 'private affairs'. They were at Abel's house. 'She asked me for £200 to get to England to get a doctor to take care of her. She was pregnant. I said I could not afford £200, but I could try and make some arrangements for her in Johannesburg. She said she had no faith in our South African doctors and wanted to get to England.'

'Did you ask her anything about the man responsible?' – 'I asked her who had got her into this trouble. She just laughed at it.'

Then, after a Sunday morning rehearsal at the Empire Theatre, Abel 'suggested going home as my wife had prepared a proper lunch. She didn't feel too well about the long drive to my home, so we went across the road to a hotel and ordered a snack. She said, "Have you done anything for me (about my pregnancy), Mike?" I told her there was nothing I could do except possibly introduce her to a doctor who could take care of her . . . '

'Have you known her to speak of her pregnancy to anybody else?' – 'Yes. The members of the cast knew.'

These reports of the young woman, promiscuous and in the family way, needed rebutting, indirectly, by the tried and tested method of blackening the character of the man in the box. Do to him what he had done to her, as the prosecution saw it. Mike Abel was the sort of imprecise witness Khaki Roberts had been munching with his morning tea for the previous four decades.

Roberts: 'You say you are a salesman: what house do you represent?' – 'I was freelancing and representing different houses.'

'Are you representing any house now?' – 'No, I am in my own business in Johannesburg.'

'What sort of business is it?' – 'Stationery and paper.'

'Is it going on now?' – 'I have just opened the place.'

'What is happening while you are here?' – 'My partner is

waiting for my return.'

'Are you over here on a holiday?' – 'No.'

'Are you over here on business, apart from giving evidence?' – 'I took advantage of seeing one or two people while I was here. I have bought some goods while I have been over here.'

'Your expenses are being found, are they not?' – 'I believe so. I know that my hotel and travelling expenses are being found. The balance is my own.'

'To come to give evidence at this court you get your passage paid each way and you get your hotel expenses?' – 'Yes.'

'It is a nice little trip for you, is it not?' – 'I didn't want it.'

'Need you have come?' – 'I was told that I would be subpoenaed to come.'

'Are you suggesting that a witness could be subpoenaed in South Africa?' – 'I don't know the law.'

'Do you suggest that you thought you could have been compelled to come?' – 'Yes.'

'I am suggesting to you that you are quite obviously not being frank with the court, and that you have come over here of your own free will, have you not?' – 'Yes.'

'Why not say so? You don't mind telling the truth?' – 'It is only the truth I am telling.'

'Then don't hesitate about it. I suggest it is a nice little trip for you?' – 'Yes.' (Character demolition completed, at least to the satisfaction of Bench and possibly jury.)

Roberts made no effort to rebut the individual incidents. 'The girl is dead,' he said. 'You know it is impossible for me to attempt to challenge or to deal with the accuracy of the statements which you make regarding the dead girl.' He reeled off a string of names from the Rand theatrical world whom Abel did not know. 'Perhaps,' he suggested, 'you were not very much in her confidence . . . you really tell the jury that this dead girl clutched you by the arm and said, "I love you, Mike"?' – 'Yes.'

'You are sure you are not romancing?' – 'No.'

'A girl of twenty-one said that to you?' – 'Yes, I spoke to my wife about it and to Mr Gilbert.'

Roberts read out a fistful of press reviews of *Golden Boy*. 'So she got through her arduous part satisfactorily whatever her state of health?' – 'Yes, she was ill on certain occasions before she went on.'

Dr Schoub was aware that the judge was not taken in by Abel. 'Anybody can look into a medical book and see the symptoms of heart disease. If he had told the truth it would have made all the difference, would have confirmed Camb's story – what used to happen when Gay had intercourse.'

Hocking, too, admits that it was 'pretty evident all the way through that the judge had made up his mind. He didn't like Camb, he didn't like me, he didn't like Webster, he didn't like the witnesses from South Africa, especially Mike Abel.'

The next witness was Dr Schoub's British husband, Henry Gilbert. A 'good-looking, wavy-haired actor-producer', said to resemble the actor Ronald Colman, Gilbert certainly would not suffer from stage fright. When he first met Gay, he told the court, 'she was a charming, nice, well-behaved young lady. During the process of my production she showed a temperament of a peculiar type. I found her often distraught and highly strung . . . she readily discussed her private affairs. She found at first that the part of Lorna in *Golden Boy* was rather difficult, as it had many facets to the character, and, of course, I did my best to guide her, as the producer, and to enlighten her as to the type of part it was. As time went on her behaviour became peculiar towards one of my cast, Mike Abel . . . she told me she was in love with him.' Gilbert spoke of her 'mauling Abel about' in his own drawing room, her 'dead faint' in the middle of a busy street, her coughing. At rehearsals she was 'very often tired and I let her off on quite a number of occasions. She told me she would get tired very easily.'

And she drank excessively at times. 'Once or twice she came to my early rehearsals and I smelt her breath and she was in an excited condition. I said, "Have you been drinking again to-night?" and she said, "I have only had a few gins."'

Casswell: 'Do you know of associations between her and other men?' – 'The first boyfriend I knew was Charles Brown. There was the occasion with Mike Abel, and then, about twelve days before my show opened, I was personally introduced by Gay after rehearsal to Charles [Schwentafsky] . . . We saw her at lunch with Mr Silver.'

Asked by Hilbery if she had said anything else to him, Gilbert answered, 'She seemed perturbed about sex. She came and cried to me that she was an unhappy human being . . . She said, "I cannot love like other people." I said, "What do you mean by that?" She said, "I am not like other girls".'

Roberts was equally brief. 'You were going to take her on to Pretoria when the theatre at Johannesburg closed down?' – 'The whole company was going.'

'And when she changed her mind, as ladies do, you can- celled the whole production?' – 'Yes.' And Roberts sat down.

Here was an oblique suggestion, perhaps, that the witnesses were biased or malicious because Gay had let them down by not going to Pretoria. But, as Casswell later pointed out, 'It is going a very long way to allege that possible resentment of a young actress's wayward temperament would lead decent, respectable people, such as the South African witnesses undoubtedly were, to traduce the name of a girl after her death.'

Last to appear was Dr Schoub, who should have been, for the prosecution, the most worrying witness of the Johannesburg trio. By then, however, one of the defence's main contentions was being played down. Dr Schoub recalls: 'The morning I gave evidence, Casswell went through the questions. He said I should not bring in the sexual part at all. He did not want my husband to say she had been fresh with the cast, probably because it would not be liked by the jury.'

Dr Ina Schoub, a 'statuesque, pleasant-faced brunette', opened by saying that she had two children, and was seven- and-a-half months' pregnant with a third. A graduate of the Witwatersrand University medical school, she had also trained in Edinburgh, and more recently been a casualty officer at the Johannesburg General Hospital.

Once again the court was told that Gay went to South Africa because of her health. 'She said she was suffering from asthma and had come to Johannesburg as she had been told it would be better for her there. She told me she had been in Durban and had had many asthmatic attacks there. She asked me if I thought the climate in Johannesburg would be better for her. I told her that asthmatic people varied very greatly. Some were better on a lower altitude and some on a higher . . . She was worried about the size of her hips and her part in the play, and she asked me for advice about diet and exercises. As I was taking a physical culture course at the time, I asked her to come along . . . she tired rather easily, became short of breath and had to discontinue the exercises while I went on. I advised her not to over-strain.'

Of their third meeting, late in July, Dr Schoub said: 'Gay discussed sex with me rather intimately. She told me she had had sexual experience and that she was expecting a period within the next week. I advised her not to come to the gym class . . . the following week she appeared at the class . . . the period had not arrived and she was rather worried. She asked me to advise her. I said it was much too early to say and that she was probably worried or excited about the show. I said, "wait some time", and if she was still worried then I would examine her. The next time I heard about the pregnancy was from a member of the cast.' When Dr Schoub broached the subject of contraception, she received a blank stare from Gay, who asked her to explain. A Dutch cap was recommended.

There was the cast party at the Gilberts': 'At first Miss Gibson was very gay, and then she became very unhappy and cried. I took her into the bedroom and tried to console her. She told me she was worried about her pregnancy and she was very unhappy. Then Mr Abel came into the bedroom, and I left her with him.'

Molony's final question: 'Did you ever see any signs of illness in her?' – 'I never saw her in an asthmatic attack, but I saw she tired easily, and got rather short of breath when she did exercises.'

Casswell was not pleased by the treatment of his witness. 'You might think,' he was to write, 'that Roberts would have accepted (the South African) evidence or, at least, have restricted himself to querying the details of it. But to my great surprise, he made a strong taunting attack on these witnesses. The inference could be drawn that all three were committing perjury with a man's life in the balance, so that they could enjoy a holiday in England at the expense of the State, which paid their expenses.

'I had closely questioned each of the witnesses separately before the hearing in order to satisfy myself that their accounts were genuine. I knew that, in fact, they were minimising rather than exaggerating the events which they had seen. I knew that all three felt very heavily the great responsibility resting on their shoulders . . . the woman doctor, for one, had been reluctant to leave her practice until it was pointed out to her that a man's life depended on it.'

Roberts asked Dr Schoub only seven questions. There was no attempt to contradict the evidence of pregnancy or ill-health. Brandishing a heavy volume, he challenged her: 'I see there is a section in the Medical Register for South Africa in Johannesburg, but there is no mention of you. This is 1947. I expect that there is a more up-to-date Medical Register?' Her quiet reply could be heard throughout the courtroom. 'Well, I qualified at the end of 1943. Is my father there? He has been a doctor there for twenty years.'

Roberts flicked through the pages. 'No, he is not in this register at all. There must be another register.' The attempt to undermine her had failed.

His last question: 'You liked her very much?' – 'Yes; I found her a very nice, charming girl.'

It had been a long journey for ten minutes in the witness box. Molony said later that 'Dr Schoub had not a great deal to say of deep value, but she gave her evidence in a way which carried conviction.' Yet, as Casswell wrote, 'No doubt, the insinuations made against (the South African witnesses) had an effect on the minds of the jury.'

The pathologist Hocking, waiting to give evidence, was disappointed. 'The objection to the South African witnesses was that they had come over to support the defence case. The judge just thought they were over for a holiday and trying to boost our ideas without any foundation. I think Abel possibly was a sort of a charlatan, but he did give essential evidence. We were anxious to know the medical history of this girl, as to

174

whether she could have collapsed as Camb said she did. That's when our South African witnesses let us down. Their affidavits were strongly in favour of asthma and all showed that this girl was not a hundred per cent well and could have collapsed. They were put forward very strongly. Our case was based on them. Then in the witness box they hedged on their very definite statements. Had it not been for these, we wouldn't have taken the matter up. But Dr Schoub testified as a responsible doctor, and her evidence as regards the missing period was far more trustworthy than idle gossip.'

Hocking wrote later to Webster that 'it was precisely shock as a cause of death that led me to advise bringing the South Africans over, and to go into the girl's sexual history. It was precisely this that the judge would not allow on any account – which just left us standing looking silly, because the jury would obviously say "What on earth were these people brought over for, their evidence (what was allowed) is not worth a row of beans, and if the defence have had to scrape the bottom of the barrel for evidence of this sort, then they must have been in a pretty poor position."

'But our evidence from South Africa was very strong, and if Casswell had been allowed to develop it, I believe it would have been of great significance. He was absolutely slammed down by the judge. It would have introduced evidence of a certain amount of sexual deviation, though not gross sexual aberration. One of the cast, not Abel, had talked of fellatio, using the words, "she sucks a cock".'

The defence also suffered severe disadvantages in the presentation of its case, due to lack of money and resources. The Poor Prisoners' Defence and grants available to bring witnesses from abroad cannot be compared with legal aid of the present day. The Assizes system, whereby judge and retinue may not be delayed overlong, meant that sometimes a defence case could not be as widely heard as counsel would have liked. In the Porthole case, where many relevant events took place in South Africa or at sea, there was not nearly enough money to mount a major, detailed, rebutting defence. As it was, the defence depended heavily on the Director of Public

Prosecutions for witness handouts – Professor Webster, Evelyn Armour and Peter Dalby – and expenses for the Johannesburg trio. Despite which, the trial's most significant piece of information was Hocking's urine find.

But whereas the prosecution, being an arm of the State, had at its disposal the services of both army and police, this benefited the defence in important, though not always apparent, ways. Roberts several times implanted 'evidence' by the manner of his questioning . . . the letter from the Durban GP, the colourful description of the Trawsfynydd show which underplayed the seriousness of Gay's condition, information obtained from Gay's flat-mate, Pat Rawlings, without her being called. And even if funds had been available, Doreen Mantle and the singing teacher, Mrs Taylor, were outside the jurisdiction of British courts and could not be subpoenaed. Nor could Charles Schwentafsky, and other men in Gay's life, who might have been prepared to testify that her experience with James Camb was not unique.

12

The Stain on the Sheet

Frederick Denison Maurice (Denis) Hocking, son of a pastor of Cornish stock, trained as a chemist, then as a medical doctor, and combined the two in the practice of pathology. In 1934 he moved to the Royal Cornwall Infirmary in Truro with a retainer of £100 a year to do police work for the county council. Ever since, he has been known to his colleagues as 'the West Country pathologist'. He was forty-nine at the time of the trial.

Hocking had been on Casswell's side before, notably in a case involving the murder of a tobacconist in Falmouth on Christmas Eve 1942, when Casswell had acted as counsel for the prosecution. As a result of their combined efforts, the defendant, Gordon Trenoweth, was sentenced and hanged. When Professor Webster came over to the defence after the Southampton hearing, Casswell recommended Hocking as the most experienced pathologist on the Western Circuit. Webster, who had been consulted by Hocking over several Cornish puzzlers, readily agreed that Hocking should be asked to assess the possibility of a natural death. And, more pertinently, to take a second look at the bed linen. Thus were the smears on the pillow found to be caused by blood/saliva, and the stain on the top sheet – urine.

The urine finding, Hocking later admitted, 'set off a whole chain of examination and cross-examination questions'. To his chagrin, the court appreciated his ability as a chemist in identifying the stain, but slighted his reputation as a pathologist by rejecting his interpretation of its relevance. For Khaki Roberts, Hocking's 'scientific and cold, passionless and impartial examination of the sheets and other exhibits exercised a profound influence upon the outcome of the case'.

Dr Hocking likened going into the witness box to walking the plank. 'One mounted four or five steps, walked six or eight feet along a narrow rail-guarded walk, and then found oneself perched four or more feet high up in the middle of the court, completely isolated. The judge was on one's left side, the defendant on the right, the jury in front, and counsel seemingly lost around their table on a much lower level.' He had the distinct feeling that he was not welcome. 'I was browbeaten by both Khaki Roberts and the judge. They didn't like me at all. They thought I was interfering quite unnecessarily with the course of justice.'

But in matters of interference, it was the judge who excelled. If Casswell asked a question Hilbery did not like, his pencil would drop ostentatiously on his desk. He rarely allowed Casswell to develop a line of argument through his witness's evidence. Thus, when Hocking told Casswell that the stain he was asked to examine contained nothing but dried urine – '. . . there was no blood in it at all . . . (and) a certain number of the cells of the type which one finds lining the external female sex organs' – Hilbery took over the questioning.

'Would the absence of blood in that stain lead you to any conclusion?' – 'It suggests that whoever passed that urine, I presume the deceased, could not have been bleeding from the sexual organs at the time, otherwise the urine could not have passed like that.'

Mr Justice Hilbery (mind perhaps focused on pyjamas): 'Do you think that there was anything between the person who passed that urine and the sheet at the time?' – 'Even if anything had been between them, the blood cells are so small that some of them would have gone through. I found these other (sex organ) cells, and if they would go through, then blood cells would go through, too.'

Good cross-examiner that he was, the judge persisted in angling for the answer he wanted. 'Did you form any opinion that anything was between, or nothing?' – 'I did not form any opinion; there may or may not have been.'

Allowed to continue, Casswell asked about the second stain

on the top sheet. No more than a 'smear' of blood, with constituents of saliva, said Hocking (indicating that the blood had most likely come from congestion in the respiratory tract, and not from any external injury to the girl).

Having identified the marks on sheets and pillowslips, Casswell asked Hocking for his conclusions. 'Dr Teare said that a violent death by strangling or throttling would produce these signs of blood and saliva?' – 'I quite agree that that is one way in which these marks could have got on the cloth.'

Before the follow-up, Hilbery was back in the arena. 'You mean that a common feature in a case of strangulation is a mark of blood and saliva on the lips?' – 'Yes, and the passing of urine.'

'Is there a further significance, in your view, in the passing of urine?' – 'I think the presence of urine shows almost certainly that the deceased was dead at the time it was passed.'

Hocking was intent on getting his answers right and was not aware of his surroundings. Afterwards, a friend in the audience, Agnes Fuller, wife of a Winchester physician, told him that 'a sigh of relief passed through the court when I said that it was almost certain the girl was dead when she was pushed through the porthole. Previously, apparently, the assumption had been that she had been pushed through alive, and might have recovered consciousness on entering the relatively cold sea.'

Hocking said the smears were not only consistent with a violent strangling, but also with heart failure due either to primary disease of the heart, or heart disease secondary to lung disease. (He admitted afterwards that the answer caused confusion in court.)

Casswell: 'In killing by pressing the thorax [he should have said "throat"], would you expect blood to come out?' – 'Pressing the larynx, the windpipe, blood is less likely to come up then because death is instantaneous.'

Hilbery intervened again: 'Dr Teare said that if the throat was closed it would be little more than fifteen seconds before unconsciousness?' – 'I agree with that; if anything, less.'

There followed a rapid exchange between Bench and witness

179

on the subject of asphyxia. The presence of blood in the saliva, explained Hocking, was less likely than in a choking death. This was 'an instantaneous death, which is rather different from a throttling death'. There was less likely to be blood in the saliva if death was instantaneous through compression of the windpipe, by choking.

Hilbery: 'Could it be instantaneous?' – 'Yes.'

'Is that not death due to choking?' – 'It is.'

'Otherwise, compression of the windpipe so as to prevent breathing, and to suffocate her?' – 'Even in that case death is very rapid, usually within a minute.'

'Is it not instantaneous if you have disease of the heart and it suddenly stops?' – 'Yes, but you would not have quite the same thing then. It is what happens before the heart stops. If the heart is going to stop, it will almost certainly go through a phase, just beforehand, of incipient failure.'

'With, you mean, congestion of the lungs?' – 'Yes, some of the fine passages of the lungs would rupture, in which case you would bring up a small amount of bloodstained froth.'

End of exchange. What the jury made of it, we can only guess. This seemed one occasion when, as hard-boiled pathologists tell you, 'they wouldn't have a clue . . . would rely on the judge's summing-up, as they always do'. Perhaps the jury would have benefited from a short lesson in the terminology of asphyxia – that 'strangling' and 'throttling' are both the compression of the larynx; the first, with a stocking, scarf, belt or other such ligature; the second, manually, usually with thumbs and fingers. And that 'suffocation' is smothering with a pillow or sheet. In cases of strangling and throttling, death is often instantaneous, as the victim dies of shock, and there is practically no blood. It may happen, however, that the victim does not die of shock, so that the larynx is compressed for longer, and death may take from one to three minutes. As a result, there is more blood, 'a lot more', said Hocking, 'than was found on Gay Gibson's sheets'.

Not having had a chance to let Hocking explain, Casswell now tried to pick up the thread.

'Would the smears you found, and the urine, be consistent

with a violent strangling?' – 'Yes.'

'Were any of the other things you found consistent with strangling?' – 'No. There is an absence of any very marked crumpling of the sheets, particularly in the regions which would become wet . . . The sheet would almost certainly have been crumpled over the mouth, and the dried saliva would have preserved its crumples.'

Mr Justice Hilbery: 'That is if it had been suggested that the sheet had been used for the purpose of smothering?' – 'I have seen many beds where violence has taken place; not necessarily strangling, but violent acts, and they have all been extremely crumpled.'

Casswell: 'Having seen the photographs of this cabin and examined the sheets, (is that) consistent with a violent death?' – 'I did not see the amount of crumpling I should have expected had a violent struggle taken place on that bed.'

The discussion moved on to fibres. Hocking: 'There are a large number of sharp edges of projecting corners in that small space, and had a violent struggle taken place, I should have expected to find blood, pieces of skin, possibly fibres from torn clothing, adhering to the edges of furniture and bruising on the bodies of any people fighting.'

'In other words, you would have expected to find bruising on Camb?' – 'I would.'

This led them to the scratches. Did Hocking agree with Dr Teare that nothing much of any importance could be discovered by looking at that photograph? He did. The jury was once again treated to graphic descriptions of gripping, digging, tearing and dragging.

Hilbery, drily: 'You, of course, can only speak of what you can discover in a photograph?' – 'Certainly.'

Hocking said that the marks on the arms were 'rather higher than you would expect . . . . if you were gripping a wrist which was throttling you. One would expect to find the scratches more on the hand, or near the wrist.' The gripping of his wrist described by Camb was caused, Hocking thought, by sudden death or the end of the sexual act.

'You have heard the accused's story of what happened in the

cabin, and you have heard the witnesses from South Africa and from England; has that led you to any conclusion?' – 'I think the story told by the accused is a perfectly possible one, My Lord, from the medical aspect.'

Camb's description of the sudden stiffening and relaxation of the body was, said Hocking, heart failure, 'most likely preceded by some congestion of the lungs as a result of a lung disease of which I have evidence'. Casswell ran through the pain in the left arm, the colour of her nails, perspiration, blue lips. All relevant symptoms, agreed Hocking. 'Heart disease may come on at any time of life, and quite suddenly, for a number of different causes. It may not be detected at any ordinary examination, yet be present and cause death afterwards . . . I have known two young soldiers in the last war who were passed "A1" into the army, and who both collapsed and died suddenly on parade. The post mortem showed nothing until microscopic sections of the heart were taken, and that showed cardial degeneration. That is by no means a unique experience.'

Casswell's final question: 'Having regard to all you have found here, can you conscientiously say that in your view this girl may very well have died from disease of the heart, or illness, in the way described?' – 'I can conscientiously say that the girl could have died in the way described by the accused.'

Enter Roberts: 'And can you say equally conscientiously that she could have died by strangulation?' – 'I can.'

Now the urine stains became the central preoccupation of the court. The exchanges gave rise to misconceptions which could easily have set the jury off on the wrong tack. The first arose from a single question-and-answer sequence.

Roberts to Hocking: 'There seems to be no doubt here, from the stains found, that the deceased's bladder had evacuated its contents?' – 'That is so.'

But . . . how could it be known for certain that the urine did pass on to the sheet at the moment of death? From the stewardess's evidence, it was clear even in a first-class cabin, the sheets were not changed every day. It was thus just possible that Gay could have wet her sheet in a moment of incontinence, brought on by drink, on an earlier occasion or during a siesta on the afternoon of her death. It is curious that the stain was on the one sheet only. When babies wet their bed, urine seeps through to the mattress if there is no protective rubber sheet. No one seems to have thought of sending the mattress for a laboratory test.

Nor could it be said for certain that the urine was Gay's. Camb spent enough time with her before she died for questions to be asked about how that time was passed. Though defence counsel would not have dared to make the suggestion, doctors did not rule out exotic practices. Dr Mervyn Glasser, the forensic psychiatrist: 'I am not mounting any sort of case, but it occurs to me that if they were up to all sorts of kinky practices, she might have urinated on him.'

Which opens up the alarming possibility that, if it had not been Gay's urine on the sheet, she may have been alive on her exit through the porthole.

The second misconception relates to Camb's trousers. Roberts to Hocking: 'There is not the smallest doubt, is there, that if his story be true (that at the moment of death he was on top of Gay), there would be penetration of urine which would encircle the part of his body which was against Miss Gibson's parts?' – 'Yes.'

'You have perhaps seen many cases where an act of strangulation had culminated an attempt to rape, and the assailant has had a patch of urine on his trousers the size of an association football?' – 'He could have, yes.'

'It is not suggested that Camb had any urine upon him. If he had not, then he cannot have been on top of Miss Gibson at the time of her death?' – 'Not if he had no urine on him.'

Camb, however, had clearly stated that her fatal attack took place 'just as intercourse would normally have come to an end'. There was no ejaculation. Even if there had been, the semen would empty high up in the vaginal canal and would not come out if urine was passed by the dying woman.

But supposing Camb had ejaculated, how can we know if he had kept his trousers on? 'I unloosened my belt and unfastened my trousers', he had said, but was not asked whether he had removed them, or lowered them to his ankles. He could have taken his time, for at that hour of the morning disturbance was unlikely. It seems more probable that Camb was naked, at least from the waist down. The nightwatchman had said that the man behind the door was wearing trousers, but by then Camb would have pulled them back up again. The ship's doctor could hardly be expected to have asked to examine Camb's trousers or, if he was wearing them, his underpants. Roberts had the chance to question Camb about his state of (un)dress, but failed to do so. He should not have been allowed to get away with the unfounded supposition that trousers would be hitched high if there had been intercourse.

And the third misconception – the urine on the sheet. Roberts to Hocking: 'The urine you found on the top sheet?' – 'Yes.'

'Showing that she was lying on her back, and, the bladder expelling its contents, it was naturally thrown up to the sheet above her?' – 'I don't know whether it was above her or not. She may have been lying on the top sheet.'

'Lying on her back then, it was expelled on to the top sheet?' – 'One would have expected it then to be on the bottom sheet, because Camb would be in the way.'

'But you must not assume things. Don't you worry where Camb was. If she was lying on her back, with the top sheet above her, you would expect the urine to be found, as it was, on the top sheet?' – 'And on the bottom sheet as well.'

'But if Camb was on top of her, Camb would receive the urine?' – 'Yes.'

'Don't you worry where Camb was', indeed! Of course they were on the top sheet. Not only had Camb admitted that they were sitting together on the bed before love-play began, it is also highly unlikely that a couple on a ship in the middle of a stifling tropical night would dutifully pull back the top sheet and get into bed, before indulging in passionate and illicit love-making.

The urine argument allows for a variety of explanations:

1) *The 'Khaki' version* – Gay is in her dressing gown, fully

fastened pyjamas beneath, lying between the sheets. Camb comes into her cabin, she resists his advances, he strangles her, she passes urine, supposedly a relatively small amount, for she would have emptied her bladder before retiring. Thus the terminal passage of urine is likely to be a dribble rather than a forcible evacuation. (Hocking later estimated the amount of residual urine he found at about two ounces.) So the urine, projected upwards but with little force, encounters pyjamas, then dressing gown, and, obedient to gravity, soaks downwards. What urine does penetrate clothing would be on the bottom sheet, with perhaps a light smear on the upper sheet. There would be more time for downward seepage if Camb's subsequent resuscitation attempts are to be believed.

Comment: The prosecution wants to win all the arguments; but either Gay was wearing pyjamas, thus blocking the flow of urine to the sheet above her; or she didn't have them on, thus weakening, by its own reckoning, the prosecution's case.

2) *The 'Camb' version* – The couple lie on the top sheet and make love 'missionary style'. As Gay is not wearing pyjamas, and the dressing gown is pushed back towards her shoulders, the urine seeps down to the sheet.

Comment: Again, it depends on whose version of events is believed. If the cabin door was unlocked, if Gay wore no pyjamas, if they were lying on top of the bed, then Camb's account seems more plausible than the Crown's reconstruction.

3) *The 'changed-mind' version* – What if Gay does agree to intercourse, and they are lying on top of the sheets, or even between them? And then she takes fright, thinks of her mother, of Charles Schwentafsky, of the Koromex in the suitcase? Camb is about to get on top of her and she resists; thwarted, he strangles her?

Comment: It is possible, if they were on the top sheet, that the urine was proof of strangling. But this was never alleged by the prosecution, which maintained that Gay wore pyjamas and showed no inclination to have intercourse, and that, despite the door being left unlocked for the hour between Camb's arrival and the nightwatchman's knock, he was an unwelcome visitor and she a staid virgin.

Thus ended Hocking's testimony. Khaki Roberts later admitted that it was unique in his experience that 'the prosecution in one way became infinitely stronger owing to the expert evidence produced by the defence'. Which is why Hocking said of the sheets, 'I almost wish I had never heard of them.'

It was 5.15 p.m. Enough time for the final defence witness, Professor Webster. But there was no sign of him. His Lordship was not amused.

Hilbery apologised to the jurors for keeping them all day on a Saturday. 'We have come within sight of the end of your labours.' The trial would end on Monday. The Rolls-Royce bore him away to the Lodge where his fellow judges were enjoying the blazing fire and a glass of sherry with their ladies.

The next day's *Sunday Express* headlined its page-one story: 'Gay Gibson died in my arms,' says Camb – Doctor says: 'I think that story is perfectly possible.' The *News of the World* teased its readers with 'The Mystery of Gay Gibson's Black Pyjamas', while on the front page it ran: 'What Happened in Cabin 126 – Camb's Story', which continued inside over four long columns. *The People* splashed the story on page three under the heading: 'Gay Gibson fainted when her love was refused', an over-stretched reference to the car scene with Mike Abel.

Camb attended morning service in the prison chapel, and in the afternoon received a visit from his wife Margaret, the first since the start of the trial.

Monday arrived, the day Gay Gibson's death would be deemed accident or murder. On the same page as its report: 'Actress Had Fainting Fits', the *Daily Telegraph* reviewed Clifford Odets' latest arrival from Broadway, *Rocket to the Moon*, at St Martin's Theatre in London's West End. 'A sad little play of human beings yearning for the happiness which always escapes them,' wrote the critic, W. A. Darlington. 'Only the girl, who, to most of the men in the play, symbolises romance, had any real hope of happiness when the play is done. Even she, young and eager though she is and full of determination to get out of life all that it has to offer, seems doomed to an ultimate disillusion.' Yolande Donlan was praised for her performance. Thoughtful readers may have been struck by an underlying irony. Perhaps, if things had turned out differently and Gay had arrived safely in England, she would have landed the part herself – thanks to her experience of Odets' work – in one of those theatreland dream sequences which occasionally happen in real life.

Josh Casswell's task on this fateful day was to extend the life expectancy of his client. As his wife drove them out of Wimbledon, he may have reflected on the rotten luck he had once experienced through the error of a scientist and the obstinacy of a judge. The Dorchester Assizes, 1936 . . . Charlotte Bryant was charged with poisoning her husband. The respected Home Office analyst, Dr Roche Lynch, had raked about under a boiler for coal ashes which, when analysed, were found to contain 149 parts to a million of arsenic. Here was damning evidence. Household coal in its natural state had 48 parts to one million of the poison, said Roche Lynch. This abnormal proportion of arsenic was corroborated by a Crown witness's story of a tin of weedkiller burnt on the fire at the Bryants' house.

Mrs Bryant was convicted and duly sentenced to death. Casswell subsequently received a letter from Professor William Bone, expert on coal at Imperial College, London. It was well known, he said, that the normal arsenic content of house coal was never less than 140 parts to the million, and usually about a thousand to the million. Casswell asked the Court of Criminal Appeal to hear the professor in person. On the morning of the appeal, the Solicitor General admitted privately to the defence that Roche Lynch had blundered; having obtained the information over the telephone, he must have misheard what had been said.

But Lord Chief Justice Hewart had other ideas. 'This court will not listen to the opinion of scientific gentlemen bringing their minds to bear on evidence which they have not heard.' There was more to come: 'This court sets its face like flint against attempts to call evidence which could have been made available at the trial' – though, as in the Camb trial, defence resources were limited by a Poor Prisoners' Defence. Nor was there reason for Casswell to suspect that 'a doctor of Dr Roche Lynch's reputation would give evidence for the Crown in a murder trial which could be inaccurate'. Without hearing the respondents, Hewart signed off with: 'It is clear that there has been no mistake.' Mrs Bryant was hanged at Exeter Prison, leaving her solicitor to divide her estate of 5s 9½d among her five children.

James Mathewson Webster, a Scot, son of a minister from St Andrew's, was, at fifty, one of the most respected pathologists of his day, the more so since the decline of Bernard Spilsbury. Unlike Spilsbury, he created a framework which lived on after him. In the twenties, Percy Sillitoe, head constable of Sheffield police – it was before he took on MI5 – made him the city's police surgeon. There he set up the first forensic science laboratory outside a university medical school. So successful was it that the Metropolitan Police followed suit. For the previous ten years Webster had been director of the South Midlands Forensic Laboratory in Birmingham as well as professor of pathology at the university which, in those days, was a part-time post, usually held by a surgeon who had failed to get the chair of surgery. Webster was not an also-ran and, even though a part-timer, put forensic pathology on the map in the Midlands.

But in spite of Hocking's opinion of Webster as 'very highly thought of as a really sensible forensic pathologist', to others he was 'blunt and unconventional, though seldom disbelieved'. He would get fixed ideas about certain things and no amount of argument could persuade him out of them. Dr Ben Davis, Webster's successor as head of forensic pathology at Birmingham University, recalls his court style: 'He had a great ability to communicate ideas to a jury. He would loll back in the witness box and address them as though they were a class of junior and ignorant students. He was blind in one eye and his glass eye gave him a peculiar squint. Quite an impressive sight. I have never known anyone else do it. And the judges used to let him get away with it.'

Apart from Camb, Webster was the star witness for the defence, the expert first approached by the prosecution to clear up the medical mystery. The fact that he now appeared for the other side should only have reinforced those opinions.

The queue for the public gallery on Monday 22 October was twice as long as on previous days. As Casswell put the finishing touches to his address to the jury, Webster told Molony that 'the account given by Camb of this girl's death could have occurred . . . There was nothing in (it) inconsistent with my own experience with regard to three deaths which occurred during intercourse.'

Molony: 'Were they people in whom signs could have been or were detected in advance of their death?' – 'One was a soldier of twenty-eight, serving with H.M. Forces at the time.'

Which, unhappily, was not the answer to the question. Molony did not pursue it, asking no more on the vital matter of previous cases, and a chance was lost of rendering an intercourse death less unusual than it seemed. Perhaps Webster had arrived too late for a thorough briefing with counsel, or he did not have details of the other cases at his disposal. Or maybe word had come down from on high that His Lordship would brook no further delay.

They moved on to possible causes of death. Webster ruled out shock – 'death would be too quick for blood to well up, and for the deceased to inflict a number of scratches which were found on the arm of the prisoner'.

Webster admitted having had 'personal experience of many cases' of strangulation. 'I want to make it quite clear . . . that I cannot exclude the possibility of (the arm scratches) having been caused during strangulation, but, in my experience, they have certain peculiarities – one, that they extend so far up the arm without there being anything on the hands; I have never seen scratches so far up the arm in strangulation. In manual strangulation, where scratching does take place is the region of the thumb, the back of the hand, and in fact the scratching of the victim's neck in an effort to relieve the pressure; these are the places where I have found scratches.'

The discussion moved from scratches to urine. The stain implied, said Webster, that 'she was dead, in my opinion, before she was put into the water. Camb's action, in my experience, fits in with medical science.' Hilbery, clearly unhappy with the witness's manner, and with his non-arrival on Saturday, seized on this as 'a rather strange way to put it, but still, we will let it pass'.

Molony asked Webster to detail possible causes of death, 'accepting for the moment the correctness of Camb's account', Webster leaned back: 'Death would have occurred from natural causes in two main ways. Both . . . give rise to blood at the mouth, the finding of urine, and the scratching of the accused's arm . . . One, the bursting of a small congenital aneurysm in the brain, a condition which is indefinable prior to death, the bursting of which occurs in young people particularly if there is an associated effort such as the act of intercourse.

'The second is by heart disease, either direct or indirect. While rare in the young, direct heart disease due to an affection* of the heart vessels, even at this age, is not unknown, and again, that type of death can give blood-stained froth at the mouth, the finding of urine and clutching.

'But indirect causes are probably more common, namely, the effect of a septic focus elsewhere in the body. In this case the septic focus was the chronic running ear. That in itself is capable of causing heart failure, and cases are known of it causing the general poisoning of the heart muscle leading to sudden death during effort or, more probably, poisoning of a special portion of the heart muscle which is responsible for the ordered action of the heart, the Bundle of His, and sudden death from that during effort is well known in both sexes.'

Webster cited the case of an apparently healthy boy of seventeen who died pushing a bicycle up a hill . . . the left tonsil had caused poisoning of the heart muscles, and the Bundle of His was swollen up within its fibrous capsule and was virtually strangled by the capsule.

* A disease of the body, a term first used in 1541 – (*Oxford English Dictionary*).

After this virtuoso mini-lecture from north of the Tweed, Webster turned from his class of Sassenachs and sipped a glass of water.

Molony: 'If any of these conditions had been present before death, would they have been diagnosed?' – 'It is quite a probability they would not.'

Was Webster aware of any other theory of death in this case which fitted the facts better than the account given by the accused? 'One cannot exclude the possibility of strangulation so far as violent death is concerned, and that appears to me to be the only other possibility, but it is no more consistent with the facts than the natural causes which I have outlined.'

Roberts stood up for his final cross-examination. For hors d'oeuvres, a slice of character assassination: 'Were you not engaged in a murder trial at Birmingham on Saturday?' – No, said Webster, it is not true. Hilbery: 'Do you know who sent the message as an excuse for your absence from this court?' – 'I have no idea.' – 'Were you in a murder trial last week?' – 'Yes, that is quite true.'

A splendid opener, like a batsman hitting a feared fast bowler's first ball for four. After which, the leading British authority on forensic medicine was permitted to give his evidence.

Roberts: 'Did you say you could not include or you could not exclude the possibility of strangulation?' – 'I could not exclude the possibility of strangulation.'

'You agree, do you not, with Dr Hocking, that all the common features of strangulation are present here?' – 'Not all the common features.' [Not having been in court on Saturday, he could not verify what Hocking had said.]

'You have the bloodstained froth from the mouth?' – 'Yes.'

Hilbery again: – 'A common feature present with strangulation?' – 'Yes, My Lord.'

Roberts: 'And the voiding of urine at the time of death?' – 'Yes.'

Bench and witness embarked on yet another fruitless analysis of the scratches. After looking at the photographs Webster grudgingly admitted that he could not exclude the possibility of manual strangulation. Roberts seemed to echo the feelings of everyone in court, bar Camb's defenders, that 'there is no particular virtue in a few inches one way or the other . . . the hand of the strangler would be round the victim's throat, but the hands of the victim would make the most violent and convulsive efforts to pull the hand of the strangler away?' – 'I accept that.'

Webster also agreed that in 'all his vast experience' he had known only the three cases of death during intercourse to which he had already referred.

They returned to the subject of asthma. Casswell said afterwards that whether or not Gay suffered from asthma, it became, in the light of Webster's conclusion and the largely corroborative evidence of Hocking, 'a matter of the gravest consequence. If the defence could satisfy the jury that there was a reasonable chance of Gay's having been asthmatic, Camb would be entitled to a verdict of acquittal. For in that event the prosecution would have failed to prove his guilt beyond all reasonable doubt.' But at the time Webster admitted that he was just assuming that Gay had asthma, without having any direct evidence of it.

The last five minutes of the testimony were in the hands of Sir Malcolm Hilbery, at his most persuasive . . . or perhaps Webster was losing his grip. The judge wanted to know more about the arching of the back described by Miss Armour of the ATS. Webster said that this could be a symptom of either strychnine poisoning, tetanus or hysteria.

'There is no suggestion that there was tetanus because she was completely recovered by the next morning?' – 'No, My Lord, nor of strychnine poisoning.'

'So it would look to you as if there was at least an element of hysteria?' – 'Yes.'

'Would we be right in thinking that the description of that episode does not suggest an asthmatic attack, or a heart attack?' – 'I entirely agree.'

'It might be, might it not, a mild attack of epilepsy?' – 'Yes, that is what I was thinking.'

'There is another possibility – it is pure conjecture – might there have been a heart condition with a hysterical complex?' – 'Yes; the pain might have been quite genuine heart pain, but the first two causes I entirely agree are completely out of it, tetanus and strychnine.'

'And asthma?' – 'Yes, My Lord.'

'Would we be right in thinking, the jury and I, that in your view, although the element of heart pain is present, the thing really indicates to you a hysterical attack?' – 'Yes, that is my view.'

What about the difficulty in breathing?' – 'It might have been a hysterical spasm of breathing.'

'And the clutching of the breast?' – 'That is consistent with pain due to heart trouble which may have precipitated the hysterical attack.'

And that was almost, but not quite, the end of the evidence. As Webster left the stand, warily treading the 'plank', Hilbery recalled him to deliver a lecture of his own to the professor. 'The greatest care should be exercised by those who have to deal with these matters on your behalf that incorrect messages about reasons for your absence should not be sent.'

What the jury made of this, and the unconscious under-mining of the value of the evidence just heard, we will never know. Webster's glass eye may not have worked its magic this time. On that sublime note, the defence closed its case.

Hocking was disappointed with his colleague's performance. 'Far too much was made of Gay Gibson's health having an effect on her heart, damaging it and thus causing it to fail at the critical moment. All this was much overdone. I did not stress, nobody stressed, that sudden death in perfectly healthy young women is a fantastic possibility. All of us, myself, Professor Webster, Dr Teare, should have been asked this. We should all have said that it is a possibility.

'There was no need to drag in all her minor diseases. Of course, if she had them it would predispose her to death in the circumstances, but they were not necessary. I think the jury might have thought that we were scraping the barrel looking for excuses. Professor Webster said that these deaths are rare, but this is not borne out by recent experience.'

As the court prepared to listen to the arguments for and against the conviction of James Camb for murder, let us consider the medical background of Gay Gibson which was not placed before the court.

13

Death in Love

On 16 February 1899, France was plunged into official mourning. Across the country the tricolor was lowered from buildings draped in black. Félix Faure, sixth president of the Third Republic, had died suddenly of a stroke in the Blue Drawing Room of the Elysée Palace. Or, as the announcement in the *Journal Officiel* put it, of a 'cerebral haemorrhage with paralysis of the face and left side'. The reality, however, was more hot-blooded. The former tanner from Le Havre had expired 'during an interview' with Mme Marguérite Steinheil, who was found naked and considerably distressed, entwined with the body of her august lover, which still grasped a strand of his mistress's blonde hair. She was ordered to dress quickly and, heavily veiled, was ushered out of the side door of the palace. The president's wife and daughter were then informed.

Death 'in the saddle' is by no means the exclusive preserve of European statesmen. Richard Nixon's vice-president, the patrician Nelson Rockefeller, likewise died in the arms of a woman not his wife. No official announcement, and certainly no post-mortem examination, has ever confirmed the circumstances of these furtive encounters. Yet they serve to show that, for an unfit man of late middle-age, be he of humble or high standing, the sexual act makes heavy demands on heart and blood vessels. Rather more men than the records would suggest have died from 'an old-fashioned coronary' while making love to a wife or lady friend.

For a 21-year-old woman, however, the odds against dying in this way are substantially higher. But how much higher, it is impossible to say. Sex, more so than death, remains a subject not to be spoken of in respectable circles. When the two come together, there is a heady cocktail. Who can blame the surviving spouse for not wishing to broadcast the unspeakable circumstances of the partner's death to friends and family? It could disturb the course of mourning, and might lead to gossip at the supermarket checkout; the more so if intercourse was adulterous. Even today, a full generation and a whole sexual revolution after the events in cabin 126, accurate reporting on sex-related deaths can break down at any one of several points – the surviving lover not telling the family; a cover-up by embarrassed relatives; the GP, if he is aware of the true facts, quite properly wishing to protect the family's good name. He is not bound to do otherwise. Only the cause, not the circumstances, of a natural death is required to be written on the death certificate.

As a result of this taboo, very little gets published on the subject in medical journals. Our knowledge is largely anecdotal. Dr Hocking recalls giving evidence at the Assizes in Exeter and saying that intercourse death is not at all uncommon. 'It caused consternation. But the prosecution pathologist, Dr Hunt, agreed. Every pathologist has them. These cases do not come out at inquests because they go down as natural causes. Nor are they very interesting from the forensic point of view.'

Dr Bernard Knight, professor of forensic pathology at Cardiff University and co-author of the standard medical textbook on pathology, *The Essentials of Forensic Medicine*, says bluntly: 'There are no statistics on death during sexual intercourse, because many are not reported as such, for obvious reasons, mainly embarrassment . . . illicit situations would inhibit such reporting. Any figures that might be available would obviously be gross under-reporting. However, in medico-legal practice, especially in a coroner's autopsy service, it is a regular, though perhaps not very frequent, experience to have a history that a person died during sexual intercourse.'

One of Britain's leading experts on the sudden death syndrome, Professor Michael Davies of St George's Hospital, Tooting, finds it impossible to say how frequently sexual intercourse does invoke sudden death, even in patients known to have ischaemic heart disease (fibrosis of the muscles of the heart). 'I have certainly autopsied an occasional male with ischaemic heart disease who died suddenly under these circumstances, but this is simply anecdotal and even if it occurred more commonly, in most instances the information is likely to be suppressed by the next of kin.'

Here is the catch in attempting to determine the rarity, or otherwise, of the manner of Gay Gibson's death as described by the defence. Demise during intercourse is never reported in the newspapers despite the fact that every detected case of strangulation, rape, or violent death associated with sex, is likely to be aired by the coroner, and usually in the criminal courts as well. Instead, the general public is given the impression by the local and national media that strangulation is a common occurrence.

The love bed is, of course, just one of the many places where death can strike out of the blue. But any form of exertion may bring it on. A man with a weak heart sprinting for a bus, an adrenalin-pumping altercation in the street following a motor collision, a nineteen-year-old policeman found dead in the shower after a jujitsu class. All these respectable ways of dying are acceptable to next of kin and mourners, and liable to be read about in newspapers and written up in medical journals.

A reliable assessment of the likelihood of Gay Gibson having died in a non-violent way is further complicated by the notorious inaccuracy of death certificates. General practitioners admit that what they write down is 'as vague as hell . . . vastly inaccurate'. In the early 1950s, a San Francisco coroner, H. W. Turkel, investigating 500 consecutive autopsies, found that clinical diagnosis was wrong in 45 per cent of cases while, correspondingly, 30 per cent of those believed to have been due wholly or in part to violence were proved by autopsy to be 'natural deaths'.

In Britain, in 1969, Professor Hugh Johnson published the results of a survey of the 5000 autopsies on unnatural deaths conducted at the London Hospital, Whitechapel, in the years 1963-7. This showed up the gap between the doctor's clinical diagnosis and the pathologist's autopsy findings. Researchers concentrated on 263 cases where the coroner's officers had either reported natural deaths or the possibility of unnatural causes was discounted by the attending doctor, police, relatives or officer himself. Professor Johnson found that, due to a mixture of deliberate deception by family, inertia by police, and 'unbelievable gullibility and stupidity of doctors (especially in abortion cases), violent deaths, often murders by poisoning or strangulation, were not referred for autopsy'.

This meant that cases which could have served as precedents for the sort of death described by Camb had no chance of seeing the light of day. For the Winchester jury, strangulation as the cause of death fitted in comfortably with preconceived notions of what could have happened – Gay had perished defending her honour from the proverbial 'fate worse than death'. The very idea of her dying of 'natural causes' during a willing act of intercourse was deeply insulting to the memory of the dead girl. Egged on by a Victorian judge and a combatant counsel, with each ambivalent clue deployed to Camb's disadvantage (bells, pyjamas, scratches, urine), the jury was not given room to appreciate the medical basis of the defence case.

On reading the medical evidence in the trial, one is struck by its comparative brevity. Yet for Professor Tom Marshall, the Northern Ireland State Pathologist, the most striking impression of the evidence was that 'nobody knows why this girl died. The prosecution seems to have done a good job in building up its case on circumstantial evidence, but having regard only to the medical aspects of the evidence it seems to me that it was quite wrong to conclude that she had been strangled. She might have been strangled, but this is only one of a number of possibilities. You should really choose a natural death before a non-natural death. Where you are working even on the balance of probabilities, a natural death in this instance must come first. And if you are talking about beyond all reasonable doubt, there is no way you could choose strangulation.' Nor did he believe that a young man was more likely to die from heart disease than a young woman.

Since the forties, much more has been learned about the

sudden, unexplained death of young people. Here, following a discussion of the Porthole case with several of Britain's leading forensic pathologists and psychiatrists, are some of the facts that are now known about death in such circumstances.

The authors of *The Essentials of Forensic Medicine*, Cyril Polson, David Gee and Bernard Knight, declare roundly that 'death may occur during sexual intercourse . . . the result of natural disease, e.g., rupture of a cerebral aneurysm'. A faulty aneurysm was favoured by Professor Webster, though not by Dr Hocking, as the likely cause of Gay's death.

The seventeenth-century anatomist, Thomas Willis, wrote a pioneering book on the human brain (with woodcuts by his friend Christopher Wren) which described how the arteries formed a complete circle at its base, subsequently known as the 'Circle of Willis'. Sometimes these arteries have little blow-outs, resulting in bleeding over the surface of the brain which produces a sub-arachnoid haemorrhage. The arteries may also burst spontaneously, during sleep. Professor Tom Marshall has called them 'little blisters on the artery wall that go pop'. Dr Ben Davis, Professor Webster's successor, has been more specific than this: it is well known, he says, 'that they can burst particularly during times of strenuous exercise, or sexual intercourse, or defecating, or anything like that. People don't know they have them. About half recover, but the rest die. Doctors can do tests and X-rays, and then clip it off surgically. But if Gay Gibson had had an aneurysm, no one would have known about it. It is feasible.'

Dr Davis recalled an inquest in Birmingham, about twenty years ago: 'A woman of about thirty saw her husband off on holiday to Jamaica, came straight home and leapt into bed with her boyfriend, who was a great friend of the husband. She died of a sub-arachnoid haemorrhage from a previously undiagnosed ruptured aneurysm.'

David Gee, emeritus professor of forensic medicine at Leeds University, talks of a 'well-recognised cause of sudden collapse and, quite frequently, death in people of this sort of age group . . . (it is) known that this could happen during sexual intercourse.' His co-author, Bernard Knight, says that sub-arachnoid haemorrhage is 'well known to neurosurgeons and accident departments as the rapid rise in blood pressure caused by the acute violent exertion of intercourse may rupture this small blister and cause rapid if not instantaneous death . . . Both males and females have an approximately equal incidence of berry aneurysm. However, it is obvious that the exertion is most often on the part of the male and therefore . . . the cause of death is predominantly in men.'

Professor Marshall admits that it is uncommon for young people to collapse and die suddenly from natural disease, but that it does happen. 'If I were to be called in this morning to do a PM on a girl of twenty-one, sub-arachnoid haemorrhage would be first in my mind. It is many times more likely than death from strangulation. If a person has developed an aneurysm (usually because of a focal weakness in the artery wall) its rupture is more likely when the blood pressure is raised, as during intercourse, although an aneurysm can rupture at any time. If it leaks before it tears, it might cause headaches. But this does not carry away young people.'

Statistics in Northern Ireland reveal that in the six years ending in 1987, sub-arachnoid haemorrhage accounted for eighty-four sudden deaths, of which six cases were under thirty years of age. Research in Austria in 1984 showed that in thirty cases of unexpected sudden death during sexual acts, most were males of higher age-groups with coronary heart disease, but there were also several with aneurysms of the basal arteries of the brain.

A second possibility worth considering in Gay Gibson's case is cardiomyopathy, said by Polson, Gee and Knight to fall into an uncommon group of causes of sudden death, 'many of which do not advertise their presence by visible changes in heart muscle'. The textbook notes, ironically in the circumstances, that one form of cardiomyopathy, asymmetrical hypertrophy, was first described by Teare in 1958 and cases occurring in Northern Ireland were cited by Marshall in 1970. This condition, say the authors, 'can affect persons in . . . ages ranged from 13 to 60 years. It is usually undiagnosed or diagnosed as sub-aortic stenosis (narrowing) in the living. More often it is the cause of sudden, unexpected collapse and death.' Marshall doubts whether the condition was known at the time of the Porthole trial. 'I started as a pathologist in 1950, but did not know about it till 1960. If there was a post mortem, they would probably say it was high blood pressure.' In a paper of 1970, Marshall noted that more asymmetrical hypertrophies seemed to occur in Northern Ireland than elsewhere. In the nine years ending 1967, he identified sixteen cases, ten in people under the age of thirty. Though eleven were males, and seven of these were under thirty, three women fell into this category.

Cardiac conduction defect, though also rare, is another condition bringing on sudden death. The heart's inherent power to beat is controlled by a system of muscle fibres which initiate an electrical impulse, causing contraction throughout each of the four chambers. Professor Marshall has seen 'a few cases where there is some damage to the conducting system. These people get fainting attacks, and they die rather as in cardiomyopathy. I had the case of a man sitting in a rose-garden eating sandwiches; he died and I found nothing at the post mortem. But I had worked on cardiac conduction defects with an American colleague who could dissect out this tissue. Under the microscope he found degeneration in the tissue. It is not common, about as common as cardiomyopathy, but the important thing is that young people can die from natural causes in this way.'

Many people have attacks of atrial fibrillation, which is fibrillation of the upper chambers of the heart and is not serious. But fibrillation of the lower chambers, the ventricles, is invariably fatal. When functioning normally, the heart contracts and blood is squirted out like a pump. But when someone collapses and is dying, they may go into fibrillation, so that instead of beating in a purposeful manner, the heart wall simply quivers without expelling any blood. Sometimes this can be corrected with an electrical stimulus, which jerks the heart and stops the fibrillation, so that the patient starts breathing again. It could, says Professor Michael Davies, conceivably happen to a young person. 'Sexual intercourse is an intense emotional and physical strain and is well known to induce angina in patients who suffer from ischaemic heart disease. Inevitably, therefore, anybody who is at risk of cardiac arrhythmias is at a particular risk of developing ventricular fibrillation during intercourse. The same would be true of a violent loss of temper or playing a game of squash.'

As to the other maladies which the defence tried to pin on Gay Gibson: asthma can cause rapid death but this usually comes about after a few minutes' difficulty with breathing; death has also been known to occur during epileptic fits, but the medical experts seemed to agree that Gay's attacks (fainting, arching of the back) were more likely to have been an hysterical manifestation of a highly-strung temperament than due to either asthma or epilepsy.

Regarding the less common causes of sudden death, Professor Marshall admitted: 'If she had any one of those conditions, it is not surprising that an ordinary army medic found nothing wrong with her. Very few of these things would have been known in 1947. But if I were asked to guess the cause of death of a woman of this age found dead in her bunk aboard a ship I would choose from the conditions mentioned above. Were I told she had died during the activity of intercourse, I would still choose from these conditions – with more expectation of being right. I do not think I would seriously consider she had been strangled.'

One other pointer as to how Gay Gibson might have died is to be found in the extraordinary story of an end-of-term rag at a Scottish university. The college janitor, fearing that the boisterous students were getting out of hand, tried to stop them. They laughed at him, and laid his head on a guillotine block for a mock execution. One of them flicked a wet towel on the man's neck and he died instantly. The towel had hit the highly sensitive vagal nerve which runs from the base of the brain, connecting with the carotid artery on the side of the neck and causing a reflex inhibition of the heart, often, as in this case, with immediately fatal results. Vagal inhibition is a form of shock, leaving no trace at autopsy, in the same way that, on the mortuary slab, no water is found in the lungs of someone who has died from drowning. 'Dry drowning' is a form of vagal reflex death. The late Professor Keith Simpson, who recounted the story of the mock execution, also described a dance-floor scene when a slow foxtrotter lovingly gripped his partner's neck, only to see her die in his arms.

Professor David Bowen, Home Office pathologist and Teare's successor at Charing Cross Hospital in London, considered the Porthole case in relation to vagal inhibition. 'If a person is frightened, apprehensive, highly-strung, hysterical, the threshold of reaction would be very low. Pressure on the neck causes the heart to slow and may even lead to death. Though I have never had a case of a girl of twenty, it probably happens more often than we imagine. It is far more likely to happen with a young woman.'

On the borderline between accidental death by vagal inhibition and homicidal strangling was the 1946 case of James Palmer, outlined in an Appendix to the Report of the Royal Commission on Capital Punishment (1949–53). 'A merchant seaman made the acquaintance of a woman on a bus and spent the next evening with her, drinking at a public house. At closing-time, they went to a nearby road, where he had intercourse with her, in the course of which she died; death was due to strangulation accelerated by shock caused by pressure on her thyroid gland, which was at that time abnormally sensitive. The prisoner said he had put his hand over her mouth or throat to stop her screaming. He had not used towards her the great violence usually associated with rape.' Like Camb, Palmer had failed to call a doctor. But here the pathologist and jury had the convenience of a body to help them reach a decision. This might have explained why the Home Secretary recommended a reprieve.

Eight years after the Winchester trial, Dr Hocking shared some of his thoughts about it in a letter to Professor Webster. The relevant passages read:

I have always thought that very odd fun and games went on in that cabin that night, and that in the course of them the girl died of shock – during intercourse, or perhaps even not . . . Your [Webster's] recollection is perfectly correct that the girl was a sexual pervert; in fact, one of the worst I have ever heard about. Your recollection is absolutely right on what was said by Eric Boon and the rest of the company. In addition, Mike Abel spread it about that she 'sucks a cock'. [Affidavits were enclosed to back up this statement.] My interpretation of her sexual goings-on was that she was a masochist, and probably a sado-masochist. To an undoubtedly highly-sexed man like Camb, this may have proved an irresistible attraction, and all sorts of things may have gone on in that cabin, leading to the girl's death by shock – or by intercourse. A damaged myocardium [muscular substance of the heart] (and I am convinced there is plenty of evidence of this) plus excitement, plus perhaps something funny might easily have led to her death, if not naturally, at least not necessarily by deliberate violence.

Is it possible that both the Crown and Camb's evidence were off-beam, that the two in the cabin indulged in non-missionary love-making, which might have led to Gay's death? We are more relaxed about these matters today, but in 1948 defence lawyers would not have dreamed of mentioning unladylike practices in a court of law. Sodomy and bestiality were one thing – Hilbery had dealt with them during the Assizes – but fellatio in the first class was unthinkable.

This down-to-earth view is shared by present-day pathologists. Thus Professor Gee: 'If one assumes she was not sexually inexperienced and he was someone who had curious ideas . . . oral sexual intercourse was practised in those days and she might well have died of choking . . . a number of possibilities, ranging from death due to the nature of sexual practices itself through to natural causes during intercourse, onwards to somebody being actually strangled because they resisted.'

Dealing with death resulting from abnormal intercourse in *The Essentials of Forensic Medicine*, the authors write: 'The victim may die of choking, especially at the moment of ejaculation during oral intercourse, or be choked by a plug of wool, or similar material, placed in the mouth to retain the seminal fluid.' The book cites an unsolved case of murder by asphyxia where a plug of cotton wool contaminated by semen was found in the woman's throat.

Among the weirdest of the death variables was that of Camb tying Gay up with the black pyjamas, partially strangling her to heighten sexual intensity but going too far, so that she died of shock. The pyjamas would have gone out of the porthole with her.

The exact nature of their love-making, so important in the search of what really happened, still eludes us after all these years. To a youthful forensic psychiatrist like David Somekh, it is 'not enough to say she was highly-sexed or a nympho-maniac. What we are interested in from the point of view of it being relevant to the sudden cessation of breathing, is perverse or sado-masochistic activities. If this were a pair of homosex-uals in 1990 it would be much clearer what might be going on. But it's the 1940s and we don't know the psychology of a gay young thing, when it was traditional to be discreet about just the sort of things we need to know about here.'

In the absence of Sherlock Holmes, the prison psycho-therapist Arthur Hyatt Williams has produced personality assessments of the two participants and offered an imaginative reconstruction of what could have gone wrong. 'He might have been a phallic man who pushed very hard with a large penis and disturbed the pregnancy and caused a reflex, leading to unconsciousness. In the first three months of pregnancy, inter-course is quite dicey, and somebody thinking only of himself and his phallic pride would be likely to do some harm. In intercourse with a woman like that, and if there was a large, aggressive penis, it would be no holds barred.'

What sort of a sexual persona did Gay have? Dr Hyatt Williams thought that 'far from being a virgin as her mother alleged, she may have been quite a sexual woman, very nar-cissistically interested in her conquests of men, quite keen on, not perversions, but variants of straight sexuality. She was rather flirtatious with a number of people . . . with the man

who gave her the first-class ticket, and she wrote in her effus-
ive, loving way to him, obviously treating him like a sugar
daddy, and whatever there was in it sexually, I'm quite certain
he didn't do it for nothing. Whether she actually liked sex, or
whether it was for her greater power or whether for her titillation, I don't know. She sounds like a loving woman, the
answer to a seaman's prayer. And the tropics – after all, she
was born in the tropics – stimulated her.'

If Gay did die a natural death, Dr Hyatt Williams thinks they
'had a long-drawn-out intercourse, exciting rather than satisfy-
ing, which would link with no seminal fluid being found,
because that is a remarkable thing. You don't expect him to
have had no condom and then to have been totally self-con-
tained. There is some evidence that she was an hysteric or a
mild epileptic. With a lot of titillation, and maybe intercourse,
and maybe without emission on his part, she could have got so
excited that her heart rate would have gone up and it is quite
feasible she would have had a syncopal attack [unconscious-
ness].'

If, on the other hand, Gay was murdered, Dr Hyatt Williams
sees a likely explanation in a wound to Camb's narcissistic
pride. 'If he were frustrated or humiliated, I think he could be
venomous. During the course of love-making he might have
said, "Well, you've never had it like that, have you?" and she
says, "Oh, yes, much better than you; you are all right, but
nothing to write home about." And yet she didn't sound like
that sort of woman . . . much more, a woman who would make
the man of the moment all-important. She was certainly no
penis teaser. I think something went wrong that wasn't
intended to go wrong.

'I don't believe either story, the prosecution's or Camb's,
completely. If you made me choose, I would say he didn't do it.
He should have been convicted for anything else they could
have got him for, like perjury and destroying evidence by
pushing the body through the porthole.'

Doctors frequently complain that lawyers expect them to
provide precise answers to every medical question which
comes before the courts, yet even if Gay Gibson's body had

been found, it is not certain that the cause of death was capable of being established. Professor Marshall says, 'It is popularly believed that when a pathologist carries out a post-mortem examination the cause of death must be revealed. Unfortunately, as all pathologists have learnt, this is not so, and in forensic practice in particular, there is a small proportion of cases in which no adequate cause of death can be found.' His department in Belfast, which is 'reasonably cautious', averaged six 'undetermined' cases for every thousand autopsies carried out.

Dr Hocking reported a case before the war of a married woman of twenty-one who died during intercourse with her husband after a dance in Bodmin. 'He was quite frank about it, and informed the police at once. I found absolutely nothing at the post mortem.'

Even if Gay Gibson's body had been eventually recovered, the deterioration might have made strangling difficult to establish. With putrefactive swelling of the neck tissues, a pathologist would be cautious about marks which at first sight indicated violence. Suspicious-looking injuries on the body might turn out to be fish- or crab-bites. After a month to six weeks in the water, the body is bald all over, toe- and finger-nails peel off, and the outer skin of the hands and feet, which thicken after a few hours in water to resemble 'washerwoman's fingers', has disappeared entirely. Identification becomes unreliable, though fingerprinting is still possible from the peeled skin shells, and there are further aids such as clothing, skull sinuses or a dental comparison.

The other answer which a corpse could have provided is whether Gay went out of the porthole dead or alive. Even here, after only ten days, putrefaction might have destroyed the best clue: water in the lungs. Later, however, the diatom test could have settled the matter. Diatoms are minute fresh- and sea-water plankton with tough shells. If a dead body is submerged in water, there will be a deposit of diatoms in the nose and mouth and even the upper air passages, but no further in. If, on the other hand, a drowning person breathes underwater, fluid will pass through the lung and heart circulatory systems into the innermost parts of the body. Diatoms will reach organs completely inaccessible to water, such as the central marrow of the bones. Being indestructible, they can be recovered, and provide strong evidence of breathing and circulation when the body first entered the water. But at the time of the Porthole trial the diatom test was yet to be developed.

So how much more difficult to ascertain the cause of death when the most eloquent exhibit, the body, is absent? Professor Michael Davies, who heads the cardiovascular pathology unit at St George's Hospital, considers it feasible that Gay Gibson simply dropped dead during extreme excitement. 'In the absence of a body it is impossible to disprove the hypothesis. It is a particularly interesting legal case and one in which I do not see how the pathologist could appear for either the defence or the prosecution. Without a body the pathologist has no basis for a view. The difficulty for the legal profession is that this view would encourage every murderer to eliminate the body totally.'

The senior forensic pathologist at St George's Hospital, Rufus Crompton, speaks for most of his colleagues: 'All I can say about this case is that I am amazed. I certainly don't think that on the evidence one can come to a conclusion about the cause of death. All Camb was convicted of was throwing the body out of the porthole.'

Dr Crompton admits that he would have written 'not ascertainable' as the cause of death on the certificate. One of his contemporaries, Professor James Cameron at the London Hospital, would have given the cause as 'asphyxia', for which he could have produced 'very good cases for the prosecution and for the defence'. In the opinion of Denis Hocking, the surviving insider pathologist, it was 'death due to shock during sexual intercourse, secondary cause – myocardial degeneration due to chronic infection'.

In the 1940s, many, perhaps most judges, had a deep-rooted suspicion of expert medical testimony. We have seen Lord Chief Justice Hewart's diatribe against the Imperial College coal expert in the Bryant case. The dignity of the court, it seemed, took priority over the relevance of the evidence. Yet the judges were not entirely to blame. The system itself was – and still is – at fault. It might seem absurd that two questions addressed to Dr Teare on the interpretation of the urine stains should loom so large in the matter of Camb's guilt. The problem is that specialist evidence is treated just like any other evidence, when by its very nature it is more difficult to comprehend and relate to the facts. All too often jurors, who are called upon to make judgments on the basis of this evidence, find it too technical and allow the judge to make the decision on their behalf. The maxim about twelve good men and true deciding on innocence or guilt is sometimes a romantic fiction.

At times, doctors feel they are kicked about like footballs in the tactical battle between counsel. Which is hardly surprising when the aim of the adversarial system is to knock the ball into the back of the court. Keith Simpson once complained that 'lawyers will not let be. They are naturally out to do their best "for" the prosecution or "for" the defence, and much as one tries to be absolutely fair in giving evidence there is always a feeling – positively encouraged by counsel – that one is giving evidence "for" them . . . Counsel will often say "How far can you go, doctor?"'

'Appearing for one side or the other is really quite unscientific,' says Dr Hyatt Williams. 'It is better that the psychiatrist and pathologist should give an objective account to the court than that the opposing counsel wrangle.' For Professor Simpson, 'the question on whose side you are appearing should not really have special significance, for a doctor or scientist ought to be quite unbiased in the views he takes'.

Khaki Roberts was genuinely puzzled by the defence's introduction of the urine-stain evidence. 'They were under no obligation to do so; and it certainly tended to destroy, and not support, the case put forward by Camb and by counsel on his behalf.' A layman might suggest that those who have to decide on guilt or innocence should be furnished with all the available facts. Not so, say the legal profession, which sees nothing unethical in a lawyer withholding information considered damaging to his client. Yet how can a pathologist offer a valid opinion when vital facts are not disclosed?

There is little doubt that cross-examination can often be relied upon to reveal the truthfulness or mendacity of a witness. But when applied to an expert – an engineer, toxicologist, psychiatrist or pathologist, testifying on abstract theory or medical principle – the arena of the courtroom is not the ideal place for arriving at the objective 'truth'. The more so in the Porthole case, where eminent pathologists were unable to agree, and the technical language of natural death was difficult to grasp.

These questions remain unanswered to this day, although the scope and complexity of forensic knowledge has increased many times over. Neither does the quest for the truth in the Porthole trial seem to have benefited from the gladiatorial tactics, tantamount to a personal vendetta, mounted by Khaki Roberts. As an expert called upon to resolve the demanding medical issues, it is absurd that the views of Professor Webster should have been disregarded when they failed to coincide with those of the Crown.

Since the Judicature Act of 1873, a judge has had the power to appoint an expert to report to the court in civil matters. Theoretically, he could do so in criminal cases as well, for a judge can summon any witness he likes, but it has never been the practice of judges to rely on the opinions of medical experts.

One alternative under active consideration is the continental judicial system, where an examining magistrate takes the evidence beforehand and establishes the strength of the case. In France, the *juge d'instruction* (the examining magistrate who decides whether a case should go to trial) has power to commission an evaluation from an expert in the field, and this report becomes part of the dossier. If there was any element of doubt remaining as to how a person had died, the expert would be called in by the trial judge to be questioned at the *'cour d'assises'*. This raises the important question of whether a *juge d'instruction* would have sent Camb for trial. And, if he had done so, what view a French jury would have taken of Camb's unchivalrous behaviour.

A final memory from Alec Hort, second-in-command on the *Durban Castle*, takes on a special significance at this point: 'I believe she died from natural causes during intercourse. It was a terribly hot, humid night. You could hardly get your breath, and it was worse in the cabins.'

Gay Gibson's army medical discharge carried a cautionary rider, the word 'tropical'. Had she wanted to stay on in the army, her service would have been restricted to the more temperate climes of Europe. The tropics were considered unhealthy for her. It was in the tropics that she died.

But on that sombre spring morning forty years ago, when Joshua Casswell rose to offer his version of the events in cabin 126, neither the influence of climate – moral or geographical – nor the resources for a thorough defence, nor the advances of medicine, were likely to strengthen his client's case.

14

Twelve Hampshire Citizens

The term 'to have the last word' means just what it says – that someone else's voice, opinion, colouring of events, has to be heard second to last. A quarter of a century before the Porthole trial, Cecil Whiteley, defending Freddy Bywaters who was to hang with his letter-writing lover Edith Thompson for the murder of Mr Thompson, complained about the Crown's un-usual privilege of addressing the jury last. Over the years this anomalous procedure has been recognised as benefiting the prosecution, the more so when followed by a judicial sum-ming-up unfriendly to the prisoner. The defence has the right to 'have the last word' only on the rare occasion when no witness other than the accused has been called. So valuable is this advantage that defending barristers have been known to forfeit the chance of calling witnesses in order to address the jury after the Crown counsel.

Now, almost at midday, Casswell went first. 'The temper of the court,' reported the *Hampshire Chronicle*, 'began to reach the highest points of almost fever heat, with the final speeches and the arguments arising from the mass of circumstantial evi-dence'. Mr Casswell, whom its court reporter had witnessed in triumph and disaster over the years, 'made one of his typical and gently persuasive addresses to the jury, underlining the defence view that the accused's story was a reasonably likely one, conforming to so many of the attendant details of the evidence as to be impossible to reject entirely'.

Casswell began loftily, reminding the jury that Pontius Pilate, called upon to make 'the most momentous decision in this world', responded with an inquiry of his own: 'Quid est veritas?' To which there was no answer. In those days, Casswell said, if a jury had been empanelled they would have been directed to find the truth. Today the jury had to decide two things: whether a death was caused by violence, and whether that violence was caused by the prisoner. It must be satisfied that guilt had been proved beyond reasonable doubt. 'In any case of this sort which comes before a jury, there is suspicion; if there were no suspicion there would be no trial; but you will realise that suspicion, and even probability, falls short of what is required before you can return a verdict of guilty.'

Perhaps, in the light of Camb's unwillingness to summon the ship's doctor, Casswell had realised that the Pontius Pilate reference was ill-advised. He continued: 'He is not the first person, innocent of crime, who has denied his presence on the scene because he wants to keep right out of it. Because of those denials, are you going to say that you are satisfied that he committed murder? . . . Would not the thought in his mind have been, "She died; I know how she died, but who will believe me? I do not know that (the body) provides evidence which will exculpate me if I am identified."'

This was a defensive speech, not surprisingly, but for all its subtlety Casswell missed out important points and stresses along the way. He made nothing of the enigma of why, if Camb was not welcome in Gay's cabin, she waited a whole hour before ringing the bells. There was also Casswell's rather lame plea that, if the pathologists disagreed, how could the jury be expected to be at one on the medical evidence.

Then Casswell raised 'the most distasteful subject': what sort of a girl was she? 'You will sympathise with Mrs Gibson. She took the only course a mother could, and no doubt she was perfectly satisfied in her own mind that there was nothing against her girl's character, that she was not easy-going with men. [Daisy Gibson was not in court] . . . you may think that she was always on her best behaviour when on leave or on holiday with her parents.' So that the Dutch cap, glossed over by Mrs Gibson and Roberts, was a sign that 'she was prepared to be intimate with a man, and that there would come a time when she would need to use it'.

With regard to her almost clean bill of health when leaving the army, Casswell pointed out that Dr Haslam had relied on information from Gay herself for her medical history. 'She did not want to be kept in the army; she wanted to go away with her mother in a week's time to South Africa; she wanted to get compassionate release. And if there was anything about her which would lead to a more careful medical examination she was not going to tell it . . . she did not mention that she had actually been in hospital for five days only a fortnight before.'

Towards the end of Casswell's speech came a damaging misunderstanding over what Dr Hocking had said regarding the amount of blood necessary to confirm strangulation. Roberts rose to say that he could not find the quoted reference in Dr Hocking's evidence and, after an exchange, the judge declared: 'Then Mr Roberts is right?' Casswell was forced to tell the jury to forget what he had just told them.

He concluded with a despairing cry of the obvious, a rhetorical device employed by lawyers when they know that the jury is not with them: 'He may be behind bars; he may be in the dock; but until he is proved to be guilty he must be considered to be innocent; and so, unless after hearing all the evidence you are then satisfied beyond all reasonable doubt that he committed that crime with which he is charged, you must acquit him, and that is what I ask you to do.'

The court adjourned for lunch. The next four hours belonged to Crown and Bench. Casswell's words faded into the outer reaches of memory. It would be an uncomfortable afternoon for the man on the high chair in the dock.

King's Counsel like Casswell and Roberts were mercenaries with interchangeable roles – at times prosecutor, then defender, but also judge (as Recorders of Southampton and Bristol) – and in no position to complain when the system did not work to their advantage. When it suited him, however, Khaki Roberts was not averse to moaning about the bias of the Bench. Once, leading for the defence, and wary of the judge's summing-up, he began his final speech cheekily: 'Members of the jury, I shall now address you on behalf of the prisoner; when I have done, counsel for the prosecution and His Lordship will then address you on behalf of the Crown.'

Now the tide was running swiftly for him. A swig of aqua pura, a tilt of the wig, and he was on his feet, ramrod-straight, hands gripping lapel. 'Magnificent and menacing', he said shamelessly of himself in the *Tit-bits* interview. 'So I must have appeared to Camb as I heaved my bulk out of my chair and stood in the centre of the court with arms outstretched, addressing the jury. I noticed the women jurors stare at me curiously. No doubt I swayed both judge and jury with my "zeal and fervour".'

He turned quickly to Camb's damning statement that he was 'fairly certain' that life was extinct when he put the body through the porthole. It was thanks only to the urine finding, he pointed out, that the pathologists were able to agree on this 'incontrovertible evidence of a terminal act of life'.

Roberts' presentation was crystalline. On the medical evidence, he said, 'There is no disagreement on the vital issue. I submit it is perfectly clear that all the doctors, Dr Teare on the one side, and Dr Hocking and Professor Webster on the other, all say there are here present all the common features of death by strangulation, and all that Dr Hocking and Professor Webster say in addition is that death may have been by natural causes . . . and Dr Teare said he could not exclude (and of course no one can exclude) the possibility of natural death . . . But, members of the jury, you have to deal with the probabilities as they accord with the known facts, and not something which would amount to a miracle.'

He reserved particular scorn for the *Golden Boy* contingent. 'Now we get to the evidence from South Africa, and in that we have the result of the visit of Mr Wells, the harvest which he brought back with him . . . Well, members of the jury, you saw them . . . for Mr Mike Abel's evidence, my learned friend thought it might assist you. It is for you to say if it does . . . Mr Gilbert said that sometimes she came to rehearsals smelling of drink, and you may think that some shame attached to people who allowed a girl of that age to drink to excess . . . You may think that Dr Schoub was not very engrossed in her job as a doctor, seeing that she has been able to come here to give evidence,' and so on, in like vein.

Tellingly, he played up the twofold defence oversight, reminding the jury that when Dr Teare was asked whether spots of blood on the sheet were greater than would have come from strangulation, he had replied that there was not too much for it to be consistent with strangulation. The same question should have been put to Hocking and Webster, but was not. 'Therefore,' Roberts concluded, 'you have had no evidence challenging that the amount of blood was consistent with death by strangulation.'

Once more with feeling, the urine on the sheet. The known facts were stretched to their limits, and beyond. 'Does that not show that he was standing by her side with the strangler's hand round her neck?' It was untrue, said Roberts, that Camb was lying on top of her because 'the contents of the bladder went on the sheet, and not on Camb . . . ' Camb, of course, was not questioned about the state of his trousers, and Roberts should have been challenged when drawing that conclusion. And, once again, Roberts took the supreme liberty of assuming that Gay had pushed the bells. 'He said she did not object to his advances, but there is a silent witness which gave the lie to that, and that is the two bells which she pressed.'

Now to the scratches. Roberts stressed the discrepancy between, on the one hand, Camb's denial that the pointed nails had marked his arms or neck, and, on the other, the defence pathologists' explanation of how those nails had caused the damage. 'I submit that neither Dr Hocking nor Professor Webster is entitled to reconstruct evidence in a way which is contrary to the evidence of the person on whose behalf they each appear.' Casswell further weakened his case by interrupting to say that Camb had indeed admitted to being scratched by Miss Gibson. The judge, having referred to his notes, was pleased to announce that Camb had twice said: 'I received no injury when with Miss Gibson; I told the truth that I had made these scratches.'

Khaki Roberts was sweetness and light. 'Members of the jury, I invited my friend's interruptions because they may help you to see the more clearly where the truth lies in this case.'

216

Rounding off his oration, Roberts asked, 'Did he panic? Panic! Do you think he is the sort of man to panic? Members of the jury, did you notice him in the witness box last Saturday? The greatest ordeal that a man can undergo, giving evidence on a charge of murder, is being cross-examined. Did you see any lack of poise, or composure, or full control of the thinking faculties? You can be quite sure that whatever Camb did when he put that body through the porthole it was not done out of any feeling of panic; it was nothing more and nothing less than an act inspired by cold calculation induced by a desire for self-preservation, to destroy the whole of the evidence against him.'

Twenty past three. He sat down.

Mr Justice Hilbery, that most potent symbol of the English judiciary, the High Court judge, had waited patiently to deliver his soliloquy, to 'sum up' the evidence of the past four days. Here now was the moment, more than any other in the trial, when the scarlet, ermine and horsehair transformed this ordinary mortal into a figure of august authority, clothing him with the power to bewitch a jury – and hang a man.

On the other hand, that populariser of forensic fiction, County Court judge Henry Cecil, once conjectured that 'if you put the prisoners walking round the exercise yard at Wandsworth prison into judicial robes and sat them on the Bench, everyone would think how learned they looked. Conversely, if you took all the members of the Court of Appeal, put them into prison uniform and walked them round Wandsworth prison yard, visitors would note their near-set eyes, receding chins and low foreheads.'

This platform of persuasion had to be subtly used. The judge would not get a jury to change its mind once it had been made up. Nor would he need to, if he knew that the jury was already heading towards a conviction. It was at the in-between stage, when there were still some 'don't-knows', that the judge's power came into play.

The judge, according to Lord Devlin, is permitted to express his opinion freely, even strongly. 'The only limitation placed upon him is that he must not put any point unfairly and must make it clear to the jury, either expressly or by implication, that on the issues of fact which are left to them they are free to give his opinion what weight they choose.'

Hilbery then told them: 'You are the judges. I do not determine the guilt or innocence of the prisoner; that question is answered by the verdict of the jury, and the jury alone are the judges. For hundreds of years, juries in this country have discharged that duty . . . '

And so on, soon stamping only too clearly on their minds his version of the events in the cabin, leaving no room for doubt that he desired a conviction. 'He put the body of that poor young woman through the porthole of that ship into the shark-infested waters . . . when she was dressing before dinner she was a happy young woman; yet by three o'clock in the morning she was dead, and her body being stuffed, ignominiously bundled, through the porthole – you may think to hide something. And the question is, "What?"'

He turned the bell-ringing into one of those children's puzzles, where, if you choose the wrong path at the start of the maze, you cannot arrive at your destination. Once the jury decided on the identity of the bell-ringer, Hilbery intimated, it led unerringly to the guilt of James Camb. 'You will probably think it right to ponder more than once, and to decide at the earliest on the evidence whether you are satisfied that young woman rang those two bells for both stewards . . . The accused man says he did not ring them. There was only one other person present there, and that was this poor woman, now dead. Did she? Do you think, when you remember Miss Field's evidence, that it was quite difficult to get between the dressing table and the bed? Do you think he could have inserted himself between the bell end of the bed and dressing table so as accidentally to get those bells and ring both of them? Because on that, members of the jury, you have heard his evidence about his movements, first, according to him, seated upon the bed, then climbing upon the bed, then lying down beside her, and finally getting on top of her, and afterwards trying artificial respiration, massaging her stomach upwards and trying to restore respiration; but in all that description never did he admit that he was ever anywhere near the bells.

'You may think, members of the jury, that it is clear that neither by design nor by accident did he ring the bells . . . '

And more, relentlessly: 'Is there any other alternative left, than that she rang them, wanting to ring them as a voluntary act? Members of the jury, I am perfectly certain it does not need me to say to you, if she did that, why? Of course you will ask yourselves, why? Then again, you will ask yourselves, "If she did it, can the account given by this man be true?"'

Hilbery's summing-up would continue for two hours more, but already he had charted the course, effectively disposed of the defence case. There were passing references, to be sure, to Camb's version, but in a language peppered with suggestive, often unsubstantiated, phrases – 'made indecent overtures to her which were resented by her, and was it not she who rang the bells to summon help? . . . thwarted lust to prompt him to violence . . . ' There was no attempt to explain what they were doing in the hour between Camb's arrival at two and the bell-ringing at three.

A slip of memory was turned to Camb's disadvantage. Hilbery: 'He has told you he went to that cabin at three o'clock in the morning. Have you any doubt that he went there expecting to have sexual intercourse with Miss Gibson?'

Casswell intervened: 'According to him, My Lord, he went there at two.'

Hilbery: 'Yes, that is true; he said two. Of course he went there at three or before, and if these incidents took place round about three o'clock, he went there before.'

The pathologists were fitted into the judge's scheme of things. 'Then you also had the evidence of Dr Teare, a man who is greatly experienced in these matters.' Teare was surely a very fine pathologist, but when it came to experience, Webster and Hocking were investigating the necks of dead women when Teare was still a boy on the Isle of Man. Had not the Director of Public Prosecutions wanted Webster as the first choice?

Hilbery went over the evidence for congenital aneurysm.

'There is the evidence about whether she had ever had asthma or had had bluish lips or muddy nails, or had hysterical fits. But those symptoms would not be present at all if she died from the bursting of a small congenital aneurysm, because Professor Webster told you that that is undiagnosable before-hand. It is entirely a matter for you, but do you think in all the circumstances of this case you can safely eliminate that?'

Hilbery's was not a theatrical voice, but the audience listened with rapt attention to the ebb and flow of his words, holding their breath whenever he broke off to refer to his notes. In the pressure-cooker atmosphere generated by the tightening noose, a woman juror became visibly distressed. Hilbery adjourned the proceedings 'to clear the air'. She fainted in the jury room. Twenty minutes and a sniff of smelling salts later, she was ready to return.

The summing-up moved on to the South African witnesses. Mike Abel, in particular, seemed to have made a poor impression. Hilbery resorted to the device of the loaded disclaimer. 'I do not know what view you take of any of the witnesses, but what you think of the witnesses and of their evidence is entirely your concern, and not mine. I may take certain views, but you are not to be influenced by any view that I may take, or any opinion that I may seem to express . . . '

He offered a view, take it or leave it. 'Whether you can derive any help from that man Mike Abel, it is for you and not for me to determine . . . [and later] you get this man, Mike Abel, who has been brought over from South Africa, having been discovered by the solicitor for the defence when on a visit in search of evidence which would support in some material particular the account of this affair which is given by the accused . . . '

As if every defence lawyer worthy of his salt, from Cicero to Marshall Hall, had not fought tooth and nail in the proper defence of his client . . .

Mrs Daisy Gibson was as useful for the Crown as she was problematical for the defence. She had to be deftly handled. Maternal licence, Hilbery seemed to be saying. She was determined to hear nothing against her daughter's character, 'and you respect her for taking that attitude; loyalty to one's own dead child is a strong motive for denying anything which could be set against that dead child's character. But it is here not a matter of her character; it is a matter of her health. It is for you to say, "Who can know the health of a child better than the mother who has borne her, and brought her up; seen her in her growing years; and had care of her until she became an adult?"'

Sometimes the jury would not know whether the judge was being sly or simply naïve: 'It is suggested that she was a young woman of such loose morals as to be willing, on the first overtures of a deck steward, to receive him willingly into her cabin at night, and that after a mere week's acquaintance, without the least sign that she had shown him that she was in love with him (if one may misuse the word as it is so often misused), without the least sign that he had excited a sex appetite in her. But it is said that her conduct in South Africa (according to Mike Abel) and her supposed pregnancy go to show that she was so degraded a young woman that she was willing to have a deck steward come into her cabin at night for the purpose of having sexual intercourse with her.'

He followed with a more tolerant view of post-war mores. 'Well, members of the jury, what is common conduct among young people of twenty or so in these days? Does the fact of a girl kissing a man in the dance room amount to much? And as to her kicking him, well, it might be thought that he deserved it. What do you think of it?'

To the judge, Charles Schwentafsky was 'a very fortunate businessman . . . lucky in everything he touched; he was backing her in her career, and she was coming over to this country with letters of introduction . . . ' Just as well, perhaps, that Charley was not called to give evidence about his business affairs or the motives for his supposedly disinterested sponsorship of Gay.

The judge noted that Camb was 'certainly a powerfully-built young man; broad-shouldered; you may think fairly heavy for his height; and powerful . . . Have you any doubt that he went to that cabin intending to have sexual intercourse with that young woman?' Left in the air was the knowledge that, yes, he could have overpowered her with ease.

Referring to the incident of the clock, when Gay came out on deck for a midnight stroll, the judge saw it as 'a very obvious moment to see whether, if he attempted to kiss her, that would be received well as a preliminary to what he had in mind later that night. There were no passengers there; was it a moment to make some sort of advance to explore the situation, and to see what reception he might look forward to if he presented himself at her cabin door?'

For the last and final time, the scratches – Camb's weakest point in the eyes of his own defence team. With a flourish of his forearms, Hilbery demonstrated how Gay could have caused those scratches. The jurors fixed their eyes on the red sleeves and ermine cuffs as he put right hand to throat and made clawing movements across the wrist with the bent fingers of his left hand. At one blow, the hesitations of the three pathologists were as nothing. The jurors now knew that there was only one way in which Camb could have been scratched. And, if any among them still had doubts, Hilbery suggested that 'you may think on the whole of the evidence that they were inflicted by that dead woman at the time when she was at the very gate of death in an endeavour to free her throat from the strangler's hand'.

Also for the very last time, the urine stains – a reminder of the seeming unawareness of a judge of the Queen's Bench that sexual intercourse may take place outside the confines of a pair of starched sheets.

Then Hilbery returned to his pet concern, the whereabouts of the black pyjamas. Camb had insisted that Gay was not wearing them on the night. 'Is that the mistake made in an apparently small detail by a man who is lying?' he asked, 'or is it true?' In the morning, the stewardess Miss Field found two things missing from the cabin, Gay's dressing gown and the black pyjamas. 'Is the fact that they were on and underneath that dressing gown, and that they were never seen by this man because he never got as far as sexual intercourse, and because they were covered by the dressing gown, and he killed her in that position, and when he pushed her through the porthole he did not observe them because of the length of the dressing gown? Is that it? Or is he telling the truth, and are the black pyjamas just missing articles, the disappearance of which is unexplained? There is the whole matter, members of the jury . . . ' On that upbeat note they were requested to 'Please consider your verdict'.

At this point Casswell rose and, in what the *Daily Mail* reporter described as 'a whispered protest', said: 'With respect, My Lord, you did not mention the bolting of the door.'

Mr Justice Hilbery: 'I have not attempted to mention all the points of the case. My duty is to point out the salient features of the case, or those which I think may be a guide to you. There are others which no doubt you will think useful, in fact, there are many other matters, and if you think they are useful, give them all the weight you think is right. I have not attempted to mention everything, and I am not bound to do so.'

Two months later, it was significant that Hilbery's fellow King's Bencher, Sir Norman Birkett, noted after summing up the murder trial of George Epton at the Old Bailey: 'I think I covered everything but always have a most anxious time afterwards fearing I have not.'

It was 6.25 p.m. The jury of twelve good and true Hampshire men and women did thereupon retire to consider their verdict.

We can have no inkling of what went on in the jurors' room that evening. The Catholic knight or one of the two ex-policemen might have opened proceedings. Did a mother speak up for Daisy Gibson? Were they inhibited by the presence of members of the opposite sex from going over all the sex evidence? What we do know of these particular people is that they were drawn from a restricted cross-section of society, and that all were over the age of thirty-five. The reason why there were only three women was that the property and residence qualifications of the time excluded most wives and other female members of a family living in the same house. So, far from being representatives of the nation as a whole, the jury was, in Lord Devlin's words, 'predominantly male, middle-aged, middle-minded and middle-class'.

In the eyes of the law, says Devlin of those days, the 'jury-man is the epitome of the reasonable man, the man in the street or . . . "the man in the Clapham omnibus". But it is an odd thing that if you stopped several men in the street or held up the Clapham omnibus while you interrogated the passengers you would very likely find that only a few of them were qualified to serve as jurors.'

Hilbery was a pastmaster at suggesting to middle-class people what they might like to think, what conclusions they should perhaps draw. He knew their limitations, that too many facts, too long a train of reasoning, tended to confuse. In this case, his summing-up was artful, but not so single-minded as to overstep the confines of legal propriety. Ten years earlier, in a speech to the Gray's Inn Debating Society, he had outlined his views on pleading to a jury.

'You wish to persuade twelve ordinary citizens, with prob-ably little or no training in consecutive thought. They will be largely if not entirely swayed by emotion. But the advocate does well to remember that in all probability they do not think so. The less training or capacity for reasoning they have, the more certain it is they will pride themselves on being suscep-tible only to strict logic and impervious to mere emotion . . . You will notice that the successful jury advocate always gives his address to a jury the form of a well-built argument, while the emphasis and appeal are at all times strongly emotional.'

It was, of course, pure chance that the trial of James Camb took place in leafy Hampshire. Had the *Durban Castle* docked at Tilbury or Glasgow or even Liverpool, the jurors might have viewed the events of 17-18 October 1947 in a more sceptical light. On the other hand, nothing suggests that the Winchester panel were unworldly-wise. They must have had their sus-picions about Gay's sexual activities while in the army and Johannesburg, and with Camb on the boat, nor is it likely that they swallowed Daisy Gibson's evidence in its entirety. But it would not have mattered much how black a picture of Gay was painted – it was their view of Camb that would be the critical factor. The prosecution made the strong point that if he was innocent, he had destroyed his best evidence by throwing her body into the sea. But to the jury, it was perhaps more simple than this. Camb had behaved in a most inhumane way in disposing of the body, whether it was marked with the hand of the strangler or still warm from the act of love.

The jury left the judgment on the medical evidence, the sheets, Gay's health, the scratches, to the Bench. If the judge was satisfied that these showed she had died a violent death, who were they to quibble? Hilbery did repeat all the medical arguments at length, but left the jury in no doubt as to what he thought of them. His bias was exemplified by a refusal to acknowledge that the unbolted door might have been a very relevant factor in crediting Camb's story – and in undermining the judge's version of events. Khaki Roberts later admitted that the unbolted door 'was a strong point for the defence'.

From observing Camb during the four days of the trial, the jury 'knew' in their own minds that he could have committed murder. There is some evidence that the defendant's personal presentation can make or break a case. The last woman to be hanged in Britain, Ruth Ellis, refused to show remorse, appearing in court in a fur coat, her hair bleached. The all-male jury convicted her of what in most other countries would have been a *crime passionnel*, a woman's desperate reaction to shabby treatment by her lover. Yet a hundred years before, Madeleine Smith, aged twenty-one, of a middle-class Glasgow family, said to have 'a most attractive appearance', was acquitted (again by an all-male jury) despite strong evidence of the calculated poisoning of her discarded lover. She pleaded 'not guilty' in a 'sweet, clear treble'. Which indicates that though juries may not always have common sense, they are unfailingly human.

Camb had no sweet treble, and though he was well turned-out, his cool, articulate, too confident demeanour discouraged sympathy. So this clever young man, the jury would have reasoned, did not call the doctor and was only 'fairly certain' that Gay was dead. Hocking remembers that Camb's 'neat appearance and supreme confidence in himself never left him throughout the whole ordeal of his trial, but in many ways he was his own worst enemy. He completely lost any sympathy the jury might have had for him by his utter selfishness in putting his job and future before the life of a young girl.' Nor, as we have seen, was he very bright when it really mattered. Even in the event of the jury wanting to listen to him, he gave them no reason to change their minds about him, by suggesting, for example, that he might have knocked against the bellpush, or that he threw the pyjamas out with the body, or by admitting, 'Yes, she did scratch me', whether in ecstasy or in her death throes.

The jury's legal responsibility is not to pronounce on the innocence or guilt of the prisoner, but to decide whether the prosecution has succeeded in proving guilt beyond reasonable doubt. This is a difficult line to draw, for lawyer and juror alike. The more so in a highly-charged drama, where the one certain fact is that he pushed her out of the porthole into 'shark-infested seas'. Were the jury, in reaching their verdict, more influenced by the facts which proved Camb a murderer, or by the terrible thing he did after Gay Gibson's death? It is unlikely that they knew the answer themselves.

Meanwhile, back in the courtroom, a trickle of spectators had left for home, and for the first time in four days there were seats available in the public gallery. Had they deserted Camb for Robert Mitchum, now playing at the Odeon in *Build my Gallows High*?

For those who waited, the news was good. Soon after seven o'clock, it was known that the jury had reached a verdict. This had taken only forty-five minutes, but perhaps they had prolonged it a while for the sake of appearances. For the last time, James Camb was taken from the cell beneath the courtroom, walked by two prison officers along a passage, up a flight of thirteen stairs, along a whitewashed brick corridor lit by naked bulbs, up a further thirteen stairs, then down four, and along a lino-covered passage with dark-brown walls. At the end of the passage he was motioned to wait before a closed door which, on being opened, he entered, stepping into the court a moment before the judge took his place on the bench.

It was eleven minutes past seven. The jurors averted their gaze from the prisoner; an ominous sign. Camb did not notice.

His eyes were on the judge.

Clerk of Assize: 'Members of the jury, are you all agreed upon your verdict?'

Foreman: 'Yes.'

Clerk of Assize: 'Do you find the prisoner at the bar, James Camb, guilty or not guilty?'

Foreman: 'Guilty.' (Camb swayed forward.)

Clerk of Assize: 'You find him guilty of murder and that is the verdict of you all?'

Foreman: 'Yes.'

Clerk of Assize: 'James Camb, you stand convicted of murder; have you anything to say why the Court should not give you judgment of death according to the law?'

Prisoner: 'My lord, at the opening of this case I was asked to plead guilty or not guilty; I pleaded not guilty, and I repeat that statement now.'

The judge's clerk balanced the square piece of black cloth on the judge's wig and said: 'His Lordship commands all persons to stand.'

Mr Justice Hilbery: (lowering his eyes to his writing pad) 'James Camb, the sentence of the court upon you is that you be taken from hence to a lawful prison, and thence to a place of execution, and that you there be hanged by the neck until you be dead, and that your body be buried within the precincts of the prison within which you shall last have been confined before your execution, and may the Lord have mercy upon your soul.'

The Sheriff's Chaplain: 'Amen.'

15

To the Rose Garden

The four days on-stage were ended. The keys jingled and the murderer was ushered out of the public gaze. He padded, zombie-like, back to the cell, where he sat on the wooden bench with his head in his hands and wept.

Geoffrey Wells drove to Southampton to see Margaret. 'Don't lose faith yet,' he told her. The Gibson family were staying in a small hotel in Lyndhurst, in the New Forest. The verdict came as a relief, but there was no hint of vengeance. For Paul, Gay was 'the best sister anyone could have. The things they said about her in court . . . it was rotten'.

People gathered in the dusk outside the Great Hall. Someone who seemed to be in the know said that two cars were waiting – green for acquittal, black for the rope. The windows of the black saloon which took Camb away were covered, robbing the public of the sight of England's newest convicted killer. He was borne swiftly across town and entered the great gates of Winchester Prison. No longer an accused prisoner presumed to be innocent, he was issued with the special clothing of a convict under sentence of death – a shirt with no tie, jacket with tapes for buttons, soft slippers. He would not be encouraged to take his life.

The condemned cell was large and bright by prison standards, whitewashed walls, a spring mattress on the bed with white sheets and three blankets, two tables and three chairs – one for Camb, two for the death-watch who would be there on eight-hour shifts until his fate was decided. Three doors led off his cell, one to the main prison, another to the toilet, and a third to the scaffold. When the governor visited the cell towards midnight, he found Camb playing solo whist with his guards. The prisoner retired in the early hours, and though the light burned through the night, he soon fell asleep. The two men sat on the hard chairs, reading, watching, dozing. In the morning Camb breakfasted on bacon and fried bread, the food cut up for him, and eaten with fork and spoon. A prison officer shaved him. Soon he was back to his immaculate, almost jaunty self again. He began to talk of his appeal.

He was allowed to read the newspapers, from which all references to the case were blacked out. So he missed the *Daily Mail*'s conclusion that 'One outstanding feature of Gay Gibson's mental make-up emerges; she could not resist men'.

The business of the Winter Assizes was completed on the Wednesday. The senior counsel present, Joseph Molony, indulged in 'the happy and pleasant' custom of saying farewell. Members of the Bar were pleased, he said, that His Lordship had been on the Western Circuit once again. Hilbery thanked counsel for the graceful references to his visit. The work-load had been heavy, but he had had the willing assistance of the Bar, and it was refreshing to have the new experience of sitting late, often very late, in the evenings.

The Sheriff of Hampshire fixed the execution for 13 April, though the date was rendered unlikely by Wells' announcement of an appeal. He was said to have received letters from people who knew Gay Gibson and were offering to provide new evidence on Camb's behalf.

For the moment, Margaret could not bring herself to visit her husband. Then, on the Friday, she received a letter, which was reproduced in the following Sunday's *News of the World*, now extracting its pound of flesh. 'Your best plan,' Camb told her, 'would be to get a divorce and then re-marry and enjoy your future as you were meant to do. In time you will forget me.'

The letter began:

I do not know what I am going to say – what can I say? Right until the judge began his short speech everyone seemed to be of the opinion that I should be freed . . .

God alone knows what agony of mind you must have

suffered that night. My heart bleeds for the torment you must be suffering now and I am helpless to do anything for you.

My darling, I must confess that I am still rather dazed by it all, and everything now seems to be hopeless, but I cannot let you suffer because of this . . .

Besides, you see, there is Tootsie [then aged three] to think of. It is not right that the stigma that is now on my name should be such a great handicap to her future.

It is costing me a great deal to say all this, but I feel that it is the least, and at any rate the most decent thing, I can do. There must be no need for you to suffer my disgrace. It is not right that you should be even asked to do so.

Whatever you choose to do – and I know your decision will be a sensible one – I beg of you to always be sure that you have been my one true love and, no matter what the future holds for me, I shall go on loving you and loving Tootsie, our sweet child.

Think this matter over carefully, little woman, and I believe that you will agree it is the best way for you and little Tootsie. I will write again unless in the meantime I receive word that you don't want me to. God bless you both, my dear wife and daughter.   Jimmy.

On the Saturday, Bob Camb came down from Waterfoot to see his son. Margaret planned to visit Camb as well, but was overcome while walking from Winchester station to the prison and had to return home without seeing him. This did not prevent the *News of the World* from claiming an exclusive: 'I came down here from Glasgow to be near him and to see him through to the end, whatever the end might be. The end has not come yet. In spite of the offer in the letter, I would not think of deserting him now.'

Early the following week, Mrs Camb at last felt able to spend an hour with her husband. Thanks once again to the Fleet Street benefactor, we know that he 'again asked for my forgiveness for all the worry and anxiety . . . I had to tell him everything I could of Tootsie's doing; how often she asked about him, what she said and how she looked.'

A petition for Camb's reprieve was launched in Southampton from the offices of Wells' friend, A. P. G. Elsom. Sympathisers queued up to sign it. Forms were despatched to trade union branches across the country. There was talk of the Home Secretary receiving 200,000 signatures. South Africa also responded well. In Waterfoot, the working men's club organised its own petition. Many signed their names at Mr Wilkinson's grocery shop on the corner of Townsend Street and Bacup Road, down the hill from where Jim was born. And at the slipper works, bus station, pubs, at Holcombe Hunt steeplechase, in Burnley and Rochdale and as far afield as Walsall. Their 4,000 signatures became part of the Southampton petition.

The death sentence was a third body blow in the life of Bob Camb. In his house up against the cliff, this solitary man sat inconsolable, comforted by his brothers, Billy and Tom, slipper clickers too. The wider family stood by him. Jenny Haslam, then in her twenties, recalls that 'our family wasn't ashamed of Jimmy. We didn't repudiate him.'

Back in the death cell at Winchester Prison, Camb bided his time with an outward show of normality. A logbook noted his conversations, meals, visits to the toilet (the door was left open). He passed the time playing dominoes, cribbage and draughts with his guards; he ordered fiction from the prison library, though thrillers were forbidden; he smoked ten cigarettes a day and divided the regulation pint of beer into a half at lunch and a half at supper, which was at four o'clock; twice daily he walked in the yard for thirty minutes when the other prisoners were at work; and though entitled as a condemned man to a generous number of visits, he contented himself with discussing the appeal with his solicitors.

Five weeks to the day since his conviction, Camb was driven to the Court of Criminal Appeal in the Strand in London to hear Joshua Casswell argue his appeal. Here was a strange process, in which three High Court judges adjudicated over the conduct in the lower court of a fourth brother. At worst, it may have

231

seemed to an outsider like a cosy club, governed by the unspoken rule, 'Don't rock my boat and I won't rock yours'. At best,
the appeal court consisted of men – there were no High Court
women as yet – of a like mind, who saw the world through the
same hand-me-down spectacles.

Yet it was an improvement on the system before the Court of
Criminal Appeal was set up in 1907, when a condemned person depended on the behind-closed-doors justice of a Home
Office pardon or the rarer consideration of a legal point by the
Court for Crown Cases Reserved. The appeals system was
created in the the teeth of strong resistance by the Bench, who
feared that their judgment and that of the jury was being
questioned. The judges had other objections. Punishment, it
was said, should follow swiftly upon sentence, or its deterrent
value was dissipated. They argued, with a pious disregard for
their own fallibility, that it was inhumane to keep the occupant
of the death cell in agony. But they soon realised that they need
not have worried. Though 98 per cent of convicted murderers
appealed, a mere two per cent were successful. You were far
more likely to get a conviction overturned on legal grounds
than on a question of fact or a judge's misdirection to the jury.
Yet, to the ordinary citizen, facts were much more important in
establishing guilt or innocence than abstruse legal points of
law.

In Camb's case, the low strike rate for a condemned man was
rendered yet more unpromising by the figure on the Bench, the
legendary Lord Chief Justice Rayner Goddard. A strong personality, with decided views on the beneficial aspects of capital
punishment, Goddard had read the transcript and was not
impressed by Casswell's arguments. His comments were
almost carbon copies of Hilbery's. The atmosphere of a retrial
was compounded by the presence of the Winchester exhibits,
including cabin mock-up and bellpush, and by Camb dressed
in the blue suit he wore at the trial. The small public gallery was
crowded.

Casswell argued that Hilbery's summing-up had 'amounted
to a speech for the prosecution'. No doubt, said Goddard, the
learned judge's summing-up was 'not favourable to the

prisoner. No one would contend that it was.' But he cited approvingly an earlier statement made by his court that it was sometime necessary for a judge to express 'extremely confident opinions' upon questions of fact. 'When one is considering the effect of a summing-up, one must give credit to the jury for intelligence, and for the knowledge that they are not bound by the expressions of the judge upon questions of fact.'

The Lord Chief Justice was indifferent to the medical evidence. 'The medical experts, of course, laboured under the disadvantage of not seeing the body. Who rang the bells, I want to know?' Casswell contended that Camb had rung them accidentally, though he was conscious that the prisoner had said nothing of the sort. 'I have done it myself in that cabin, and it is quite easy to depress the bells with the hip.'

Goddard thought otherwise. 'If she died a natural death, what reason was there for concealing the body in the way that was done? If she died an unnatural death, was there not every reason why the body should be disposed of in the way it was? Those were matters for the jury and, as I have occasion to say nearly every time this court sits, this court does not sit to re-try cases thereby usurping the functions of the jury.' It seemed to him that 'the evidence on which the jury returned their verdict might almost be described as overwhelming'. Appeal dismissed, without bothering to call Khaki Roberts.

Deliverance was at hand, however. By now, Camb would have learned from his solicitor that he was unlikely to hang anyway. By a quirk of fate, the trial had coincided with a periodic outburst of conscience in the House of Commons over capital punishment. The Labour back-bencher, Sydney Silverman, had given notice in March 1948 of an amendment to the Criminal Justice Bill to suspend hanging for a trial period of five years. At the time of the Porthole trial, before the clause was voted on, a Home Office minister had assured the House that there would be no automatic reprieve for those awaiting execution. 'Each case is considered on its merits and there has been no change of policy or practice.'

But matters did change after the clause was adopted in a free vote of the House on 14 April. The Home Secretary, Chuter

Ede, announced that it was his duty to recommend commutation of capital sentences during the period before the Bill became Law. By the day of the appeal, 26 April, Casswell knew that his client would be granted an automatic reprieve. Otherwise, Camb would certainly not have been saved. The Labour Cabinet was divided on hanging, and public opinion, then as now, was overwhelmingly against liberalisation. Winston Churchill, Leader of the Opposition, with scant regard for accuracy, complained that 'the House has, by its vote, saved the life of the brutal lascivious murderer who thrust the poor girl he had raped and assaulted through a porthole to the sharks'. In the free vote, Churchill was joined in the 'no' lobby by Harold Macmillan, Rab Butler and the future Lord Chancellor, Quintin Hogg, though three other future prime ministers, Eden, Wilson and Callaghan, did not vote. The Labour stalwarts – Attlee, Herbert Morrison, Ernest Bevin, and Chuter Ede himself, who was by no means a reforming Home Secretary – were also against the amendment.

When, seven weeks later, the House of Lords threw out the amended clause, the narrowness of Camb's escape was starkly apparent. But with abolitionist MPs still hoping to work out a compromise, it was not until late July that the English judicial system was able to return to the comforting certainties of mandatory hanging for murder as it had been for centuries. Camb was one of eleven convicted murderers destined for the gallows – but for the temporary respite of the Silverman clause. Capital punishment for murder was suspended in 1965 and abolished four years later.

So Camb lived, thanks to a fortunate conjuncture brought about by the South African witnesses and the House of Commons. Had Wells not sought out witnesses in Johannesburg, the trial would have gone ahead in the late autumn of 1947, with Camb being hanged in Winchester Prison well before the vote.

All of which was a far cry from Lord Chief Justice Stanhope's sentence on Sir Walter Raleigh in the Great Hall, Winchester, on 17 November 1603: 'to bee drawn upon a hurdle through the open streets to the place of execution, and there to bee hanged till you are halfe dead, your members to be cut off, your bowels to be taken out and cast into the fire before your face (you being yet alive), your head to be cut off, your quarters to be divided into foure parts, to be bestowed in foure severall places, and so the Lord have mercie upon your soule.'

Once the appeal had failed, Captain Patey formally altered the entry for character assessment in Camb's discharge book from 'VG' (Very Good) to 'DR' (Decline to Report).

At the end of May, Camb was sent to Parkhurst Prison, on the Isle of Wight, to start his life sentence. He was then lucky enough to be transferred to Wakefield Prison, one of the more progressive penitentiaries which housed long-term but not violent prisoners, and conveniently situated across the Pennines from his family. It began life in 1594 in Love Lane as 'a house of correction of idle apprentices, whores and beggars'. Master Key, appropriately, was the first governor. When the present prison was built in the 1840s, it was described as the most striking building in the country with the exception of York Minster. A foreigner suggested that 'the English must be great people when they can even make their prisons beautiful'. In some respects, the regime was more humane than it is today. Single cells, with WCs, were the rule rather than the exception, until Sir Edmund du Cane, the first chairman of the Prison Commissioners, ushered in a soulless late-Victorian regime. Since the twenties, however, Wakefield had been an enlightened place, a test-tube for reform, with hard but creative work the rule, and an unusually high rate of non-returnees. Camb was not the most notorious prisoner; that was left to two men who passed atom secrets to the Russians, Dr Allan Nunn May and Klaus Fuchs.

Prison governorship was the prerogative of ex-army, navy and RAF officers who needed to be found suitable peace-time jobs. In the years immediately after the last war, most prison officers were probably ex-NCOs and warrant officers, and as a result rarely rose though the ranks to the top jobs. Wakefield's governor, Major Bruce S. K. G. Gyse-Moores, had fought in two world wars, and half-a-dozen others. He ran a civilising 'regiment', offering artisan and engineering training. His assistant governor, Alastair Miller, recalls a relaxed training prison, with freedom within the walls. 'We were not a hardline regime, nobody said, "stand to attention, take your hands out of your pockets." If it hadn't been for the walls it could have been called an open prison.'

But Camb was not in the mood for any discipline at all. He was unable to accept that he was termed a murderer and being treated like a real convict. The natural resentment of authority reared up. Miller: 'If a governor thought somebody was recalcitrant, a bloody nuisance, not so much upsetting the staff as the other prisoners, he would ask another governor to take him in for a while, not necessarily to sort him out, but to change the environment, try new warders.'

One day Camb found himself at Dartmoor, most uncongenial of Britain's prisons, on the bleak heights of Devon. He complained about the mist which swept across the moors. Nobody came to visit him. Flogging and birching were on the list of punishments, and there was work in the quarry. Most of all, he was shocked by his first contact with hardened criminals. In a letter he wrote to his cousin, Florrie Stone, she recalls two anguished words: 'Remember me!' The short sharp spell in a really tough gaol showed him there were worse places than Wakefield. After a few months he requested a transfer. Those who made the decision must have been satisfied that the medicine had worked. He returned from 'the Moor', chastened, to a centrally-heated cell in Yorkshire.

He became a model prisoner. It was just as well, for here James Camb would spend eighteen of the remaining thirty years of his life. In some ways, prison was not that different from life at sea; the long periods away from home, the double life and dual personality, strangeness with family and friends, the guarded letters home and the restricted sleeping accommodation. Ship's captain and prison governor were absolute masters of their domain, with the power to impose instant punishment. Camb moved from well-oiled cog on the ocean wave to well-oiled cog in an urban house of correction. He found a job in the prison library, where he catalogued and bound books and made up picture scrapbooks for illiterate prisoners. Every morning he walked the corridors collecting requests for books left by prisoners on a slate outside their cells. At times, he worked in reception, logging in new arrivals, emptying their belongings into a large envelope.

So Camb swung across the pendulum, first resisting, then embracing, the prison system, until he became a 'trusty', requiring little supervision. He was friendly with warders, much as he had once preferred the company of passengers to seamen. Though not unpopular, he was rarely seen in the prisoners' common room. In the curious morality of prison, he did not become a target for abuse because of what he had done to a woman. His was 'an adult crime', not in the despised category of assault on children. One report from those days: 'Even in the drab grey prison clothing Camb, dark-haired and good-looking, managed to look well dressed. His cell was always spotless. Towards the warders his manner was deferential, tempered with easy charm.'

In December 1948, Margaret Camb changed her name by deed poll back to McCombie, and soon after divorced him. The grounds – his adultery with Gay Gibson. Presumably the jury's verdict, which implied that no sexual intercourse had taken place, was not offered as proof. To the surprise of those associated with the defence team, Margaret later married James Weekes, a clerk in the office of Camb's solicitors, Woodford & Ackroyd. He was in his forties, and his son, also called James, was an articled clerk with the firm. In October 1958, Mr and Mrs Weekes formally adopted Tootsie. Camb signed the consent paper, agreeing 'not to remove the infant from the care and possession' of the Weekeses. He had earlier agreed not to approach mother or daughter on his release. Camb also changed his surname by deed poll. Significantly, he chose Margaret's second name, Clarke, with an added 'e'.

In those days, nine years was the average sentence served by a reprieved murderer. By 1956 Camb was talking hopefully of parole. 'I think I might soon be released,' he wrote to his father, mentioning a visit by Home Office officials to review sentences. Professor Webster approached the Home Office in a bid to reconsider the case, but nothing seems to have come of that. Camb spoke of getting on to a ship 'which will take me far away from here', though he did 'not expect to find a berth in a passenger liner!'.

In April 1959, he was given a trial run outside prison, acclimatising himself as a storeman in Stan Griffiths' garage in Dewsbury. He was paid union rates, travelling by bus to and from Wakefield every day where he lived in a prison hostel just outside the walls. Few people in the garage knew his true identity. Ron Carbutt, the parts manager, recalls his 'smart appearance, black sleek brushed hair and courteous manner . . . I remember being a little uneasy about his attentive and flattering attention to women . . . He could charm women, some felt uncomfortable with him but could not explain why, but with others he was popular and he was not short of female company.'

A *Daily Express* reporter shadowed him, and Camb, irate, 'belted him one' and called the police. A long article followed, without the murderer being named, and with a picture, face blacked out, of him walking down a Wakefield street. 'A disturbing reform, some people might think', commented the newspaper.

He was released in September, together with his friend Edward McKinney, who had been reprieved after murdering an Egyptian policeman in 1954. Now he could leave prison gently, confident of a solid re-start in life. A moral philosopher might have seen Camb's eleven-and-a-half-year sentence as an injustice for a murder flimsily proved, but as just deserts for throwing Gay Gibson's body out of the porthole. Old Bob was now eighty-one and ailing. After a tearful reunion, he told a newspaper that his son still felt badly about the verdict. 'Ever since he was sentenced he has maintained that he was innocent. He has nothing at all to gain by telling me that story, but he has stuck to it and I believe him. He always said he would not have been convicted if other witnesses had come forward and he is sure he can clear his name by finding them.'

Camb called at the Seamen's Union offices in Liverpool but was warned that going back to sea was too great a risk. The wife of a Greek shipping tycoon was rumoured to have promised him a job, but nothing materialised. Nor could it have done. He had in his pocket a letter from the Home Secretary, Rab Butler, reminding him that he was out on licence and subject to the supervision of a probation officer, whose permission was needed to change job and lodgings. So he went back to the garage, and a room in a public house in Batley was found for him by the prison authorities.

He bought an old Wolseley out of the £2,500 paid for a series of articles about his life and trial written by Harry Ashbrook in the *Sunday Pictorial*. Though revelations were promised, the 'amazing statement' offered little more than 'I swear I did not murder Gay Gibson'. With the money and a steady job, Camb lived it up. Cousin Florrie says that Jimmy could take a drink or leave it, but when he took it he never knew when to stop. 'He'd been eleven years away from society with no fun, so probably wanted to make up for lost time.' He was once found drunk in a pub car park. In July 1962, a local paper reported that James Clarke, aged forty-five, of Park Street, Radcliffe, had been fined £5 and his licence endorsed at Dewsbury Borough Court for driving without due care and attention.

He was still a comparatively young man and women of all ages were attracted by his easy charm. Florrie Stone recalls an outing to Cockerham Sands near Morecambe soon after his release, when a girl of thirteen came up to him, 'and the next thing she had her arms round his neck and was loving him. I was horrified. I told her mother to stop it. The girl pleaded: "Don't take my man away."'

Soon afterwards he met Irene, a barmaid in Dewsbury, and prepared to remarry. Cousin Florrie asked whether she had been told about Gay. 'He said she had, but I didn't believe him.' Old Bob was dead by now, and Uncle Billy, the only Camb relative at the wedding, was probably sworn to secrecy. 'He would have been all right with Irene if he had stuck with her,' says Mrs Stone. But the 'homely Yorkshire lass wasn't fancy or glamorous enough for our Jimmy. Nobody could get him out of that fantasy world. Like his Granddad Camb, he was always looking for fresh fields to conquer.' And yet, the marriage worked well enough for Jim to adopt Irene's six-year-old daughter, Jackie.

Then, in May 1967, James 'Clarke' hit the headlines. He had landed a job as the steward of the working men's club in Bishop's Stortford, the Hertfordshire market town where the insatiable businessman of Empire, Cecil John Rhodes, was born. Here the magistrates were wont to deal with offences no weightier than heifers straying on the highway, or cycling under the influence. Now Camb came up on a charge of indecently assaulting an eight-year-old girl. He pleaded guilty. Being out of prison under licence, at the Home Secretary's discretion, his freedom was dependent on good behaviour. He could be sent back to prison even without being convicted of a subsequent offence. Now he had a second stroke of luck.

The job had been a marvellous chance for him. The club was rather like the one in Waterfoot: male dominated, Labour supporting, and a diet of snooker, darts and cards. Perhaps he forged the letter of recommendation, but the claim that he was one of the finest Union-Castle stewards was not far off the mark. He had settled in well and came to be highly regarded. His rehabilitation had seemed complete.

The girl in question was a school friend of his daughter's. She sat on his knee, and he showed her pictures of a naked female. Gilbert Pusey, the probation officer in charge of the case, recalls that 'he allowed his hand to wander a bit on the little girl and she told her mother who complained to the police and Clarke was arrested and held in custody for a week till the trial'. His solicitor, John Parry-Williams, pleaded that he had not been out of work since leaving Wakefield prison. 'I seem to recall that a GP gave us a letter that Clarke was complaining of impotence at the time, and was taking "Yobinol" to improve his performance. He and wife were having emotional difficulties.' (Yohimbine hydrochloride, or salt of Yohimbine, was said to work on the sympathetic nervous system and stimulate an erection, but there is no evidence of its value as an aphrodisiac.)

Pusey told the Bench: 'If you give him an opportunity, his wife will stand by him. He could go back to where he worked before he came to Bishop's Stortford.' The chairman of the magistrates, Mrs E. M. Smith, was about as different from Sir Malcolm Hilbery as could be imagined, the wife of a railway porter who lived in a railway cottage. She saw it as a borderline case which had little to do with Camb's previous offence and, as the Home Office was not going to exercise its right of recall,' she put him on probation for two years. Irene was led sobbing from the court, saying that her marriage had been happy until then.

Pusey found Camb a quiet man, very uncertain of himself, 'unable to control his emotions with this child, but who within himself was not evil, though very weak'. The next day's reports in the London and local papers made mention of the Porthole case, but mysteriously referred to him as Clarke, not Camb.

After the publicity, Camb had no option but to leave Bishop's Stortford. Accompanied by his family, he moved to a head waiter's job in Kendal in the Lake District. Now Camb was back on his old form, unable to put down roots, moving expectantly to greener grass, to Fleetwood, Blackpool, Oban, and other posts. After a while, mother and daughter returned to Dewsbury, but Irene stuck by him and there was affection between the three of them.

His transgressions were next in the news in May 1971 when, as head waiter at the Waverley Castle Hotel, Melrose, a respectable establishment in Roxburghshire, he pleaded guilty at Jedburgh Sheriff's Court to 'lewd, indecent and libidinous practices' towards three members of a school party at the hotel. He had followed a girl of ten into her room and locked the door. There, according to the procurator fiscal, 'he pushed her on to the bed, lay on top of her and started to kiss her. The girl tried to push him away and he finally got off her when noises were heard in the corridor.' He then went into a room shared by two eleven-year-olds, kissed one of them, but left when she objected. Later that night she was awakened by her room-mate crying. Camb was under the bedclothes.

Those who were convinced about the events a quarter of a century earlier in cabin 126 on the *Durban Castle* might have been excused for saying, 'Leopards don't change their spots.'

Camb's lawyer argued that the offences might be explained by the fact he was now living apart from his wife, while 'his sojourn in prison could mean that something happened in his sexual life'. It is feasible that Camb's rampant sexuality was twisted by the many years in prison. By now he was a disturbed and isolated man, terrified of his sexual powers waning. At fifty-four, his hair streaked with grey, dressed in waiter's striped trousers and black jacket, he was a pathetic sight in the dock. Not for the first time, reporters used the term 'No emotion' as the offences were described. He was sent to the High Court in Edinburgh for sentencing. This time there was no escape. The three-year sentence he was imposing, the Lord Justice Clerk, Lord Grant, told Camb, was to some extent academic. His licence was revoked.

After a lapse of twelve years, he passed once more through the familiar portals of Wakefield prison to find a radically tougher regime. Where once prisoners in other gaols would scoff at Wakefield as a soft option, now the spirit of enlightenment had been tarnished by changes effected by the Mountbatten Report, in the wake of the escape of George Blake, the Soviet spy, from Wormwood Scrubs in West London. Dangerous men were no longer concentrated in a few top-security prisons, but dispersed around the country. No more could Wakefield prisoners work outside the walls, as cooks, cleaners, gardeners, or waiters in the Prison Staff College. But in two important respects, nothing had changed – the chamber pot and the military governor, now Major Michael Oldfield.

There were other signs of the times. Frank Stagg of the IRA died in the prison after a sixty-two-day fast intended to win political status and a transfer to Northern Ireland. He was survived by Father Patrick Fell, 'evil genius behind the IRA terror campaign in Britain', and, a temporary phenomenon, by James Greenfield, of the anarchist Angry Brigade, serving ten years on bomb charges. James Camb would have kept his distance from them, and from the 160 prisoners who, in 1974, staged a peaceful 'demo' over pay.

He was a broken man. When the assistant governor, Trevor Gadd, first saw him he did not realise this was James Camb. 'I made inquiries and was flabbergasted. He was seedy, grey, rather shrivelled, a crusty, irritable old man. A lot of it stemmed from his frustration and feelings of injustice that he had been recalled. He always claimed that he had done nothing to justify his recall. And then the reviews by the Parole Committee did not get him out.' He became Gadd's 'tea boy'.

Irene was bitter at not being informed about the Scottish offences. She wrote to Camb saying that she would never live with him again. 'I've faced most of my problems but you didn't. I never said anything about the Club affair but I didn't forget it either. I learned to live with it but I don't want to live with this. You didn't have the courage to tell me yourself. You left that to the newspapers.' But she was a kind woman, and for a while carried on visiting her husband. On his first Christmas inside, Jim asked Cousin Florrie to give boxes of chocolates to his wife and daughter. At first Irene thought these were from Mrs Stone, but when told they were from Jimmy, she flung them across the room. And she was not a violent woman. She even allowed Jackie, now aged fourteen, to write to him and visit him in prison occasionally. The divorce went through in 1974.

When finally released in 1978, suffering from heart trouble, Camb was still hoping for a bit of enjoyment after the eighteen lost years. He found a flat in Leeds and a job at Moortown Golf Club, before leaving for what would be his final position, at the Jesters public house in the prosperous north of the city. Soon he was running functions in the dining room and doing the things he was best at. He was called 'Jimbo' by the staff and clientele. They knew nothing of his past.

Life revolved around working, coming home, washing, going to bed. But there was still time for women. His pocket diary for 1979 has a page of phone numbers – Betty, Lydia, Iris, Eileen, Debbie, Lily, Alison – and a note about Fine Blue for the last race at York.

Once Florrie Stone asked him about his crimes. 'In the name of God, Jimmy, why?' and he replied, 'I must have needed my head tested.' According to Max Moore, the probation officer who supervised the final period of his life on licence, Camb was reluctant to talk about his past, but when it came up he always denied murdering Gay Gibson, right to the end. He had 'a sort of military precision about everything he did. He washed his own clothes and polished his shoes. I'm sure he would have made an excellent butler. But there was a nasty side to his nature, and he could be pig-headed. I got locked into this thing about him not having live-in jobs, because of the risk to himself and to young people, but again and again he would come to my office and say, "Oh! I've got a job", and I would say OK as long as you are not living in. He would threaten to write to the Home Office about me because he felt I would queer his pitch. I offered to give him the address. He would back off in the end.'

He died one morning at the pub; it was a Saturday, 7 July 1979. He was sixty-two. There was more than one drinking glass on the table in his flat, suggesting company the night before. Was it male or female? Unlike Gay Gibson, James Camb had the benefit of a post-mortem examination. The death certificate recorded that he died of 'myocardial infarction, coronary occlusion, coronary atheroma'; the old man's coronary.

Tom Stone, working part-time for an undertaker, brought the body to Rochdale, where it was cremated and the ashes strewn across the rose garden. Florrie said that the family thought it best. 'There was only room for two in our grave.' A dozen mourners turned up, the publican and his wife from the Jesters, a policeman friend from Leeds, Jenny Haslam, other relatives and friends, Cliff the undertaker. Those who knew that the Porthole murderer was on his last voyage kept it to themselves. Those who didn't know had probably never heard of Gay Gibson and James Camb anyway. There was a slap-up lunch at the Broadfield pub afterwards.

'In a way,' say Florrie, 'it was a wasted life. I couldn't say he was a bad man. Apart from the women side, he never did any thieving or robbery. Just women. Daft, isn't it, how you can get involved through women . . . '

The cast of the Porthole drama went on to play other roles, some even improving on their performance. Sir Malcolm

Hilbery never did get over his prejudice against the defendant. In May 1960, Gray's Inn threw a dinner to mark the silver anniversary of the judge's elevation to the Bench. Lady Dorothy was there, and Robert Menzies and John Diefenbaker, the Australian and Canadian prime ministers. The Inn magazine reported that 'so enthusiastically were the speeches received that a passing stranger, attracted by the beauty of the Hall lights shining through the jewelled windows, would have been puzzled to know what could possibly be occasioning so many successive gales of laughter and applause.' Hilbery continued to be a 'reliable' judge until his retirement in his eightieth year.

Some years after the Porthole trial, Hilbery tried a case in which a young wife was suing British Rail for injuries to her husband, who, as a result of a train accident, could not have sexual intercourse. Midway through the trial the judge called counsel to his chambers. The case was causing distress, he said, and should be settled. He had damages of £2,300 in mind, not knowing that British Rail had paid £2,750 into court. Noting the hesitation of plaintiff's counsel, Hilbery remarked: 'Well, I suppose sexual intercourse means much more to the working class than to you or me.' The wife was awarded damages of £3,000.

On his death, *The Times* obituarist wrote that Hilbery's work as a judge brought 'a deep knowledge of human nature'. In 1948, said the paper, it had fallen upon him to try James Camb in 'one of the most sensational cases of that time . . . Camb was convicted and, on his appeal to the Court of Criminal Appeal, the direction which Hilbery had given the jury met with the full approval of the Court.'

In his will, Hilbery left his Chippendale writing desk and chair to Gray's Inn in the hope that it might be used in the Benchers' Library. His portrait, painted by William Dring in the year of the trial, hangs in the Inn. He is suitably accoutred in wig and ermine.

To the last, Joshua Casswell remained convinced that Camb had been wrongly convicted. 'If I had been a member of the jury I should have refused to convict,' he wrote in his ghosted memoirs, though admitting that he could not be regarded as unbiased. Several contemporaries believed that Josh had made 'a bit of a botch' of the Camb defence. Casswell's memoirs, entitled *A Lance for Liberty*, were renamed *Only Five Were Hanged* in the paperback edition – five, that is, out of nearly forty defended.

The doughty, intelligent fighter would have made a good judge, all seemed agreed. So why was Casswell not appointed? There might have been no vacancy at the critical time. But his clerk, Sidney Newlands, recalls that 'he and I asked ourselves many times' about the appointment that never came. 'In the early days he was in the same chambers at 2 Mitre Court Building as William Jowitt and they were not great friends. As Lord Chancellor from 1945–51, when Casswell was eligible, Jowitt was influential in recommending names for the Bench.' In 1951, Casswell became an Official Referee, and subsequently spent his days adjudicating on complicated building disputes. A low-key end to a noteworthy career. After a heart attack he was no longer seen on the golf course at Wimbledon, but he remained a consummate ballroom dancer.

He might have left the law just in time. When, in 1957, the Homicide Act reduced the categories of capital murders to six, Casswell sorrowfully declared that modern murder trials had 'lost their sting . . . With the knowledge that a man is no longer on trial for his life has come a slackening in the tension, a falling off in the drama.' He died in 1965.

Khaki Roberts missed out on the Bench for other reasons. He simply rubbed too many people up the wrong way. 'He opened his mouth and words came out,' recalls his clerk of many years, George Snow. 'He would regret them afterwards, but he did upset people in certain circles. It was part of his downfall . . . '

As Recorder of Bristol, Roberts conducted trials expeditiously, if at times hastily, and the sentences were always fair. He would clear a roll of twenty-five cases in a day. A critic observed that 'he did not hesitate to take a strong line one way or the other and he was apt to be impatient of any faults in advocacy'. While not quite a bully, the great bulk and boisterous manner of this old-style Bailey barrister of fiction made him seem a threatening figure in court.

In *Circuit Ghosts*, the history of the Western Circuit, Roberts elicited the following comment: 'One of the sad things at the Bar is to see a man who in his time has been a busy and skilful advocate gradually overtaken by old age, deserted by his clients for younger men and suffering with dignity the bitter pangs of disappointment.' His first wife died young, and he was unlucky with his second, a German widow, Margot Von de Muhlen, who left him in 1950 after less than two years of marriage. She ran up enormous bills, which he was obliged to settle. His charming third wife, Louise, was the one he should have married instead. There were times when City of London constables would help the mellow eighteen-stoner up the four cramped flights to his flat in King's Bench Walk. He died at the age of eighty, deaf as a post, and the recipient of occasional handouts from illustrious members of the London Bar and Bench who had looked up to him in his prime.

The Assizes – along with several centuries of justice, and some injustice – were swept away in 1971, to be replaced by the Crown Courts. Among the last to be tried in the Great Hall at Winchester were the Price sisters from the Irish Republican Army. Since 1974, trials have been held in an unremarkable purpose-built complex. Trumpets still sound on opening day. Wine still matures in the cellars of the Royal Hotel, but the Grand Nights are not what they used to be. One of the of last big shindigs was the dinner in 1961 to mark Khaki Roberts' retirement after forty-nine years at the Bar and fourteen years as Leader of the Circuit.

With the abolition of the death penalty in 1965, the demise of the Assizes and their flamboyant practitioners, the art of advocacy became rather more low key. Since the advent of legal aid, in 1960, cases often took the longer road. An eminent silk, finding his case suddenly ended when his client pleaded guilty, was heard to complain that 'it does not help me, I've got public school fees to pay'. The photocopying machine arrived at the same time. Before then most legal documents were typed with two fingers by a detective sergeant in the back room of a police station. Nowadays the machine churns out reams of needless paperwork for the perusal of lawyers. What once took a day, may now take a week. Malcolm Hilbery would have fumed.

In 1973, jury rolls were democratised so as to coincide with the electoral roll. At last, James Camb could have been a juror at his own trial.

Denis Hocking, a low nonagenarian at the time of writing, still appears in court to offer the benefit of sixty-five years of professional practice. He no longer cuts up bodies. He believes as strongly as ever that James Camb should not have been convicted.

In the years after the Porthole trial, Professor Webster developed high blood pressure and heart disease which affected his brain – and his judgment. After resigning his Home Office appointment, he was left high and dry financially and would take on any sort of defence case that had money in it. He came up with some extraordinary opinions, which, judges were eventually warned, might well lead to an innocent person being hanged. It was a sorry end to a fine pathologist. He died in 1973, aged seventy-five, a forgotten man.

The last of the three Porthole pathologists, Donald Teare, scaled the heights of his profession, well-liked and respected. When lecturing, he would sharpen attention by announcing: 'This afternoon I am going to lecture on a subject that will interest you – rape.' His students would brighten, until Teare shuffled his papers. 'Ah, sorry, I was wrong. My subject I see is "Staining".'

In June 1948, Roberts, Moloney, Elam and Hocking took part in a Medico-Legal Society dissection of the trial. Henry Elam declared that he had lain down on the bed in cabin 126 and succeeded in ringing only one of the bells. Khaki Roberts repeated the chestnut that Camb could not have been lying on top of Gay Gibson because of the urine on the top sheet. The doctors present voiced disapproval at the finding. Professor Keith Simpson said, 'The medical aspects of the Camb case can only raise grave doubts in the mind of any doctor'. Since the trial Dr Hocking has lectured widely on the Porthole case: 'My

248

medical audiences have been almost unanimously in favour of Camb. The legal audiences have been almost a hundred per cent against him. The lay audiences have been about fifty–fifty, but the outstanding feature was that they were confused with the medical evidence, and would have taken the advice of the judge, which is exactly what the Winchester jury did.'

Most of the other actors in the drama are dead. Dr Schoub lives in retirement in Wembley and Dr Haslam in Richmond. Mike Abel died in 1956, having, his widow says, once visited James Camb in prison. Wing Commander William Bray, who dined at Gay's table on the *Durban Castle*, became mayor of Chichester but died at the early age of forty-eight without recovering from his wartime consumption. Minden Plumley, the detective inspector who had to endure Casswell's withering cross-examination, emigrated to South Africa and was thereafter sued by his wife for maintenance arrears of £94 10s for their two children. Sammy Davis Jnr starred in the Broadway musical version of *Golden Boy*. Charles Schwentafsky, Gay's generous benefactor, died penuriously in South Africa. He is remembered in Nairobi as 'Porthole Charlie', while the shy Captain Patey was nicknamed 'Porthole Patey'. He became commodore of the Union-Castle fleet, honoured on his retirement with a CBE.

The young girls on the *Durban Castle*'s outward journey who had made their belated complaints against Camb were not called as witnesses at the trial, although their stories were later leaked to the press. They may have been telling the truth – Camb, after all, must have been inside dozens of female cabins without causing alarm bells to ring – but it seems more likely they were seeking notoriety once Gay Gibson's plight had been made public.

The *Durban Castle* continued to be an unlucky ship for a while. On an outward passage soon after the murder, an ex-RAF officer shot himself in his cabin. Later, a stewardess jumped overboard. Six months after the trial, the Union-Castle directors invited the prosecution team to a 'thank-you' lunch in Fenchurch Street. Henry Elam jokingly suggested that they should charge a premium for passengers boarded in cabin 126.

The company let it be known that cabins on the Shade or 'B' Deck had been renumbered, but the truth was that 126 remained unaltered. South African coastal voyeurs paid stewards half-a-crown a time for a sniff around Gay Gibson's cabin.

Winston Churchill, accompanied by his wife, three secretaries and an 'equerry', travelled on the *Durban Castle* as far as Madeira. Alec Hort, still chief officer, recalled him as 'a nuisance from the moment he came into Southampton . . . he delayed the mailship's sailing by half an hour, and he had to do his V-sign on the gangway and another five minutes were lost. Captain Gorringe went on the bridge . . . he didn't want to have anything to do with him.' But the half-smoked cigars scattered on ledges around the ship were snapped up during the three-day voyage as souvenirs by the passengers.

Churchill had a comfortable suite, but preferred the small lounge made available for his daytime use. At 2.00 a.m. on the first night out Hort was summoned to the lounge to find Churchill pacing up and down in his siren-suit. The ship was in the Bay of Biscay, rolling uncomfortably. 'Do you realise there is no squeak in this cabin?' he said. 'I am going to sleep here.' Hort woke the ship's carpenter and by four o'clock the former First Lord of the Admiralty was in his new bed. 'He was up two hours later telling everyone he'd had a good night's sleep.' Next he asked Hort to stop the squeak in his cabin. 'The carpenter came in again and I told him to make a hammering noise somewhere, as though knocking in a wedge. I waited a while and went into his bedroom. It was stifling. He was in bed with a big shawl on, an extra heater, there were books, a bottle of whisky and a siphon, and a cigar was going. I said I'd fixed the squeak, knowing full well I hadn't done a thing. The ship rolled and there was no squeak. Fate was on my side, but if he had gone on to Cape Town I would have been a nervous wreck.'

In 1950, the *Durban Castle* returned to the round-Africa run for which she was built. For a dozen years she sailed uneventfully, before being 'scrapped' in Hamburg.

The once mighty Union-Castle Line has disappeared, its ships riding the waves under other names or recycled into tankers in Korean shipyards. After being subsumed into the anonymous monolith of British and Commonwealth Shipping, the company went into liquidation following a spectacular collapse.

Alec Hort could recall no public announcement or internal memorandum to Masters about improving security aboard ship. But the post of master-at-arms was soon introduced on Union-Castle passenger liners, certainly as a result of the Camb affair. One of his duties was to keep stewards out of cabin areas.

Before the word 'Castle' was removed from the hulls of ocean-going liners, however, another sex drama led to a murder trial in Winchester's Great Hall. Once again, a body had been thrown overboard. Stephen Marley, a teenage engine-room boy on the cargo vessel *Rotherwick Castle* was charged with killing a fifteen-year-old South African girl who had stowed away with a friend. The girls slept around in different cabins. Ten days out from Cape Town, Michelle Kirkwood, drunk and noisy, broke a model boat Stephen was bringing home for his mother. He strangled her with radio wire, 'panicked', and tossed her overboard. This time the nearest landfall was the Portuguese island colony of Cape Verde. Those members of the crew who knew what had happened said nothing, but after docking at Southampton, Michelle's friend, hitching a lift, told her story to the driver who went to the police. The jury of ten men and two women convicted Stephen Marley of manslaughter, even though Mr Justice Lawson described him as a young man of 'excellent character and excellent record and good family background and everyone speaks highly of you . . . There was a good deal of provocation about what happened.' Marley did, in fact, have a record – a fine at fourteen for stealing metal from a scrapyard. He was sentenced to five years for manslaughter. One wonders what Camb's jury and judge would have made of that.

Some years after the Porthole trial, a hand was found in the stomach of a shark caught off the coast of Florida. The fingers matched those of a young sailor who had been lost from a US naval vessel. No trace of Gay Gibson was ever found. The judge accepted the newspaper headlines of 'shark-infested waters', and it is possible that she was eaten by a great white, a shortfin mako, or an oceanic whitetip. Equally, her body could have dropped to the seabed and there been cleaned up by more effective scavengers. Or perhaps she was picked up by the Guinea current and washed on to the reefs of the Bissagos archipelago, and there buried quietly by the islanders.

After the Porthole trial, Daisy Gibson gathered herself together and opened a nursing home for the elderly in Rock Ferry. Sunny Lodge was a nineteen-roomed semi overlooking the ramshackle pier, with views across the Mersey to Liverpool's Anglican cathedral. She was respected as a fine nurse and a good mother. Old Joe Gibson was not seen about much. Gay's death was only the start of their woes. Young Joe never got over the death of his sister. He took to religion and lived at home with his parents until, one day, he jumped off a cooling tower at an oil refinery. His brother Paul, who was married with young children, was killed in a motorcycle accident soon afterwards. Within ten years all three Gibson children were gone. Daisy adopted two Irish girls, but she never gave up her life's task of clearing the name of her only daughter.

Postscript

This book must have lain long in my subconscious. As a boy of twelve in Cape Town I read the reports of the Porthole trial with salacious interest and discussed them avidly with my mates. Later, there were trips on Union-Castle ships around the African coast and to England. Then, after law school, I worked my passage to Southampton as a second-class dining-room steward on the *Capetown Castle*.

It was five years ago, when selling my house in London, that Stephen Gilbert, a young man who worked in the office of my solicitors, mentioned that his mother had given evidence for James Camb. When I met Dr Ina Schoub, I found her memory of the dramatic events in Johannesburg and Winchester un-dimmed by the intervening decades. The idea of a book began to take shape, but still I had my doubts.

Then a sad, but revealing, episode strengthened my resolve. The son of friends, a strapping, uncomplicated boy without any serious record of ill-health, returned home from his first term at university. One morning he woke up, chatted to his mother, and died. The pathologists could find no cause of death. His parents, for their own peace of mind, were deter-mined to find out why their son had died. As a last resort, they consulted Professor Michael Davies at St George's Hospital, perhaps the country's foremost authority on sudden death. He wrote back to say that the hospital was doing research into sudden deaths associated with heart disease 'during which it came to our attention that in some cases we were unable to find a clear cause of death, despite every effort on our part to do so. This problem,' he admitted, 'is a considerable embarrassment to both the legal and medical profession and we believe it may be more common than either profession has cared to admit.'

I knew then that Gay Gibson's death could have happened in the way that James Camb described it. Other pieces fell into place. The largest of these was supplied by Dr Hocking, whose contribution to this book is everywhere apparent. The other key 'piece' was the greatest *trouvaille* of my twenty-five years in journalism – the discovery of the ship's log of the voyage. Dr Camille Wolff, purveyor of antiquarian crime books, casually produced it from a crumpled Marks & Spencer shopping bag. How Dr Wolff obtained the log is a mystery. Though not mentioned at the trial, I must assume that the prosecution studied it, and Captain Patey refreshed his memory before giving evidence. After the trial it must have been locked in the Union-Castle strongroom, to be pried loose years later when the company was taken over. For myself, finding the log almost made up for the disappointment of learning from the Home Office that the James Camb records had been destroyed, though even then I might have had to wait until 2048 before being allowed to peruse them.

One problem in writing about the Porthole case is that the story is neither fish nor fowl. It falls between history and living memory. While most of the protagonists are dead, there are still survivors whose recall of events may be quite different from what my research revealed. For the trial, I have relied heavily on the version by Geoffrey Clark in the 'Notable British Trials' series, itself based on the transcript, which I was unable to locate. But these were the bare words of the courtroom, without a feeling for the drama as it unfolded, and sometimes Clark (who was a minor cog in the prosecution team) has omitted what he must have considered extraneous incidents, such as the judge's ticking-off of Professor Webster. The *Southern Daily Echo* in Southampton and the *News of the World* carried excellent reports of the trial, but those sitting side by side in court did not always hear things the same way. Thus Clark records Casswell, in his opening speech, saying, ' . . . not one isolated attack, but several; not one instance of infatuation, but several'. The *Echo* reported it as ' . . . not one isolated seizure – but seven; not one isolated instance of infatuation with men – but seven.'

Some of those who have contributed ideas might be distressed and/or embarrassed by the treatment of Gay Gibson or James Camb, but responsibility for the total presentation is mine. My researches have taken me halfway round the world. Those sources named in the text will, I hope, accept this book as a token of my thanks; others deserving special or additional mention include:

From furthest afield – Tony Hubbard of *The Dominion*, Wellington, New Zealand, and Rod Usher, of the Melbourne *Age*. In India, thanks to Mr John Peacock of the Baptist Missionary Society, Calcutta, and to his colleague in New Delhi, the Reverend G. H. Grose. Ian Jack briefed me on India. Donald Vincent corresponded with me on tapes for the blind from Mahé in the Seychelles. In Nairobi, Mrs Errol Trzebinski and Glyn Davies recalled the style of 'Porthole Charlie'. The South African Library in Cape Town provided valuable help with my research, as did: Frank Marriott (seaman), Ralph Mundel (solicitor), Judith Shopley (welfare worker), Margaret Young (travel agent), Percy Baneshik of *The Star*, Gerald Shaw of *The Cape Times*. The prompt – and friendly – response from the South African Police Museum and Archives in Pretoria constituted my first conscious communication with the Force since I was expelled from that country in 1976 for my reports to the *Guardian*, the *Sunday Times* and the BBC.

From Waterfoot, Robert Willetts and Willie Howorth helped me to build up a picture of Camb as a boy, as also did Jean Gillatt of the Rossendale *Free Press*. Thoughts on Gay Gibson's Wirral childhood were vouchsafed by Norman Foster and Flora Green (née Jacobs). Enid Foster, the British Theatre Association librarian, generously shared her knowledge of wartime entertainers. Special thanks are also due to: Alec Hort, since deceased, Joe Chidgey, in his nineties in King's Lynn, and John Havers, who warmed to the task of casting their minds back to the days of the Union-Castle Line and, in particular, to life aboard the *Durban Castle*; Bob John at the Department of Transport who filled me in on shipboard law and custom;

Professor Alan Usher at Sheffield University; James Chambers of the Natural History Museum in London, who described the fate of a body in the sea; Francis Bowker at Gray's Inn; Peg Durrant, now retired from the Jurors' Office; Barbara Carpenter Turner, Winchester's historian; Dr Arthur Hyatt Williams and Professor Tom Marshall; Henry Elam, sole survivor of the Porthole lawyers; and to Sir Leonard Hoffmann, a modern Queen's Bench judge, for his comments on the book in manuscript form. Indeed, everyone I have approached for help has been most cooperative, with one exception. Julian Lee, chief executive of the Bricom Group, inheritors of Union-Castle, refused my request to peruse the minutes of the company during the Camb affair forty years earlier, on the grounds of 'confidentiality'. He looked forward 'to reading the book when it is on the bookstands'.

I am also greatly indebted to the libraries and librarians at the Hampshire Record Office in Winchester, the London School of Economics, the Imperial War Museum, London, the Foreign Office, the General Register and Record Office of Shipping and Seamen in Cardiff, and to those wondrous British institutions, the British Library and the Public Record Office; and to the British Petroleum archives and Rex King of the Rugby Football Union. The *News of the World* library opened its voluminous crime file to me. Among the newspapers which carried appeals for information on the Porthole case were *The Seaman*, *The Stage*, *NAAFI News*, *Southampton Evening Echo* (successor to the *Southern Daily Echo*), *Hampshire Chronicle*, *Hampstead & Highgate Express*, *Birkenhead News*, *Liverpool Daily Post*, *Wakefield Express* and the Durban *Daily News*.

I should also like to thank Messrs William Hodge of Glasgow for kindly agreeing to the use of extracts from *The Trial of James Camb*, published in 1949; to Mrs J. D. Casswell for the portrait photograph of His Honour J. D. Casswell QC; and to the Honourable Society of Gray's Inn for the portrait of Sir Malcolm Hilbery. And more than the regulation thanks goes to my agent, Elaine Greene, and to Ion Trewin and Jane Osborn at Hodder & Stoughton.

The final word is personal. Soon after the trial, Wendy

Noakes was at a dinner party where Joseph Herbstein, judge of the Cape Supreme Court, declared roundly that James Camb was guilty. Had Camb been tried in Cape Town, and had my dear uncle been on the Bench, I might have been deprived of the chance of writing this book.
Denis Herbstein,
London,
September 1990.

Bibliography

Among the books which have helped me in my research or in my inspiration are:

G. D. Roberts, *Law and Life* (W. H. Allen, 1964)

G. D. Roberts, *Without my Wig* (Macmillan, 1957)

J. D. Casswell, *A Lance for Liberty* (Harrap, 1961)

Julian Symons *A Reasonable Doubt* (Cresset Press, 1961)

Michael Williams, ed., *Facets of Crime* (Bossiney Books, Bodmin, 1975)

Sir Travers Humphreys, *A Book of Trials* (Pan Books, 1956)

Benjamin Bennett, *Too Late for Tears* (Howard Timmins, Cape Town, 1948)

Anthony Harwood, *Circuit Ghosts* (privately published, 1980)

W. Lloyd Woodland, *Assize Pageant* (Harrap, 1952)

Henry Cecil, *The English Judge* (Arrow Books, 1972)

David Pannick, *Judges* (Oxford University Press, 1987)

W. R. Cornish, *The Jury* (Allen Lane, 1968)

Michael Gilbert, ed., *The Oxford Book of Legal Anecdotes* (Oxford University Press, 1989)

Colin Wilson and Patricia Pitman, *Encyclopaedia of Murder* (Pan Books, 1984)

E. Spencer Shew, *A Companion to Murder* (Cassell, 1960)

Keith Simpson, *Forty Years of Murder* (Granada, 1980)

Robert Jackson, *The Crime Doctors* (Frederick Muller, 1966)

Eugene Block, *Fingerprinting* (Franklin Watts, 1969)

J. D. J. Havard, *The Detection of Secret Homicide* (Macmillan, 1960)

Douglas Browne and Tom Tullett, *Bernard Spilsbury: His Life and Times* (Panther Books, 1963)

Tom Tullett, *Inside Dartmoor* (Frederick Muller, 1966)

Jack Sadler, *Discipline at Sea* (Brown Son & Ferguson, Glasgow, 1983)

A. W. Brian Simpson, *Cannibalism and the Common Law* (Penguin Books, 1986)

W. H. Mitchell and L. A. Sawyer, *The Cape Run* (Terence Dalton, Lavenham, 1987)

G. R. Berridge, *The Politics of the South Africa Run – European Shipping and Pretoria* (Clarendon Press, 1987)

Marischal Murray, *Union-Castle Chronicle 1853-1953* (Longman's Green & Co., 1953)

A. Gordon-Brown, ed., *The South and East African Year Book & Guide* (produced for Union-Castle Mail Steamship Co. Ltd, 1947)

Martin Biddle and Beatrice Clayre, *Winchester Castle and the Great Hall* (Hampshire County Council, 1983)

Clifford Odets, *Golden Boy* (Heinemann Educational Books, 1981)

Margaret Dady, *A Woman at War* (The Book Guild, Lewes, 1986)

Hans Habe, *Gentlemen of the Jury* (New English Library, 1967)

Charles Boswell and Lewis Thompson, *The Girl in the Stateroom* (Gold Medal Books, New York, 1951)

Some outstanding works of true crime which I read while writing this book:

René Weis, *Criminal Justice* (Penguin Books, 1990)

Brian Masters, *Killing for Company: The Case of Dennis Nilsen* (Coronet Books, 1986)

Gordon Burn, *Somebody's Husband, Somebody's Son: The Story of Peter Sutcliffe* (Heinemann, 1984)

James Fox, *White Mischief* (Penguin Books 1984)

Jonathan Goodman, ed., *The Pleasures of Murder* (Allison & Busby, 1983)